SINGAPORE

ARCHITECTURE OF A GLOBAL CITY

SINGAPORE

ARCHITECTURE OF A GLOBAL CITY

Robert Powell

With photography by Albert Lim K.S.

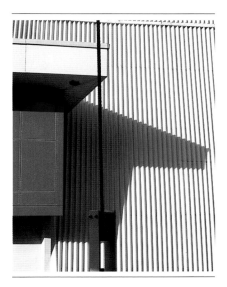

With essays by

Chee Li Lian • Chew I-jin
Campbell Iain Cumming • Ann Gerondelis
Hee Limin • Nirmal Kishnani • Anand Krishnan
Leong Teng Wui • Vincent Lim • Look Boon Gee
Peter Sim • Tan Boon Thor • Tan Hock Beng

ARCHIPELAGO PRESS

AUTHOR'S NOTE

This is a book about Singapore architecture and not exclusively about Singapore architects. In Singapore, the title "architect" is legally protected and applies only to a professional registered with the Board of Architects (BOA). Accordingly, architects registered elsewhere but working on projects in Singapore are referred to in some other way—for example, design consultant or master planner. The authorship of a design is, in some cases, disputed and I have tried with difficulty to negotiate this tricky terrain. I apologise if the outcome is not in all cases satisfactory to all parties.

SILVER SPONSOR

Rider Hunt Levett & Bailey

TEXT © Robert Powell 2000
Individual essays remain the copyright of the contributors
EDITOR Geraldine Mesenas
DESIGNER Nelani Jinadasa • Annie Teo Ai Min
PRODUCTION MANAGER Edmund Lam

PHOTOGRAPHY BY
Albert Lim K.S. • Robert Powell/Akimedia
With additional photography by Peter Mealin • Amir Sultan • Ian Lloyd • Dennis Gilbert
• Frenchie Christogatin • ARCAID • MAPS Image • Xiao Photo Workshop • Tan Kah Heng
• Tim Nolan • Tim Griffiths

COPYRIGHT © 2000 Editions Didier Millet

Published in 2000 by Archipelago Press
an imprint of Editions Didier Millet
64, Peck Seah Street, Heritage Court, Singapore 079325
Tel: 65-324 9260 • Fax: 65-324 9261
E-mail: edm@pacific.net.sg • Website: www.edmbooks.com

COLOUR SEPARATION BY Colourscan Co Pte Ltd
PRINTED AND BOUND IN Singapore by Tien Wah Press Pte Ltd

The publisher acknowledges the support of PWD Corporation Pte Ltd
in the preparation of this book.

Pontiac Land
Private Limited

The publisher acknowledges the support of Pontiac Land Private Limited in the launch
arrangements for this book. The launch was held at The Ritz-Carlton, Millenia Singapore.

ISBN 981-4068-05-5

Page 2: **Temasek Polytechnic**
Page 3: **Singapore Discovery Centre**
Left: **Lem House**

ACKNOWLEDGEMENTS

This book has had a long gestation period. It was originally conceived in 1995 as a Guide Book to Singapore and came within three months of publication in that form. But with the economic downturn in Southeast Asia in 1997, the project was abandoned. When the project resurfaced in 2000, the publisher changed, the format changed and more than half of the projects were superseded or updated. That fact alone says much about the dynamism and the rate of change and obsolescence in Asia.

Many architects and their clients in the private and public sectors have assisted in the preparation of this book and have been enormously patient in waiting for it to come to fruition. I wish to thank particularly: Ernesto Bedmar, Chan Soo Khian, Chan Sui Him, Patrick Chia, Chua Ka Seng, Fung John Chye, Aldo Giurgola, Goh Hup Chor, Vikas Gore, Richard Hassell, Richard Helfer, Justin Hill, Kerry Hill, Helmut Jahn, Koh Seow Chuan, Kisho Kurokawa, Robert Kwan, Kwee Liong Phing, Lai Chee Kien, William Lim Siew Wai, Liu Thai Ker, Ken Lou, Geoff Malone, Zack McKown, Meng Ta Cheang, Mok Wei Wei, Ng Weng Pang, Michael Ngu, Ong Tze Boon, IM Pei, Dominique Perrault, Didier Repellin, Kevin Roche, Edward d'Silva, Siew Man Kok, Tan Hock Beng, Tan Kok Hiang, Tan Teck Kiam, Tan Kay Ngee, Tang Guan Bee, Kenzo Tange, Tay Kheng Soon, Neil Troiano, Michael Wilford, Wong Mun Summ and Yang Soo Suan.

Many of the plans, sections and elevations have been redrawn from original construction drawings provided by the architects. The majority were redrawn by Sim Choon Heok and Sian Chong Ping, with additional assistance from Christina Low, Chow Li May and Yap Meng Chuan. Others were redrawn by Foo Li Ching, Joan Lee Ling Mun, Chun Kian Chong, Ng Say Peng, Juliana Lai Sin Ling, Tan Chia Chia and Lee Kim Teck. Other drawings were supplied by Kevin Roche John Dinkeloo and Associates, Tsao and McKown, Kisho Kurokawa Architect and Associates, The Housing and Development Board, Michael Wilford and Partners London, Akitek Tenggara, PWD Consultants Pte Ltd, the Urban Redevelopment Authority and P and T Consultants Pte Ltd. I am deeply indebted to the Japan Information and Cultural Centre, the Australian Trade Commission and Le Conseiller Culturel Scientifique et de Cooperation Technique of the French Embassy in Singapore for their assistance.

As the book moved into "fast forward" mode in mid-2000, I invited a number of young architectural critics and writers to contribute short articles which, in most cases, involved the substantial rewriting and reworking of critical essays they had published elsewhere. I am indebted to Chee Li Lian, Chew I-jin, Campbell Iain Cumming, Ann Gerondelis, Hee Limin, Nirmal Kishnani, Tan Boon Thor, Anand Krishnan, Peter Sim, Leong Teng Wui and Vincent Lim. They represent the best architectural writers of their generation and their contributions have added immeasurably to the value and richness of this book, giving it a depth and range of critical viewpoints that would have evaded me as sole author.

I have benefitted greatly from the continuous dialogue that I enjoy with my former colleague in the National University of Singapore, Tan Hock Beng, who was associated with the original draft but had to withdraw to concentrate on his flourishing practice, MAPS Design Studio. Some of his original contributions are retained. I must give a special word of thanks also to Mark Tan of Page One Books for his encouragement.

My first opportunity to participate in the discourse on architecture in Southeast Asia was offered by the Aga Khan Award for Architecture (AKAA) in 1985 and I still remain indepted to Suha Özkan, the secretary general of the Award for that introduction. Later, William Lim Siew Wai involved me with the Singapore Heritage Society which he initiated in 1986 and AAAsia, of which he is president. A third forum, the Asia Design Forum set up by Ken Yeang in 1990, also stimulated my interest.

I take this opportunity to thank the National University of Singapore for affording me the opportunity to travel and write about architecture in Southeast Asia whilst in their employment from 1984 to 2000. I would particularly mention, for their advice and critical comments, my erstwhile colleagues, Norman Edwards, Ho Pak Toe, Wong Chong Thai, Pinna Indorf, T.K. Sabapathy, Lam Khee Poh, Chua Beng Huat and Joseph Lim. The Singapore Institute of Architects (SIA) must also be mentioned. From 1986 to 1998, I served on the publication committee of the institute, the last two years as editor of *Singapore Architect*, under the diplomatic chairmanship of Tan Kok Hiang. This gave countless opportunities to review new projects, as does my current role as the editorial consultant of the magazine *SPACE*. For the latter, I thank the publishers Panpac Lifestyle Magazines.

As with my previous publications, the text of this book and its countless revisions were typed by my research assistant, Lynda Lim. She has shown immense patience. Lastly, I have to thank Didier Millet, Charles Orwin, Timothy Auger and editor Geraldine Mesenas of Editions Didier Millet (EDM) for their enthusiasm for this book and Antoine Monod, also of EDM, without whom the book would surely not have seen the light of day.

In 1989, I wrote the very first book on contemporary architecture in Singapore entitled *Innovative Architecture of Singapore*. It featured just 25 projects and I was hard pushed to find others worthy of inclusion. In this book, there are 90 projects and the difficulty has been to decide which to omit.

Inevitably, there will be controversy about the choice of buildings. For this I am entirely responsible. The projects illustrated are, in my opinion, the most thoughtful and visually exciting produced in Singapore in the last decade of the 20th century. There is no hidden agenda, except that I hope that gathering together this collection of completed works and those that are in progress will add fuel to the critical discourse about architecture and that this will ultimately raise the level of appreciation of good design.

CONTENTS

Singapore: Architecture of a Global City illustrates 90 projects completed in Singapore in the last decade of the 20th century and others that will be completed in the early years of the new millennium. These buildings have been selected to illustrate the extent to which globalisation has penetrated the economy of the island city-state, the manner in which globalisation has dramatically shaped the city skyline and the fact that works by internationally-renowned architects stand side by side with the products of Singapore architects.

ARCHITECTURE OF A GLOBAL CITY

Above: **Tampines North Community Centre (1989), designed by William Lim Associates. (Later renamed Pasir Ris South Community Centre.)**

Opposite: **The Colonnade, designed by Paul Rudolph, in association with Archiplan Team, was completed in 1985.**

I n the last decade of the 20th century, the notion of the Global City entered the language of political, economic and socio-cultural discourse. John Friedmann is credited with the first attempt to define the attributes of a "global city" in a seminal essay entitled "The World City Hypothesis" (Friedmann 1986).

Friedmann defined a hierarchy of so-called global cities in which Singapore was seen to play a vital role. Singapore does not have the population size of "primary" global cities such as London, Tokyo, New York and Los Angeles, all with populations in the 10 to 20 million range, but in terms of its importance as a major financial centre, a headquarters for transnational corporations, the extent of its business service sector and its position as a transportation node, Singapore has acquired the status of a regional metropolis.

It is important to grasp this connection with the interlocking system of production and markets which compose the global system, for this has a significant effect on the architecture and urban forms of the island of Singapore. It has drawn Singapore into a world arena and created that "social schizophrenia between, on the one hand, regional societies and local institutions, and on the other hand, the rules and operations of the economic system at the international level" (Friedmann 1995).

"Furthermore", states Friedmann, "in such cities, the traditional structure of social and political control over development, work and distribution have been subverted by the placeless logic of an internationalised economy enacted by means of information flows among powerful actors beyond the sphere of state regulations."

In other words, Singapore cannot act independently of the world economic system or, at least, it is severely constrained. In

this contemporary world system, there are "flows of material cultures that encompass everything from architecture and interior design through to clothes and jewellery" (Knox 1995). Architecture in this international arena is simply a commodity which flows across national boundaries.

It is not surprising, therefore, that when one looks at the skyline of downtown Singapore, the creative endeavours of many of the world's so-called signature architects are prominent. Architectural critic Deyan Sudjik in his book *The 100 Mile City* (Sudjik 1992), implies that it is almost *de rigueur* for aspiring global cities such as Singapore to have towers designed by the likes of Helmut Jahn and Richard Meier. This is a measure of the cosmopolitan culture of a world city and the shift from a more territorially based community.

RAPID TRANSFORMATION

In a sense, Singapore has always been plugged into the global economy. The earliest entrepreneurs who arrived on the island after Sir Stamford Raffles claimed the territory for the East India Company in 1819 were a mixture of British and other Europeans, Chinese,

Armenians, Arabs and Indians, who settled alongside the indigenous Malays. The trade networks they set up stretched from China to India, the Mediterranean, Europe and the New World.

But the transformation of Singapore since the island achieved independence has been remarkable. The city-state is the brainchild of a remarkable man, Lee Kuan Yew, who, in 1959, ushered in the first independent government. Even today, although nominally the "extra man" in the government, Lee still wields enormous influence. The island became an independent nation in 1965 and has since established itself as the major growth node in Southeast Asia. It has moved from under-developed to developed status in the space of 35 years. Possibly no other city in the 20th century has been so rapidly transformed. And this has not been a chaotic transformation, for everything in Singapore is planned. To quote Rem Koolhaas, "Even the chaos is planned chaos."

Several United Nations reports in the 1960s formed the basis of government planning. The aim was to create a favourable investment climate and to build up the island's strategic strength as an entrepôt. Slum clearance and urban renewal became the highest priority. The government initiated tough legislation to acquire land and properties for public purposes. The government's Home Ownership Scheme, which was introduced in 1964, has succeeded in creating, through the Housing and Development Board (HDB), large numbers of reasonably priced housing units.

Architecture became the visual symbol of Singapore's economic achievements. The earliest symbols were the NTUC Conference Hall (1968), designed by Malaysian Architects Co-Partnership; Jurong Town Hall (1970), designed by Architects Team 3; and People's Park Complex (1970), conceptualised by Design Partnership.

Since the mid-1970s, however, the architecture of the city downtown area has been dominated by foreign architects. Part of the reason for the influx of famous names was the Urban Redevelopment Authority's Land Sales Policy, introduced as part of a strategy for the comprehensive redevelopment of the central area. Proposals and schemes were submitted and a key factor in winning these "competitions" appears to have been the choice of interna-

tionally recognised "names" to do the design, albeit in association with a local practice.

Some of the resulting buildings are examples of architecture which compare favourably with the best in the world. OCBC Centre, the result of the Second Sale of Sites in 1968, designed by I.M. Pei and Partners in association with BEP Akitek, is one such building.

John Portman was responsible for the Pavilion Inter-Continental (renamed the Regent in 1988), in association with BEP Akitek. Completed in 1982, it was his first hotel design outside the United States and was the result of the URA's Sixth Sale of Sites in 1977.

The Marina Square Complex (1984–85) was also designed by Portman and was based on North American models. It was the largest development of its kind in Southeast Asia, with three international hotels, Pan-Pacific, Marina Mandarin and The Oriental, utilising the Portman trademark—the internal atrium first developed in his Peachtree development in Atlanta, USA. This development was a result of the URA's Seventh Sale of Sites in 1978.

Others include: Raffles City (1984–85) by I.M. Pei, in association with Architects 61; OUB Centre (1990) by Kenzo Tange, with SAA Partnership; and Moshe Safdie's Habitat (1984), in association with Regional Development Consortium.

The wish to express progress and modernity was reflected in these international symbols of modern corporate architecture. However, the influx of foreign architects in the role of "design consultants" was met by cries of alarm from local practitioners. The changing social values of the latter half of the 1980s brought a questioning of Western values, references to the plural cultural roots of Singapore and an increasingly strong conservation movement which contrasted sharply with the mood at the beginning of the decade. "The large scale introduction of International Style buildings", commented William Lim, "may provide a superficial image of progress and modernity. However, it destroys the fragile experiment in the evolutionary development of localism and identity."

The Singapore government was pragmatic in its response. In 1991, at the Singapore Institute of Architects annual dinner which I attended, the then Minister of State for National Development Dr

Above: **Raffles City (1985) was designed by I.M. Pei in association with Architects 61 Pte Ltd.**

Opposite left: **Habitat Ardmore Park (1984) was designed by Moshe Safdie in association with RDC Architects Pte Ltd.**

Opposite right: **OCBC Centre, designed by I.M. Pei and Partners in association with BEP Akitek, was completed in 1975.**

Right: **Chee Tong Temple, designed by Akitek Tenggara, was completed in 1986.**

Opposite: **Unit 8 by William Lim Associates was completed in 1983.**

Lee Boon Yang said, "Singapore will be better off by judiciously tapping the experience, expertise and creativity of selected internationally recognised architects." It might be argued that this is the equivalent of what Australians call a "cultural cringe", an attitude that anything that comes from Europe or the United States is better than can be produced by home-grown, locally trained professionals. Buildings by foreign architects then become the equivalent of the BMW, Mercedes or Volvo car, Armani or Versace suit, Rolex or Guy Laroche watch, Chanel, Gucci or Elizabeth Arden accessories.

Singapore's Marina Centre area might be dubbed "Little America", given the proliferation of buildings designed by American architects and its distinctly American urban spaces. In addition to the three hotels by Atlanta-based John Portman, the Ritz Carlton Millenia (1996) was designed by Kevin Roche of Connecticut and the Conrad International (1997) was designed by John Burgee from New York. Millenia Walk (1996), a shopping mall, was designed by Philip Johnson and a convention centre at Suntec City (1994) was designed by a New York practice, Tsao and McKown.

Other international architects whose buildings grace the skyline of Singapore include Paul Rudolph, Helmut Jahn, Kisho Kurokawa, James Stirling and Michael Wilford, Aldo Giurgola, Dominique Perrault, Arquitectonica and Hugh Stubbins.

Knocking at the door are Rem Koolhaas and Shin Takamatsu, who have made high profile visits to the city-state. Gwathmey Seigal & Associates has completed a new polytechnic and Edward Larabee Barnes Lee was the consultant for staff housing for the National University of Singapore. Many of the Mass Rapid Transit (MRT) System stations were also designed by foreign consultants.

There is a downside to this. Many of the buildings by foreign design consultants frequently do not adequately consider the climate and the culture of Singapore. Many are temperate models transferred to tropical Asia without substantial reassessment and are therefore inappropriate for the tropical climate (the staff housing at the National University of Singapore is one project that can be criticised in this respect). The overseas consultants are not alone in this, however. Many local practitioners do not adequately consider the climate as a generator of form.

Several large Singaporean architectural practices are associated

with a substantial proportion of the major projects on the island. Some of their works are featured in this book. They include RSP Architects Planners and Engineers Pte Ltd, DP Architects Pte Ltd, SAA Architects Pte Ltd, Architects 61 Pte Ltd and RDC Architects Pte Ltd. They frequently work in association with foreign architects although, when commissioned directly, they have shown themselves capable of producing architecture that is of a high standard. Examples are Capital Square (1998) and The Heeren Building (1996) by Architects 61, Capital Tower (2000) by RSP Architects Planners and Engineers, and Bugis Junction (1997) by DP Architects.

One should also include the work of PWD Consultants Pte Ltd (formerly known as the Public Works Department), a former government department which was privatised in 1999. It has produced a wide variety of buildings of consistently high quality, including Changi Airport Terminal 1 Extension (1999), Singapore Art Museum (1995) and Crescent Girls School (1993).

REGIONALISM AND/OR GLOBALISATION

In 1986, in a review of the book *A History of Singapore Architecture* (Beamish and Maitland 1985), I took the authors to task for their prediction that Singapore architecture would adopt an increasingly international image. I argued then that, given the rising regional consciousness in the mid-1980s, attitudes were changing; that the growing confidence and innovative ability of a generation of Singapore architects since independence indicated that the "countries of the Asian region (Singapore included) stand poised to assert a regional identity in architecture, which is endogenous and finds its inspiration in the cultural past and ecology of the region."

This observation was based upon the fact that parallel with the "globalisation" of architecture, there was an apparent shift towards Critical Regionalism in architecture. This translates into an architecture designed by natives to a place which simultaneously absorbs the benefits of modernisation and modern technology.

I was wrong, for at the dawn of the third millennium, the influence of foreign design consultants on the largest projects in Singapore is arguably even greater than in 1986. Camden Medical Centre, designed by Pritzker Prize winner Richard Meier, was completed in 1999. Philip Cox from Australia was the design consultant for Singapore's Expo 2000 project and RIBA gold medallist Norman Foster is the designer of the Expo MRT station, due to be completed in late 2000. Singapore Exchange Building, designed by Kohn Pederson and Fox (KPF), will be completed in 2001. The conceptual designer for the Esplanade: Theatres on the Bay (completion due 2002) was Michael Wilford and Ken Yeang designed the National Library Board (NLB) Building, due to start on-site in 2001.

Given that this is a characteristic of global cities, there is nevertheless a strong local consciousness evident in the work of a number of Singapore architects. The most consistent practices in this regard are Akitek Tenggara, William Lim Associates and Tangguanbee Architects. The most important projects by William Lim Associates in the 1980s were Unit 8 (1983) and Tampines North Community Centre (1989). Lim describes his current work as "contemporary vernacular" and a celebration of "pluralism". It is best exemplified by Marine Parade Community Centre (2000) and Gallery Evason (2000), the latter a collaboration between William Lim Associates and Tangguanbee Architects. Tang Guan Bee's Abelia Apartments (1992) and Windsor Park House (1997) are also noteworthy.

Akitek Tenggara's best work embraces the benefits of modern technology in a design language which emphasises "line, edge, mesh and shade" rather than "plane, volume, solid and void". The development of this language can be traced through Parkway Builders Centre (1985) and Chee Tong Temple (1986) to ITE Bishan (1993) and Kandang Kerbau Hospital (1997).

The works of these practices, although by no means forming a coherent school of ideas, can be seen as a resistance to the domination of Western practice. Architects Vista is also responsible for a number of well-designed buildings, including ITE Balestier (1997).

Several foreign architects are long-time residents in Singapore. Kerry Hill Architects, headed by Australian Kerry Hill, has built a reputation for producing a minimalist modern architecture, which is sensitive to local cultures throughout Southeast Asia. Examples in Singapore include Genesis (1997) and Cluny Hill House (1998). Hill

is currently working in Japan, India, Sri Lanka and Australia. Another expatriate is Argentinean designer Ernesto Bedmar, whose forte is exquisite houses such as Eu House No I (1993) and Victoria Park House (2000). Both make convincing modern interpretations of vernacular architecture. Another Australian, Geoff Malone, runs an international practice from Singapore and is one of the world's foremost designers of multiplex cinemas. Yishun 10 (1992) is one of more than a hundred cinemas he has designed in locations throughout the world, including Taipei and Paris.

THE NEXT GENERATION

A younger generation of architects and designers are also doing impressive work. Among them are Mok Wei Wei of William Lim Associates, whose work has been described by Leon Van Schaik as "second order modernism". Mok has produced several projects, including Lem House (1997), Morley Road House (1998) and Paterson Edge (1999), which mark him as arguably the leading designer of his generation.

Tan Teck Kiam of KNTA Architects, along with his London-based partner Tan Kay Ngee, are the architects of Check House I (1996) and Check House II (1999), two provocative residential projects.

Yale graduate Chan Soo Khian, who heads SCDA Architects, established his practice in Singapore in 1994 and has produced a number of houses of remarkable sensitivity and sophistication, including Sennett House (1999) and Coronation Road West House (2000). Tan Kok Hiang, who honed his skills with Akitek Tenggara, has also produced a number of notable projects since breaking away to set up Forum Architects: the best to date is Henderson Community Club (2000).

Wong Mun Summ and Richard Hassell of WH Architects/WOHA Design have also designed a number of exemplary projects. Their project at 62 Emerald Hill (1998) won them the Royal Australian Institute of Architects International Award in 1999 and in 2000, the practice won a major competition for the design of Museum and Boulevard MRT stations against a talented field of international architects. Other young architects whose work is attracting atten-

tion are Tan Hock Beng of Maps Design Studio (Gentle Road House, 1999), Look Boon Gee of Look Architects (Lam Chuan Industrial Building, 1995), Han Yip Lee Associates (158 Emerald Hill, 1996) and Siew Man Kok and Cheng Pai Ling of MKPL Architects.

The conclusion could be drawn that, while foreign architects, in the role of design consultants, have established a firm foothold in the Central Business District and the tourist belt, the works of local architects dominate the island and a younger generation of Singapore architects are producing work of increasing sophistication and maturity which is attracting patronage.

ERASURE OF MEMORY

In the process of acquiring the status of a global city, Singapore has not been able to avoid the consequences. In addition to the influx of foreign architects as design consultants these include rapid change, constant re-zoning of land at higher plot ratios, frequent obsolescence of uses and the escalation of land prices as users compete for locational advantages. For example, three 35-storey luxury apartment blocks at Ardmore Park, completed as recently as 1978, were replaced by three new blocks at a higher plot ratio. Demolition was completed in December 1997 and by 2000, three new blocks were reaching completion.

Another consequence is unremitting pressure on the urban landscape, which has led to the erasure of memory through the loss of historical heritage. Every rural village has been demolished and their inhabitants rehoused, usually in high-rise apartments. The last village, Kampong Wak Selat, was bulldozed in May 1993. It signified the end of the country's rural heritage and a way of life which predated the arrival of Sir Stamford Raffles in 1819. Agriculture was adjudged to have not made the most effective use of limited land. The emphasis was initially placed on manufacturing industries and more recently on information technology (IT).

The economic restructuring of the country permitted little time for sentiment about the built heritage. Many fine buildings were lost and communities dispersed in the years that followed, as ideas on conservation were slow to gain acceptance.

Check House I, designed by
KNTA Architects, was com-
pleted in 1996.

Authority (URA) took the lead in the conservation of a number of historic areas—rather than their redevelopment—and conservation soon became an integral part of government policy. In 1988, guidelines for the conservation districts of Chinatown, Little India and Kampong Glam were published and rent de-control was introduced, followed shortly by guidelines for other areas. The Planning Act was amended in 1989.

By the early 1990s, visitors to Chinatown, Little India and Kampong Glam were being confronted by the sight of feverish activity as dozens of shophouses were being conserved and adapted for new uses. It became apparent that large profits could be made. Prices of old shophouses escalated and a new problem surfaced— conservation was happening too quickly. Insufficient time was being devoted to proper analysing, researching, documenting and surveying of old buildings. Often, the solution was tearing out the interior, leaving only the façade and then rebuilding within a concrete frame structure within the existing party walls. Many architects and engineers versed in modern construction processes were insensitive to the nuances of an old structure and were unable to "read" the building or to sense its inherent qualities.

There has been a tendency to over-conserve on the one hand, and on the other hand, to create an overall blandness erasing the patina of age. The intangible qualities which created the ambience of, for example, Bussorah Street and Duxton Hill, have been largely ignored and ten years of vigorous conservation has resulted in many replicas of the past; with containers emptied of life and with cultural memory expunged.

Conservation done in this manner has erased the former economic landscape dominated by small family businesses. The rewriting of history and the invention of tradition often follows. The supreme irony is that the Singapore Tourism Board (STB) is currently promoting a scheme in Chinatown to attract tourists. This scheme involves the development of thematic zones where consultants have the licence to be creative and innovative and to recommend specific strategies to make the Chinatown experience one which is "truly memorable and world-class". It is an ironic statement, considering

By the early 1980s, misgivings were being expressed. References were subsequently made to the loss of memory that accompanies physical change. It found support in government circles. The then Second Deputy Prime Minister S. Rajaratnam, in the foreword to the book, *Pastel Portraits*, notes that "buildings are a record of our ancestors' aspirations and achievements."

But even as reservations were being expressed, the urban renewal process continued unabated. Significantly, following the decline of tourist arrivals in 1985, the Singapore Tourist Promotion Board (STPB), now known as Singapore Tourism Board (STB), began to lobby for heritage conservation. The Urban Redevelopment

that most of the traditional activities, the very activities that created the diversity which gave these areas their "spirit of place" have been expelled. The emotional and adverse response to the STB's "Disneyfication" of Chinatown was forcefully conveyed at a public forum in January 1999. Conservation is much better when the process happens gradually. Keong Saik Street and Ann Siang Hill are two examples, where old uses still prevail alongside new activities.

PUBLIC HOUSING

Singapore's land area cannot be increased much more. Hence there is a need to optimise its use. Once out of the city centre, the predominant image is of high-rise, high-density public housing, for 87 percent of Singaporeans live in apartment blocks designed by the Housing and Development Board (HDB) and more than 90 percent of these households own the apartments they live in.

Singapore's public housing programme began in 1960. Building homes was a priority and by 2000, the HDB had designed and constructed over 800,000 housing units. Most of these are located in self-contained New Towns. Singapore adopted the New Town typology for development, probably because of its close alignment with British planning practice in the 1950s and 1960s. The ring plan for Singapore (1971), with its planned dispersal of population to outlying areas, was not unlike the 1944 British New Towns strategy.

Each of the 21 New Towns is planned for between 250,000 and 300,000 residents, with essential facilities provided. These include commercial facilities such as cinemas, shopping complexes and supermarkets; institutional facilities such as libraries, schools and community centres; and recreational facilities such as sports and swimming complexes. Each town is divided into neighbourhoods of about 24,000 residents and each neighbourhood is further divided into precincts of between 2,000 and 3,000 residents. The larger facilities are sited at the town centre, which is also the transportation hub where the bus interchange and MRT station are located. In the town centres, one finds a wide range of inexpensive local eating establishments and every conceivable international franchise.

The earliest designs of apartment blocks were kept simple to facilitate speedy construction but Singapore's younger generation is now more demanding. The basic housing provision that satisfied their grandparents and even their parents is no longer sufficient. This has presented a challenge to the HDB which has responded with a programme of upgrading of public housing since 1992, starting with blocks which were almost 30 years old. Various means have been explored to achieve identifiable character; the composition of buildings of different heights to achieve a special silhouette, articulated roof forms and special architectural features in the buildings. Natural features are also incorporated to enhance the character of each new town.

Public housing has also become increasingly integrated with the private sector. The most recent development is the concept of a waterfront town in the north of the island, called Punggol 21, which will have a planned mix of public and private housing development.

Some obvious efforts have been made in the urban design of HDB new towns to improve legibility. Special buildings such as religious buildings are located at prominent sites to act as landmarks. There is an attempt to define clear edges through change in landuse (from residential to open space) and form of development (from high-rise public housing to low-rise private housing). Green reserve zones are employed to strengthen the edge. They are developed into linear parks, where the edges of two new towns coincide.

High-rise housing in other parts of the world has generally received bad press but, in Singapore, it seems to work and, in 1991, the "quality of life" in Tampines New Town was recognised with a United Nations World Habitat Award. To quote Rem Koolhaas, "The Singapore model stands out as a highly efficient alternative in a landscape of near universal pessimism about a makable future, a pertinent can-do world of clearly defined ambitions, long-term strategies, a ruthless determination to avoid the debris and chaos that democracy leaves in its wake elsewhere." To many Western observers, HDB blocks still look monotonous but over the years, public housing in Singapore has become a model studied with immense curiosity by planners around the world to determine just why it is so successful.

STABLE GOVERNMENT AND RATIONAL PLANNING

The People's Action Party (PAP) has governed Singapore since 1959. Since achieving independence in 1965, Singapore has established itself as a major growth point in Southeast Asia. In the process, it displays an almost visible "angst". Almost daily, Singaporeans are urged by government ministers and the media to maintain the country's global competitiveness.

Singaporeans have been persuaded that there can be little nostalgia for the past and constant change must be embraced, with an emphasis on high value-added sectors, such as disc drive production and IT. If buildings and traditional trades have to be phased out and communities relocated, it is accepted as a necessity.

In sharp contrast to neighbouring Malaysia where planning is development-led, with huge private initiatives such as the Petronas Twin Towers, Singapore has a tightly controlled centralised planning system. This sees the steady release of land for development, which prevents over-heating of the economy and ensures steady, if no longer spectacular, growth.

In 1991, the Urban Redevelopment Authority (URA) published the Revised Concept Plan for the island, which provided a vision for Singapore's physical development into the 21st century. Singapore was divided into 55 planning areas and a Development Guide Plan (DGP) for the next decade was prepared for each area. In this way, the broad vision of the Concept Plan has been translated into proposals. By December 1998, all the DGPs had been completed.

The planning methodology adopted tends to lead to the homogenisation of the Singapore landscape. The impression is that there is very little difference between urban and rural; there is a seamless merging of one New Town and another, although many areas in the central area do manage to retain a unique "genius loci".

In 1996, the URA issued plans for the New Downtown at Marina South, entitled "Ideas for the City of Tomorrow". Several million square metres of residential, commercial and recreational floor space are planned, together with major developments in infrastructure, including a Light Rail Transit (LRT). The first sale of land for commercial development was launched in 1997 and a new National Trade Union Congress HQ tower block will be among the first buildings to appear.

THE NEW MILLENNIUM

In 2001, the URA will reveal a new and revised version of the Concept Plan for the island, catering for a population of 5.5 million by the year 2040. This estimation has been revised upwards, as the target of 4 million, which formed the basis of the 1991 plan, was achieved by September 2000.

According to the Dutch research group MVRDV, Singapore, with a population density of 5,771 inhabitants per square kilometre, is already the most densely populated country in the world. (Hong Kong and Macau may be more dense but they are part of China.) When the population reaches 5.5 million, it will be 7,237 inhabitants per square kilometre (assuming the land area is extended to 760 square kilometres (293 square miles).

In 1984, the population was 2.3 million and HDB floor area ratios (FAR) were around 2.1. By the late 1980s, the population had grown to 2.87 million and FARs in the HDB estates to 2.8. Now as the population passes 4 million, FARs are being specified as 3.5. In the new situation, FARs of 6 and higher will have to be considered. The challenge for URA planners is to manage life at extreme densities. Pressure on land will be severe, particularly land for recreation or areas designated for conservation of nature. Related problems of a high population include provision of water supply and electrical power. Recycling and tidal/solar generation of power become increasingly important. Will life be tolerable?

Even now, when one drives to the north of the island, it is no longer possible to tell where one New Town ends and another starts. Ang Mo Kio merges with Hougang, which runs seamlessly into Punggol and then into Sengkang. The landscape is undifferentiated. The legibility of the landscape will be an important challenge for URA planners, who must now explore the idea of cities over water. A precedence for this can be found in the Tokyo Bay proposals.

Architects must rise to this challenging new situation and must aim for several benchmarks:

- **Ecological awareness and sustainable development**
  One aspect that has been largely ignored in the bid for continuous high economic growth has been the question of resource conservation and sustainability. Architects (and their patrons) must become more aware of how to design buildings which protect the environment, use minimum resources and do not pollute the atmosphere. In this respect, Singapore has some way to go, for the island consumes a huge amount of energy, 50 percent of which is devoted to air-conditioning. The building regulations in Singapore do not always encourage ecologically responsive architecture. The calculation of gross floor area in relation to plot ratio has anomalies and has resulted in the almost total disappearance of external balconies from contemporary apartments and offices.

  In 1990, Tay Kheng Soon proposed a radical new form of tropical city—The Kampong Bugis Development Guide Plan (DGP) which was premised on sustainable urbanisation. It was never implemented by the government but it is now more relevant than ever.

  There are signs that attitudes are changing. In 1999, Dr Ken Yeang, who has consistently stressed an ecological approach to design, won the competition for the design of the new National Library Board building, which should commence on-site in 2001.

- **Conservation of memory**
  It is increasingly important that sites of cultural memory need to be conserved. Singapore has lost many of its authentic visual symbols and the planning process is not always helpful in this respect, as it arguably creates greater homogeneity of landscape through the DGP process. One consequence is that the younger generation, deprived of sites of cultural memory, struggles to recall its own history.

- **Public spaces suitable for the tropics**
  The city-state lacks distinctive and memorable tropical urban spaces. There are signs that attitudes are changing and several memorable public spaces—streets and squares—emerged in the last five years of the 20th century. More effort needs to be con-

centrated on improving the quality of urban design and it must be appropriate to the tropics—shaded, cool, naturally ventilated and unpolluted.

- **Regionalisation of the Singapore economy**

  Many Singapore practices are now designing projects in China, India, Vietnam, Indonesia, Sri Lanka, Brunei, Mauritius and Australia. This is in line with the country's drive to export its expertise to the region. This brings with it a need to question if what has worked for the island city-state of Singapore is appropriate for other cultures and other economies. Singapore architects could otherwise be accused of transporting inappropriate architectural solutions.

- **Globalisation and regionalism in architecture**

  Tied to the issues of resource conservation, sustainability, conservation of memory and public space in the tropics, there must be the continuing search for an architecture appropriate to Singapore measured by its relation to culture and climate. This, according to Davidson (1995), implies an architecture that mediates the universal with the particular, an architecture that resists Westernisation as well as the superficial imagery of a nostalgia for an unrecoverable past.

Robert Powell

Robert Powell

Singapore

September 2000

Conrad International Centennial Hotel was designed by John Burgee Architects working as design consultant with DP Architects Pte Ltd.

chapter 1

THE CENTRAL
BUSINESS DISTRICT

A sleek and finely detailed tower, the UOB Plaza demonstrates the manipulation of a simple geometric form to create a visually commanding landmark office building, a symbol of Singapore's emergence as a global centre for finance and banking.

UOB PLAZA

Architects 61 Pte Ltd
Concept and Master Planner:
Kenzo Tange Associates
1993–95

The imposing $340 million UOB Plaza is located in Singapore's Central Business District. Conceptualised by Japanese master architect Kenzo Tange, in association with the Singapore practice of Architects 61, the tower impressively fronts the Singapore River. It terminates a row of restored shophouses along South Boat Quay opposite the Civic District and the historic spot at which Sir Stamford Raffles landed in 1819. The south façade of UOB Plaza fronts the busy Raffles Place, the financial hub of contemporary Singapore.

With a total floor area of over 115,000 square metres (1,237,848 square feet), the UOB Plaza consists of a six-storey podium linking the 66-storey, 280-metre (919-foot) high UOB Plaza 1 and an existing 20-year-old 38-storey tower. The older tower, formerly UOB Building, now known as UOB Plaza 2, has been transformed to resemble a shorter version of UOB Plaza 1. Because UOB Plaza 2 was

Opposite: **UOB Plaza impressively fronts the Singapore River.**

Right: **Site plan**

Pages 20 and 21: **Caltex House**

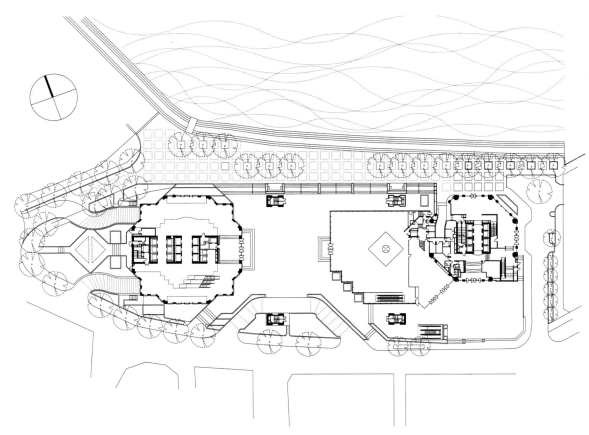

originally an octagonal tower, the new tower reflects the same leitmotif by having octagonal plans juxtaposed at 45-degree angles to each other. These are superimposed in a succession of geometrical rotations while simultaneously tapering towards the top of the tower. The curtain wall system is composed of a truly state-of-the-art, unitised "'thin-skin performance wall" envelope of white and arctic-grey granite, aluminium framing and insulated grey glass.

The building is divided into three zones, each serviced by six lifts. High speed, double-decker lifts bring passengers from the first and second storeys to sky lobbies located at storeys 37 and 38.

The 12-metre (39-foot) high public plaza links the two towers and forms a "grand" arch that visually connects Raffles Place and the Singapore River. Stainless steel trusses suspended from the podium structure hold the glass envelope of the banking hall. UOB Plaza demonstrates the manipulation of a simple geometric form to create a visually commanding landmark office building.

UOB Plaza and other mega projects, such as Hitachi Tower/Caltex House (design consultant Murphy Jahn Architects), have earned Architects 61 a sound reputation for producing finely-detailed, well-constructed corporate towers. These buildings have been instrumental in enhancing the practice's reputation as one of Singapore's top corporate design firms.

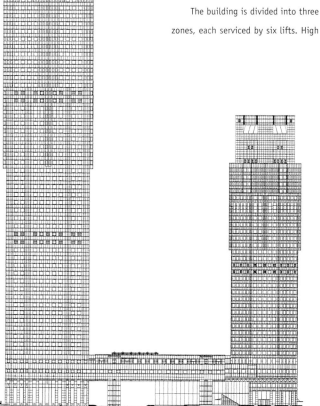

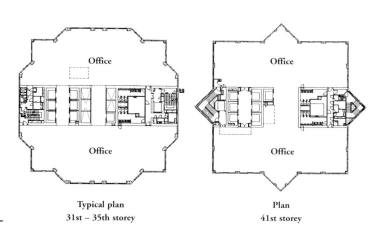

**Typical plan
31st – 35th storey**

**Plan
41st storey**

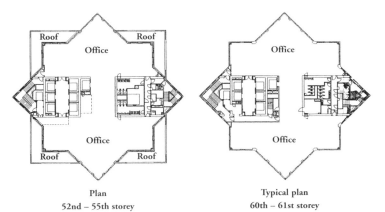

Plan
52nd – 55th storey

Typical plan
60th – 61st storey

Above left: **The curtain wall system is composed of a state-of-the-art, unitised "thin-skin performance wall" envelope.**

Above right: **UOB Plaza 2 *(right)* was originally an octagonal tower. UOB Plaza 1 *(left)* reflects the same leitmotif by having octagonal plans juxtaposed at 45 degree angles to each other.**

Far left and left: **Typical floor plans of UOB Plaza 1.**

Hitachi Tower and Caltex House stand out for their architectonic qualities as well as the use of "high-tech" imagery. Both towers are conspicuously well-crafted corporate buildings. An arcade cuts through the podium of Caltex House and Hitachi Tower, linking Raffles Place to Collyer Quay.

HITACHI TOWER/CALTEX HOUSE

Architects 61 Pte Ltd
Design Consultant:
Murphy Jahn Architects
1993

BY TAN HOCK BENG

Right: **Caltex House has a 29-storey glass tower rising to a roof finial, which is crowned by radiating fins.**

Below: **Hitachi Tower faces Collyer Quay and signals a gateway to Raffles Place.**

Hitachi Tower faces Collyer Quay and consists of a cylinder extending out of two colliding glass planes. As a counterpoint to the adjacent buildings with distinct podium and set-back towers, Hitachi Tower's base is a carefully orchestrated composition of the podium structure and canopies which gesture towards the arcade entrance. The geometry of the first storey reinforces pedestrian movement in and around the site and results from the existing urban structure along Collyer Quay.

At the top of Hitachi Tower, a double-storey volume, complete with radiating fins and a navigation beacon, terminates the roof line. Hitachi Tower provides an identifiable image on the skyline when viewed from the East Coast Parkway (ECP), as well as from the various commercial shipping lanes converging at the southern tip of the Malaysian peninsular. The tower signals a gateway from Collyer Quay to Raffles Place.

The design for Caltex House provides a signature building on Raffles Place as a counterpoint to the OUB Centre's Tower. The project has a four-storey retail podium, with a 29-storey glass tower rising from a column-supported base to a roof finial which is also crowned by radiating fins. The rounded end of the tower generates the roof form and signals a four-storey entry portico alongside the retail arcade. This portico provides access to the MRT station below as well as the third floor office lobby.

The two towers are significant in the way they address the site forces and urban fabric. They are a continuation of an evolving urban fabric and reinforce the surrounding urban patterns with a naturally ventilated arcade that cuts through the podium of Caltex House and Hitachi Tower, linking Raffles Place to Collyer Quay. This link, animated by shops and street cafés, creates an urban space where interior and exterior, public space and private space are ambiguous. This link was originally the route of the historic Change Alley, a narrow public shopping street which was an important venue for money changers.

Below left: **The rounded end of Caltex House forms a four-storey entry portico alongside the arcade.**

Below right: **The new urban street is a private space connecting Collyer Quay to Raffles Place. It was originally Change Alley, a narrow public shopping street.**

Left: **Typical office floor plan in Caltex House.**

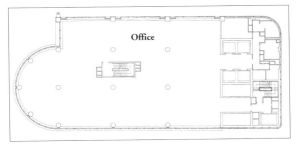

Office

The six-storey podium block of OUB (Overseas Union Bank) Centre occupies a strategic location on the west side of Raffles Place. The podium overlooks the historic square which has been a significant urban space since 1823, when Sir Stamford Raffles had a hillock near Battery Road levelled and the earth used to fill the marshy ground that was the south bank of the Singapore River.

OUB CENTRE

SAA Partnership
Design Consultant:
Kenzo Tange Associates/Urtec
1990

Opposite: **The larger prism is 63 storeys high and rises to a height of 280 metres (919 feet) above ground level, while the smaller prism rises to a height of 48 storeys.**

Below: **Externally finished with anodised aluminium cladding and double-glazed windows, the precise geometric form of the OUB Centre tower creates a strong presence in the dense business district.**

Right: **Section**

The early name for Raffles Place was Commercial Square. Also known as Hua Hoi Kak (flower garden corner), on account of the trees and shrubs that were planted there, Commercial Square soon contained the Telegraph Office and major banks, as well as the offices of established trading companies. It was renamed Raffles Place in 1858. In 1864, it was lit for the first time by gas. It has, at various times, been a car park and an ornamental garden, with an underground car park housing 250 cars. Today, cars are not permitted to enter the square, which has been given over to pedestrians. Beneath is the Raffles Place MRT station.

The OUB Centre is built on the site of the old Robinsons Store, which was established in 1858 and was once regarded as the premier departmental store. OUB Centre is bounded by Malacca Street to the south and Chulia Street to the north, with a link to Market Street at the rear. It houses the headquarters of the Overseas Union Bank and is linked directly to the MRT station at the basement.

The OUB office tower rises out of the podium and consists of two triangular prisms of different sizes attached to each other. It is an exceedingly elegant skyscraper. The sharp corner of the tower is positioned in such a way that it aligns with Battery Road and draws pedestrians into the foyer of the banking hall.

The typical floor plan up to the 48th storey is a rectangular column-free office space, with the service ducts and elevators housed in the projecting pointed ends of the larger prism. Above the 48th storey, the typical floor space is also column-free but triangular on plan.

The conceptual designer of the OUB Centre, Kenzo Tange Associates, was also the design consultant for the UOB Plaza on the opposite side of Chulia Street. Tange has contrived to connect Raffles Place to the Singapore River via the 12-metre (39-foot) high public plaza beneath UOB Plaza.

Kisho Kurokawa is an acknowledged master in the manipulation of the sculptural form of the high-rise tower. The elegance of Republic Plaza sets it apart from the fussy detailing of lesser designs. It is a strictly functional object, yet crafted and cut like a diamond to reflect the sunlight. It is a sparkling focus in the city skyline.

REPUBLIC PLAZA

**RSP Architects Planners
and Engineers**
Design Consultant:
**Kisho Kurokawa Architect
and Associates**
1996

The obelisk-type structure
of Republic Plaza is
chamfered and cut to
form a slender column
that reduces in cross-sec-
tional area as it ascends.

The pencil-slim 66-storey, 280-metre (919-foot) high Republic Plaza sits on a 6,764-square-metre (72,807-square-foot) site at the southern end of Raffles Place and asserts its individuality in the heart of the Central Business District (CBD). The main entrance to the tower is at D'Almeida Street, which skirts the square. Faced with the usual developers' stipulation that floor plate size and lettable area be maximised, RSP Architects Planners and Engineers and design consultant Kisho Kurokawa opted for a simple, square plan form with chamfered corners at the base, which taper in a series of geometric manipulations.

The design challenge appears to be how to achieve a slender, visually elegant form manipulated around a central service core. In some ways, it is the equivalent of designing a distinctive shape for a state-of-the-art pen. Certain functional features had to be accommodated at the core, including high speed lifts in various combinations, fire escape stairs, toilets and service ducts, service lifts and refuse chutes, kitchenettes

and storage. These vertical services are themselves the subject of constant technical research and refinement, with elevator manufacturers seeking maximum speed without passenger discomfort.

The tripartite form of this vertical sculptural object has proportions of approximately 5:4:4:1—the latter figure being the height of the "stub'" at the summit. It is planted like a tri-

umphant stake to claim its territory in the city.

The requirement to maximise floor plate size in addition to the need to allow the main structure to proceed in advance off the wall cladding determines that the external skin of a skyscraper be kept as thin and light as possible, while complying with safety requirements in regard to structural stability and wind loading.

Left: The external skin of a skyscraper has become a specialised field of design and has led to the emergence of "façade engineers" who are highly skilled at achieving a desired architectural effect while meeting increasingly stringent requirements for energy conservation.

Below: **Axonometric**

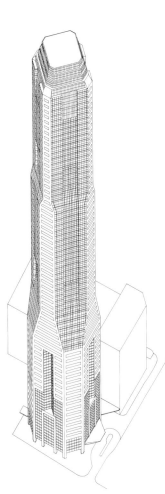

Inspired by successful foreign examples such as Covent Garden in London and Faneuil Hall Market Place in Boston, local professionals both in the public and private sectors championed the adaptive reuse of Telok Ayer Market to inject night-time activities in the downtown commercial area.

TELOK AYER MARKET

Quek Associates
1996

Below and right: **The recycled Telok Ayer Market has succeeded in bringing life back to the CBD after office hours.**

The first Telok Ayer Market, a timber-framed building, stood at the end of Market Street on the waterfront. It was designed by G.D. Coleman in 1824 and was substantially rebuilt in brick in 1834. The reclamation of Telok Ayer bay was carried out in 1879, the shallows filled with rocks taken from nearby Mount Wallich. Telok Ayer Market was then re-sited on the reclaimed land nearer the new shoreline. Designed by James McRitchie, the municipal engineer from 1883–95, the cast-iron structure was manufactured in Glasgow by P and W MacLellan and was erected by Riley Hagreaves and Co (now United Engineers Pte Ltd).

When the new market was completed in 1894, Coleman's structure was demolished. The Singapore Free Press commented on 9 January 1894: "No legitimate expense has been spared in making it the most handsome building of its kind in Singapore....Architecturally...the new market is a valuable addition to the city's public buildings...the elegant iron structure is of novel and effective design. The ground plan is that of an octagon with radial alleys...in the centre is a fountain. The slender cast-iron columns with moulded composite capitals, the cast-iron trusses with filigree infills, the fretted cast-iron archways and cantilevered eaves brackets reflect a leisurely, more meticulous period in architecture." (Seow 1974)

The building was originally a wet market selling fresh fish, meat and vegetables, with adjacent eating stalls to serve the local population.

With rapid urbanisation and economic development in the 1960s and early 1970s, land prices of the sites adjoining the market escalated and development intensity increased. Many high-rise commercial buildings were constructed. In the 1960s, the demolition and redevelopment of the market appeared to be unavoidable, but it was converted to a food centre in 1973 and gazetted as a National Monument in June 1973.

The market was closed from 1985–86 as it was affected by underground work on the MRT line. It was dismantled by the PWD and after the completion of MRT works, the market was re-erected on the same site and offered to developers for adaptive reuse. It was initially acquired by Renaissance Properties, who adapted it to a festival market similar in concept to those in the United States.

Architectural Restoration Consultants Pte Ltd and William Lim Associates carried out the initial renovation work, with consultant Garth Sheldon advising on the restoration of the cast-iron structure. The market reopened in February 1992. With a small gross floor area and a high financial investment, commercial use of floor spaces had to be maximised. It proved unprofitable, however, and the market

Above: **In the adaptive reuse of the market, the intention was to play up the beauty of the cast-iron.**

Below left: **Section**

Below right: **Plan**

was closed again in 1995, to be reopened a year later as Lau Pa Sat Festival Market. The wheel has come full circle and the building is once again used as an eating place.

In the adaptive reuse of the market, the intention was to play up the beauty of the cast-iron. The most recent conservation work was carried out by Quek Associates. The recycled building has succeeded in bringing life back to the Central Business District after office hours. The adjoining roads are closed and eating stalls spill out onto the roads in the traditional Asian pattern of "dining in the street".

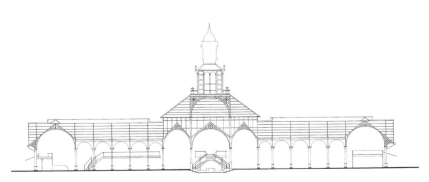

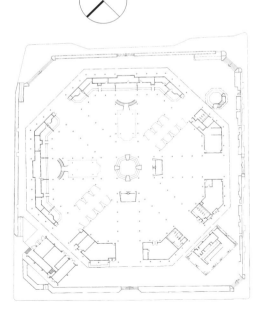

Sir Stamford Raffles landed on 28 January 1819 on the north bank of the Singapore River, which was then home to a settlement called Temasek. Here, Raffles set up a trading post for the British East India Company.

SOUTH BOAT QUAY CONSERVATION AREA

Urban Redevelopment Authority (URA)
1994

Boat Quay is the soft front to the "hard-core" banking and financial district immediately behind it. The eating places on the quay serve the well-heeled business crowd of the area.

The Singapore River became the commercial heart of Singapore on Raffles' last visit to the island in 1822. Contrary to his instructions of 1819, he found that Colonel Farquhar had allowed merchants to build on land reserved for government buildings on the north side of the river. To set things right,

he ordered the levelling of a nearby hill, creating the site for Raffles Place. The earth from the levelling was used to reclaim the swampy south bank of the river. The resulting Boat Quay and Circular Road were then divided into plots and auctioned off or given to merchants who had been evicted from the north bank. Godowns

soon arose, overlooking the river traffic or the commercial street behind the quay.

By the 1860s, three-quarters of Singapore's shipping business was transacted from Boat Quay. Goods were carried from ships anchored in the roads to Boat Quay by lighters, or *tongkangs*. At its zenith in 1865, there

were as many as 150 boats moored on the water, trading in everything from rubber, tin and steel to silk, porcelain, rice, opium, spices and coffee.

More than a century later, the heritage of the quay was recognised by Dr Goh Poh Seng and William Lim Siew Wai who, with a number of associates, produced the Bu Ye Tian conservation proposals in 1982. However, their plans did not go beyond the conceptual stages.

A year later, as part of the government's project to clean up the Singapore River, the lighters, which had transported cargo to the riverside warehouses for 150 years, were moved to a new anchorage off Pasir Panjang. This move was not totally unexpected, as the days of riverine traffic had been numbered for some time. The highly-mechanised container port at Tanjong Pagar replaced the laborious and often hazardous lighter system.

From 1983 to 1990, South Boat Quay stood forlorn and fretting, the river deserted. In July 1989, the Boat Quay Conservation Area was gazetted and in the 1990s, its resurgence began. By early 1993, practically every shophouse was in the throes of reconstruction. As was the case in 1822, the frantic activity was the result of private commercial initiative. But that is where the similarity ends. The Boat Quay of today, filled mainly with restaurants, pubs, wine bars and galleries, is a far cry from the work-a-day godowns, offices and lodging places where clerks and coolies laboured.

Today, Boat Quay is the soft front to the "hard-core" banking and financial district immediately behind it. This seems to support the argument that conservation, in the Singapore context, is inevitably consumed by big business; cultural continuity being a by-product rather than the *raison d'être* of the schemes. Perhaps this is the reflection of Singapore values at the beginning of the 21st century.

Above left: **Kinara, a North Indian restaurant.**

Above right: **The Boat Quay Conservation Area was gazetted in July 1989 and is now filled with restaurants, wine bars and galleries.**

One Fullerton is a prime waterfront development adjacent to Collyer Quay overlooking Marina Bay. Born out of an Urban Redevelopment Authority (URA) sale of sites, One Fullerton's plot amounts to one-third of a larger land parcel that includes The Grand Fullerton (a five-star hotel developed by Hong Kong-based Sino Land and local property developer Far East Organisation) and a new underpass below Fullerton Road that links the two buildings.

ONE FULLERTON

Architects 61 Pte Ltd
2000

BY CAMPBELL IAIN CUMMING

From the outset, Architects 61 conceptualised One Fullerton as an "object" designed to stand out. The architects drew their inspiration from the sea, calling upon a wave analogy for the building's roof form. Much emphasis has been placed on the importance of the roof, which can be considered as the fifth elevation of the building when viewed from The Grand Fullerton or from the skyscrapers in the CBD, which form an impressive backdrop to the site. The roof form was originally conceived as two curves (one large and one small), but, as is evident in the final roof composition, the number of curves was increased to four (one large curve and three smaller sister curves). This was a result of the combined desire of both the architects and the Urban Redevelopment Authority (URA) to make the building more theatrical and to increase the visual impact of the project.

The orientation of the building on the site, coupled with its long slender plan form, maximises the building's frontage along Marina Bay. The introduction of a full-height glass curtain walling system ensures unobstructed views across the bay and enhances the commercial viability of the project by ensuring that, in a development with a 15-metre (49-foot) height limit imposed by the URA, prime waterfront accommodation is maximised. To this end, the architect has chosen not to use sunshading on the east façade that overlooks the bay, relying instead on façade engineering and the employment of solar control glass to minimise solar heat gain.

The building presents a more solid façade along Fullerton Road, where aluminium cladding panels concealing the service cores act as barriers to traffic noise and offer protection from the afternoon sun. The building does not become a fully impenetrable barrier to the bay, however; a limited number of carefully considered openings offer welcome visual relief.

The building boasts a mixture of prime office, retail and restaurant accommodation. A partially covered roof terrace offers a panoramic view of the city and Marina Bay, while at ground level, the waterfront promenade and the introduction of shops and restaurants provide the opportunity to create an exciting urban space at the mouth of the Singapore River.

The complexity of the building's form has ultimately resulted in many complex details and junctions which, on the whole, have been handled well. The architect's choice of roofing material has helped resolve many complex external constructional details. The malleable nature of zinc titanium proved to be a vital factor in helping to mould the shape of the roof. Other materials used for the project include

This development is intended to bring life back to the waterfront. One Fullerton overlooks Marina Bay.

Far left and above: **The roof form was conceived as a number of curves, the architects drawing their inspiration from the sea.**

Left: **A projecting canopy offers protection from the elements.**

Below: **Aluminium-framed glass curtain walling and aluminium louvres are the principal materials used for the façades.**

grey granite, which is used throughout the external areas (view corridor, drop-off porch, waterfront promenade), and polished black granite flooring, which is used internally in combination with timber wall panelling to give a softer touch to the lift lobby areas. The principal materials used on the outside of the building are a combination of aluminium-framed glass curtain walling, aluminium louvres and aluminium cladding panels.

Architects 61 has tried to create a building that imparts a grand statement but One Fullerton is not a large institutional or public building. Only time will tell if One Fullerton will be able to compete with the megascale of the proposed new downtown development or even with the bold form and composition of the new Esplanade: Theatres on the Bay, presently under construction on the opposite side of the bay (see chapter 10).

The bottom line for any commercial office development is the efficiency in terms of floor area ratio (FAR) or, as it is known in Singapore, the plot ratio. With a gross floor area of 95,000 square metres (1,022,571 square feet) on a site area of 7,100 square metres (76,424 square feet), the FAR for Capital Tower is 1:13.44. The floor plate sizes are between 882 square metres (9,494 square feet) and 1,950 square metres (20,990 square feet).

CAPITAL TOWER

RSP Architects Planners and Engineers
2000

Right: **The square boasts a dynamic water feature, with a glass sculpture by artist Han Sai Poh. Curiously, the playful nature of the fountain and pool seems at odds with the formality and dignity of the building.**

Below: **The building has a distinctive profile and it assists in orientation as one enters the business district from the south and west.**

Capital Tower occupies a prominent corner site flanked by Cecil Street and Robinson Road, two prime commercial and banking locations. The 52-storey building, which is linked by an underground walkway to Tanjong Pagar MRT station, serves as the new corporate headquarters of developer Pidemco Land Ltd. Other tenants include the Government of Singapore Investment Corporation (GIC), which has acquired 19 floors of the tower, and Chase Manhattan Bank, which has leased six floors that house their investment and commercial banking businesses. The building is in close proximity to major financial institutions, such as The Monetary Authority of Singapore (MAS) building, the Central Provident Fund Board (CPF) headquarters and a host of banking and finance houses.

Capital Tower is reputedly the first in Singapore to have wireless local area network (LAN) and Internet screens in high-speed lifts. Other state-of-the-art facilities include video conferencing capabilities, a 230-seat auditorium, a heated swimming pool and a penthouse restaurant. For motorists who have searched in vain for parking spaces in the cavernous basements of downtown office blocks, Capital Tower offers an electronic parking guidance system.

The tower is in the form of a huge "wedge" shape—of the type that one associates with the skyline of Manhattan—determined by zoning requirements. The lower part of the tower is rectangular on plan and is extruded to a height corresponding to two-thirds of the total height. The upper part of the tower is gradually tapered and is topped by a rectangular "cap". The vertical proportions of the

245-metre (804-foot) high skyscraper are in the ratio 8:3:1. Scale-giving embellishments to this simple form include a projecting triangular element halfway up the lower section, on the "front" elevation, that has some affinity to a classical *voussoir* stone—it does not of course serve the same purpose in this situation. Similarly, an eight-storey-high portico opens out to a new urban "square", which gives prominence to the entrance.

The building's "thin-skin", an essential part of the technology of a high-rise tower since it determines the OTTV (Overall Thousand Transmission Value) and has a substantial effect on the overall aesthetic, was designed by RSP Architects, Planners and Engineers, with the technical assistance of Arup Façade Engineering. The façade employs Asahi heat-strengthened, blue-tinted double glazing.

The elegance of Capital Tower confirms the ability of RSP Architects Planners and Engineers to design high-rise buildings that are comparable with those by reputable architects elsewhere in the world.

Capital Tower has quickly become a landmark in the Central Business District.

chapter 2

MARINA CENTRE
AND
THE CIVIC DISTRICT

Grand. Commanding. Pure. Tranquil. Millenia Tower stands as the centrepiece of Singapore's Marina Centre landscape. Its powerful presence is attributable to numerous factors; not least of these is its sheer size. The tower stands 41 storeys tall—a component of the Pontiac Marina development whose 80,231-square-metre (863,598-square-foot; 8.02-hectare) landsale remains one of the largest in the downtown area.

MILLENIA TOWER

DP Architects Pte Ltd
Design Consultant:
Kevin Roche, John Dinkeloo and Associates
1996

BY ANN GERONDELIS

Opposite: **Appearing to support the tower at its corners are four 15-metre (49-foot) high cylinders of opalized glass.**

Below: **First storey plan**

Page 40: **Millenia Walk**

Page 41: **CHIJMES**

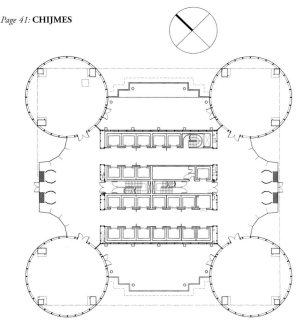

Kevin Roche of Kevin Roche, John Dinkeloo and Associates (KRJDA), in association with the Singapore practice of DP Architects Pte Ltd (DPA), masterplanned the large parcel of land at Marina Centre owned by Pontiac Marina. Roche's intention was to foster integrative relationships with the adjoining Marina Square development and Singapore Suntec City.

The project's high-rise components match the existing grid of the neighbouring developments and generate relationships extending west across the Singapore River towards the new downtown through matched alignments. The Pontiac Marina masterplan intensifies the activity at the Suntec border and the retail element is designed to be the corridor naturally connecting Suntec City and Marina Square: the plan attempts to integrate the three developments. It was not an easy task, for Marina Square has an elevated street at second storey level and Suntec City has its principal pedestrian plaza below ground. In addition, the three land parcels are separated by wide boulevards.

Given these circumstances, the Pontiac Marina parcel masterplan is not totally effective in generating a truly integrative connectivity, which remains possible in such a large parcel. Architect and critic Rem Koolhaas articulates the possibilities inherent in large-scale environments; he speaks of the value of "bigness" as supporting genuinely new relationships between functional entities that expand rather than limit their identities. (1)

Instead of internal programmatic integration supporting the creation of new events, the Pontiac Marina masterplan is the result of clarified and isolated identities of pre-defined activities—office, hotel and retail. The creative use of repeated architectonic elements and materials creates visual integration within the parcel; however, it cannot overcome the lack of programmatic integration and cross-influence advantageous to such a large development. The introduction in 2000 of park and dine facilities in the newly named Time Square, designed by Jerde Partnership, will go some way to remedying this situation.

Millenia Tower, though an isolated entity, exudes a powerful presence. It achieves this through a pure minimalist architectonic language, large efficient floor planning and the use of the grand scale, even at ground level.

The architects have generated a pure geometric massing for the tower: a tight skin over a monolithic shaft on four massive cylindrical volumes at the base, capped by a brilliantly lit skeletal pyramid top (2). The parti appears

By night, the cylinders of opalized glass exude a brilliant glow onto the plaza.

as a further development of Kevin Roche's prior vocabulary. Its immense volume houses an efficient, finely tuned plan, which boasts a floor plate of 1,950.9 square metres (20,999 square feet)—the largest in the downtown area to date. The tower is a highly ordered, pure expression of the modern efficient office tower—a temple to the multinational corporation tenants it is designed to serve. It acts as a beacon when approaching the city from Changi Airport.

The urban high-rise often exhibits a strong image on the skyline, but lacks a potent street presence. Here, however, the tower's greatness is

brought to the street level by celebrating its quantity, its "bigness", in a large-scale, highly composed combination of form, space and light. Appearing to support the tower at its corners are four 15-metre (49-foot) high cylinders of opalized glass. The scale is monumental. By day, the cylinder's interior defines a silent space bathed in light. By night, the cylinders exude a brilliant glow onto the exterior plaza space. The plaza is the setting for several commissioned sculptures by Roy Lichtenstein.

The plaza level of Millenia Tower offers internal and external environments of reflection, surrounded by

polished stone, reflecting pools and entry glass walls. The design of these surfaces magnifies the project's grand scale through images that are transient and fragile, resulting in a subtle complexity contributing to the tower's tranquil, yet commanding presence.

Notes
1. *Koolhaas, Rem, "Bigness or The Problem of Large", L'Architecture d'aujourd'hui, Volume 298, April 1995, pp 84–85.*
2. *The square plan parti with corner cylinders first informed Roche's design for the Knights of Columbus Headquarters in 1969. Variations of the pyramid form appeared in 1971 in the College Life Insurance Company of America Headquarters before re-emerging in 1992 as a high-rise skeletal cap in Atlanta's NationsBank Plaza.*

 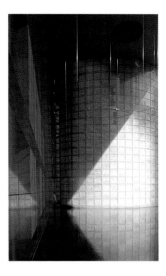 

Far left, centre and left: **The plaza level of the Millenia Tower offers internal and external environments of reflection—surrounded by polished stone, reflecting pools and entry glass walls.**

Below: **The entrance lobby boasts an entire wall covered with a painting by renowned artist Frank Stella.**

The Suntec City project is one of the largest privately-owned commercial developments in Singapore. The complex comprises a convention and exhibition centre, an 18-storey office building, four 45-storey office towers, an extensive three-storey retail and entertainment mall, and two basements providing more than 3,000 car park lots.

SINGAPORE SUNTEC CITY

DP Architects Pte Ltd
Design Consultant:
Tsao & McKown
1994

The central plaza integrates the building. From a large circular fountain at the centre, it radiates out, extending the plaza by carving away the bases of the buildings.

The challenge for the architects of Suntec City was to design the development in "a context of very little context", both urbanistically and architecturally. The site was part of a large stretch of land reclaimed from the sea, surrounded by highways and with one neighbour, Marina Centre, that was very inwardly focused (like many of its contemporary counterparts). The result was an area with a daily pedestrian traffic of thousands but completely lacking in urban street life. A great deal of activity occurred inside the neighbouring buildings (hotels and a shopping complex) but all was hidden from public view.

From the outset, therefore, Tsao & McKown realised that they would have to draw life from the existing buildings and provide an urban focus for this entire section of the city. Only then could they succeed in creating vibrant urban street life for Suntec City itself.

The central plaza is the hub of circulation within the project. On grade, vehicles and pedestrians flow around and through the plaza and into the buildings at various points. Below grade, under the central plaza, very public and active shopping and restaurant promenades radiate out from the four corners of the Fountain Terrace, interconnecting each of the buildings of Suntec City and its neighbour, Pontiac Marina.

At the heart of the development is the fountain, a water feature with a diameter of 40 metres (131 feet). Developers are increasingly conscious that architecture should contribute to the public domain. They are aware of the crucial link between the quality of a complex's public spaces and its marketability in an increasingly competitive world. It is unfortunate that the only access to this fountain is via four viewing stairs. How much more exciting it would be if the public could experience the cooling effect of the fountain and sit with their feet in the water (think of Piazza d'Espagna in Rome or Trafalgar Square in London), instead of just viewing it from a glazed walkway.

It was intended that the expressive multi-pyramidal roof of Suntec City would become a symbol for the complex. The space-frame roof structure rises 50 metres (164 feet) above the street level. Essentially consisting

of a 7.2-metre (24-foot) deep double layer offset orthogonal space-frame of tubular steel sections connected by steel nodes, the roof has a clear span of 170 metres by 69 metres (558 feet by 226 feet)—one of the longest spans in the world. Three Boeing 747-200s, wing tip to wing tip, could be fitted inside it.

The building is not intended to be understood only in terms of quantifiable, material facts, however. The triumph of technology is also conveyed in the spaciousness that is evident in the huge column-free convention hall under the expansive roof.

Outdoor/indoor spaces are evident throughout the project. At the Temasek Avenue, Raffles Boulevard and Nicoll Highway entries to the Convention Centre, there are three-storey-high covered porticoes—here, formed by extensions of the street space carving out the base of the building—which provide completely open exterior vestibules. Just above the portico on the Temasek Avenue side is a five-storey-high atrium leading to the exhibition/convention halls. The atrium is essentially an outdoor room but enclosed with glass. The two retail atria are also large outdoor/indoor rooms with glass roofs. The lobbies to the office towers themselves are outdoor/indoor rooms that capture part of the space carved away by the extension of the plaza.

The transitions from these outside spaces to those inside are often blurred, and intentionally so, according to architect Zack McKown (1). Most of the internal public spaces have a feeling of being part of the outside captured by the building's semi-enclosure.

Notes
1. From explanatory notes on the design of Suntec City by Zack McKown of Tsao & McKown.

Top left: **The multi-pyramidal roof of the convention and exhibition centre is the symbol of the complex.**

Top centre: **The water feature at the heart of the development has a diameter of 40 metres (131 feet).**

Top right: **The transition from outside spaces to those inside are intentionally blurred.**

Above left: **Overall development plan of Suntec City.**

For a consumerist society, Millenia Walk is the ultimate symbol of arrival on the world stage. Its retail outlets are stocked with the most exquisite modern artefacts and expensive designer clothing from the fashion capitals of the world.

MILLENIA WALK

DP Architects Pte Ltd
Design Consultant:
**Philip Johnson and
John Burgee Architects
1996**

Right: **The Great Hall leads north and south to a 16-metre (52-foot) wide shopping galleria with 14 bays of smaller pyramidal roof structures.**

Below: **Section through the Great Hall of Millenia Walk.**

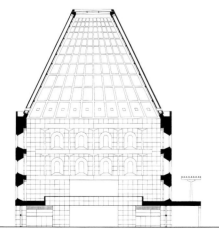

Philip Johnson, the 94-year-old, New York-based design consultant of Millenia Walk, is no stranger to controversy. Credited with the introduction of modern architecture to America, his most famous building is undoubtedly the Glass House, designed for his own use in 1949. Johnson has frequently been the target of criticism and his later buildings, such as the AT&T Building (1978–84) in New York, which is topped by a huge "broken" pediment, have been less enthusiastically received. Charles Jencks described it as "signifying fastidiousness and boredom, that combination of good taste and uncreativity which has made prestige commissions so remorselessly funereal."

Jencks would have found similar aspects to criticise in the design of Millenia Walk. It is a historically derivative post-modern solution, with echoes, in its pyramidal roof forms and arched window niches, of Boullée and Ledoux. But this liberal borrowing of historical precedents has never dulled Philip Johnson's popularity and he has won a wide array of architectural awards. including the prestigious Pritzker Prize. The question is, what is its relevance to Singapore except to show that it too can have a shopping mall with the Johnson signature? But let Johnson describe the project himself. He writes: "Millenia Walk is 'T' shaped in plan, with entrances at the ends of each wing and also directly to the main central space. The Great Hall (Johnson originally called it the Great Court) ends an axis made by an entrance road and a courtyard. This main entrance is a 22-metre (72-foot) high cube topped by a 22-metre (72-foot) tall pyramidal

roof. The exterior is clad in a dark red granite in an ashlar pattern and the roof with lead coated copper in a fish scale pattern.

The interior is a single vast volume with the walls clad in the same red granite articulated within a column and beam structure. The entire area is naturally lighted by a top skylight, small clerestory windows and deep cut arched windows with gold leaf coated angular side jambs. The assembly is striking in its use of colour and materials.

The Great Hall leads north and south to a 16-metre (52-foot) wide shopping galleria with 14 bays of

smaller pyramidal roof structures, giving a total height of 30 metres (98 feet) to this space. The galleria is flanked on both sides by retail spaces at two levels."

The shopping mall is camp in its use of gold coloured structural columns, black and white marble floors and decorative iron street lamps. The false perspective incorporated in the ceiling design is intriguing although the architectural language of "Great Halls" and "gallerias" is difficult to justify in the Singapore climate, with towering internal volumes, all requiring to be air-conditioned.

Above: **The design is a historically derivative postmodern solution with echoes, in its pyramidal roof forms and arched window niches, of Boullée and Ledoux.**

Below: **A dramatic change of scale between Millenia Walk and Millenia Tower.**

Ritz Carlton Millenia is one of five hotels in Marina Centre: the area might be dubbed "Little America", given the proliferation of buildings and urban spaces designed by architects from the United States. The 32-storey hotel has a slender rectangular form, floating on four structural piers, 35 metres (115 feet) above the ground.

RITZ CARLTON MILLENIA

DP Architects Pte Ltd
Design Consultant:
Kevin Roche, John Dinkeloo and Associates
1996

The design consultant described the conceptual design of Ritz Carlton in the following words: "As visitors approach the centre of Singapore from the airport, the highway bends to the left in a large curve before going over the (Benjamin Sheares) bridge, permitting a glimpse of Marina Bay and the city beyond. Since the hotel is placed on direct axis with the heart of Singapore, that dramatic view is preserved by raising the hotel so that the towers of the Central Business District (CBD) can be seen under the raised portion of the hotel." Concept perspectives illustrated a view of the city skyline that would be framed.

It has to be said that this claim was hyperbole, for there is no possibility of catching such a view of the city from the East Coast Parkway (ECP). This unfulfilled promise generated some controversy at the time although this has long since subsided. Indeed it could be argued that the view was not sacrosanct and that the dramatic view of the CBD is simply delayed until one crosses the Singapore River estuary.

The slender slab block annexes the stupendous view across the bay for the exclusive delight of the hotel guests, thereby earning Ritz Carlton the distinction of being one of the highest rated five-star hotels in the city, catering to top-tier corporate travellers and independent visitors. The 610 guest rooms include 22 suites; a quick calculation against the total construction cost of S$450 mil-

lion puts a S$738,000 price tag on each room. The rooms are said to be 25 percent larger than equivalent hotels and bay-view bathrooms also enjoy the stunning panorama.

The contrast between the massive east façade overlooking Marina Bay and the slender gable which visually terminates Bras Basah Road is dramatic. Under certain conditions, the external play of sunlight on the "eyelids" that project above the bathroom windows is exquisite; at night, the façade is reflected in the waters of the bay. The reverse elevation also enjoys a sea view, looking out to Kallang Bay.

One further view is embraced by the hotel for private consumption. A glass roofed barrel vault, which projects out above the main entrance, focuses in the middle distance on the financial heart of the CBD. The hotel in effect "borrows" this view and it becomes an extension of the traveller's experience of the city.

The hotel foyer is flanked by high-vaulted public rooms, a coffee shop and a bar. Several large original artworks commissioned by Pontiac Marina are displayed in the public areas of the hotel.

Opposite: **The 32-storey Ritz Carlton Millenia has a slender rectangular form, floating on four structural piers, 35 metres (115 feet) above the ground.**

Above left: **The barrel vault provides a magical backdrop for the hotel swimming pool.**

Above right **A glass roofed barrel vault which projects out above the main entrance focuses in the middle distance on the financial heart of the CBD.**

Left: **Site plan**

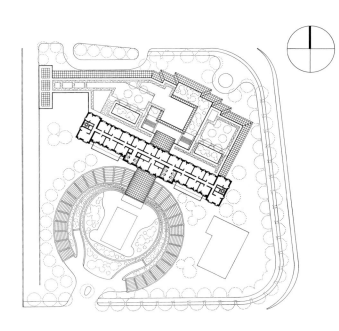

The history of Raffles Hotel dates back to 1887. Its first owners were the Armenian Sarkies brothers from Julfa (Turkey)—Martin, Tigran, Aviet and Ashak—who were proprietors of the Eastern and Oriental Hotel in Penang and, later, the Strand hotel in Rangoon. The main entrance and dining rooms, which were restored in 1989–91, evoke the spirit of the great Asian hotels of the 19th century and are an experience to be cherished.

RAFFLES HOTEL

Architects 61
1991

The site of Raffles Hotel, at the junction of Bras Basah Road and Beach Road, was originally occupied by a bungalow known as Beach House. One of the earliest guests to Raffles Hotel was Joseph Conrad and a young Rudyard Kipling, who visited the hotel in 1889. That same year, two new wings flanking Beach House, designed by Henry Richards, were constructed. Five years later, in 1894, the Palm Court wing was added. Raffles Hotel was the first building in Singapore to use electric lights and fans.

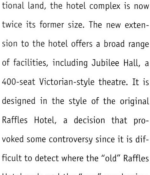

In 1899, the main building of the hotel was completed. It has a three-storey façade and the centre portion is surmounted by a triangular pediment. At each end of this three-storey façade are splayed wings, each of which contained a carriage porch. In 1904, the Bras Basah wing was built and in 1913, a cast-iron verandah, with stained glass, was added to the front of the main building.

In 1987, the hotel was declared a National Monument and, in March 1989, it was closed for two and a half years for conservation work. The owners, Raffles Hotel (1886) Pte Ltd, a subsidiary of DBS Land, decided to return the hotel to its 1915 appearance. This necessitated removing the ballroom, which was an addition in the 1920s, and the northeast corner entrance created by the Japanese during their wartime occupation of the hotel, which was then known as Syonan Ryokan and was used as an officers' mess.

Raffles Hotel (1886) Pte Ltd spent S$160 million to restore the building to the ambience of the 1920s, when the hotel was in its heyday, and to develop an adjoining land parcel. Over four hundred items of furniture from the existing building were restored. The original Greek Revival cast-iron verandah that was removed in 1920 has been replaced with a replica. Drawings of the original verandah were found in the Singapore National Archives and details of the cast-iron were on microfilm in the Mitchell Library in Glasgow, United Kingdom. The new structure was cast in a foundry in Alabama in the United States.

On 16 September 1991, the hotel reopened to the public. With the additional land, the hotel complex is now twice its former size. The new extension to the hotel offers a broad range of facilities, including Jubilee Hall, a 400-seat Victorian-style theatre. It is designed in the style of the original Raffles Hotel, a decision that provoked some controversy since it is difficult to detect where the "old" Raffles Hotel ends and the "new" one begins.

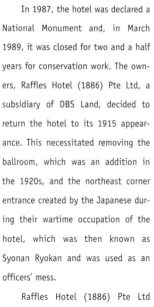

Opposite: **In 1899 the Main Building of the hotel was completed. The plans were signed by R.A.J. Bidwell who dominated the work of the architectural practice of Swan and Maclaren from 1895 to 1914.**

Above: **The cast-iron verandah is a replica of the original Greek Revival structure that was removed in 1920.**

Below left: **At each end of the Main Building façade are splayed wings each of which originally contained a carriage porch.**

Below right: **The restored Raffles Hotel retains the spirit of Asia's great hotels during the 19th century.**

Any review of the Singapore Art Museum (SAM) at the old and much loved St. Joseph's Institution (SJI) on Bras Basah Road must extend beyond space and form. It must deal with the question of what conservation and revitalisation should and should not encompass. And, in relation to this, how old and new architecture should respond to a newly adopted programme of a museum. As we look to the next century, there is also the future of the museum as a building type to consider.

SINGAPORE ART MUSEUM

**PWD Consultants Pte Ltd
1995**

BY CHEE LI LIAN

Right: **The architects have performed admirably, giving the nation a piece of history that will continue to be loved and admired for many, many years to come.**

Below: **The popular Dome Café assists in making art accessible to a dramatically changed audience.**

On 20 January 1996, the Singapore Art Museum opened its doors to the public. PWD Consultants' architectural team repaired, restored and converted three buildings and built two new ones at the old St Joseph's Institution, a Catholic boys' school run by the La Salle brothers since 1855. Gazetted as a National Monument in 1992, it was decided that the educational institution (also the site of Singapore's first Catholic chapel) would be given a new lease of life as home to Singapore's art collection and a venue for promoting regional and international contemporary art. Occupying an area of approximately 10,000 square metres (107,639 square feet), the museum boasts 13 exhibition galleries, all fully equipped with state-of-the-art climatic controls and lighting.

Upon entering the museum, one senses the public's protective attitude towards the old school. Commemorative plaques and leaflets remind one of its past, as does an informative

Above left: **The principal gallery space.**

Above right: **Both architects and curatorial staff admit that it was mind-boggling (and it continues to be) to "tame" the curvilinear configuration of some of the spaces into a showcase for modern art.**

account of the restoration process lining the courtyard corridors. Yet beyond the technical chutzpah and SJI's restored dignity, how does SAM really fare as a contemporary art museum?

The key to a contemporary museum's success lies largely in its ability to order, classify and celebrate art on a highly public basis. And since it has become desirable, from the age of Pompidou, to make art, especially modern art, as accessible, visible and readable as possible, the appeal of SAM to a dramatically changed audience becomes crucial.

Conceived originally as a school, the building exudes a formality befitting an alma mater. Its most distinctive feature, two curved "arms" that extend paternally forward in a welcoming gesture, in fact becomes the stumbling block to the museum's layout. The planning of the old school is centrifugal in nature, with a central point of control branching out to two wings kept under its surveillance. For a school, this arrangement is acceptable, but for a Modern Art museum, it raises some fundamental problems.

Recent contemporary museums are distinguishing themselves from the former big and anonymous white boxes. Spaces are becoming more varied in size, either very intimate or very monumental in scale. The post-modern audience demands diversity. On a more pragmatic level, these inclusive spaces allow objects to come alive as well as serve as catalysts for new art. At SAM, both architects and curatorial staff admit it was mind-boggling to "tame" the curvilinear configuration of the old school.

Given the difficult mould of SJI as a Modern Art museum, one then examines how the new additions to the old have attempted to address these misgivings. PWD's intervention to the Queen Street wing reflects the massing, form and scale of the original block. Yet, it is somewhat disconcerting that this new wing looks remarkably similar to the older blocks. Could the new additions not have made the museum appear more open in organisation and more populist in image, in place of the staid archives?

There is the question of growth.

This refers to SAM's ability to stage a series of temporary exhibitions, moving shows on loan from elsewhere. Has this museum space that is plastic and malleable enough to physically (and psychologically) house these treasures? This point may justify the need to change the scale of the new additions, perhaps make them much larger to accommodate future expansion of both collection and audience. In the stubborn refusal of policy-makers and the public to link recycling and conversion to contemporary needs, SAM may live to bear the difficult consequences of this folly.

SAM must recognise the new conditions under which it must function: at once an archive, a laboratory for the new and a city "square" where public debate is continually fuelled. Pregnant in this agenda is a duality that has both neutral and specific parameters to allow SJI to flourish as a monument and to allow the museum to become a catalyst for art but not to subsume the works. Being a relatively new player, only time will tell if SAM can achieve the second criterion.

The Convent of the Holy Infant Jesus (CHIJ) was founded by Father Jean-Marie Beurel in 1852 in a house opposite the Cathedral of the Good Shepherd originally built for H.C. Caldwell to the design of G.D. Coleman. The Gothic style chapel within the convent walls was erected in 1890 and an arcade linked it to Caldwell's House.

CHIJMES

Ong and Ong Architects Pte Ltd
Design Consultant:
Didier Repellin
1996

Below: **The Convent of the Holy Infant Jesus Chapel is the focal point of the development.**

CHIJ is one of the leading girls' schools in Singapore. In 1983, the school moved to a new site in Toa Payoh. Shortly afterwards, the chapel was severely affected by tunnelling works for the Mass Rapid Transit (MRT) line which passes beneath it. The convent might well have been demolished, like the adjoining Raffles Institution, had it not been for a fortuitous change of attitude to historic buildings in the mid-1980s.

In 1990, the 1.4-hectare (3.5-acre) site was tendered out and CHIJMES Investments, a consortium comprising construction group Low Keng Huat, jeweller Je t'Aime Investments and Lei Garden Restaurant, paid $26.8 million for it. In 1996, after $100 million dollars had been sunk into the enterprise, it reopened its doors. Said to be Singapore's biggest conservation project, it is marketed as a wedding and convention venue. Principal consultant for the conservation of the convent building was French expert M. Didier Repellin.

Raffles Institution, situated on an adjoining site, was replaced by an 83-storey-high hotel and retail development, Raffles City. The dramatic physical contrast between Raffles City and CHIJ might, in the capitals of neighbouring countries, be read as signifying the different spaces of two economies. In the Singaporean context, they signify the same economy where corporate profit is the bottom line—a rental income of $12 million was projected for CHIJMES in the first year of operation (*Business Times*, 18 May 1996).

Following its conservation, the Convent of the Holy Infant Jesus (CHIJ) has been reincarnated as CHIJMES. A sunken courtyard has been introduced and the chapel is now the focal point, as the courtyard visually raises it onto a podium. An ambulatory tiered on two levels gives constantly changing views of the chapel, juxtaposing the new with the old in a way that creates a theatrical yet serene space. The ground level acts as a historical datum: above it are the conserved buildings of CHIJMES while below it is the new construction. This is an ironic inversion of the usual archaeological topography.

CHIJ may have retained its physical form, but it has become no less a symbol of consumerism.

Bottom: An ironic role reversal at CHIJMES is that while many Christian churches in Singapore hold their Sunday worship in hired hotel function rooms, the beautifully restored chapel of the former convent is used for mainly secular functions. It is evidence of the gradual process of erasure of memory accompanying rapid cultural change. The link with the girls' school founded by Father Beurel in 1852 remains only in name.

Managed until September 1995 by the Practice Performing Arts Co. Ltd, The Substation is a symbol of the gritty fight of creative artists and performers in Singapore to establish recognition for the arts in a society dominated by economic goals and political expediency. Ten years after its founding by Singapore's drama doyen Kuo Pao Kun, it still does not have any government representatives on its board of directors.

THE SUBSTATION

PWD Consultants Pte Ltd
1990

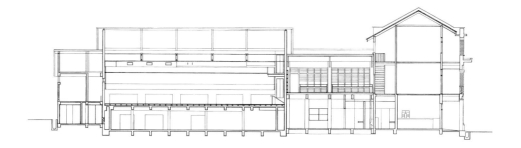

The Substation, located in Armenian Street, is a modest early modernist structure originally erected in 1928 to house an electric transformer and ancillary machinery. It became redundant in the late 1970s and stood empty for two decades until 1990, when the building was renovated and adapted for use as a centre for the arts. The original transformer room has been converted into a 150-seat experimental theatre with back-of-house facilities. In addition, there is a small art gallery, craft shop, dance studio (built on the original flat roof), two rehearsal rooms, a central booking office and administration offices. A lively cafeteria, The Fat Frog, operates in The Substation's large paved garden at the rear of the premises.

The original construction methods were researched and materials were acquired and refurbished so that the conservation of the building was deemed authentic. For example, seagreen glazing in metal angle windows and timber louvres help retain the original proportions and sense of scale. Nevertheless, new features were added with a simple modern language, without attempting to copy or compete with the old style. New elements in vibrant colours were picked to contrast with the existing fabric.

Performances and exhibitions at The Substation range from the distinctly amateur to the highly professional, with the exploration of issues affecting Singapore society through theatre. The Substation has been described by Ho Kwon Ping, a former chairman of the Board of Directors, as "one of the early crucibles for creative thinking and 'out-of-the-box' artistic development."

The Substation has provided a lifeline for many young artists and performers, including Zai Kuning, visual artists Tang Mun Kit and Sanjot Sekon Kaur, and experimental groups such as Theatre Ox. The current joint artistic director Audrey Wong notes that the advantage the Substation has over mainstream venues in presenting avant garde work is that it is "small, flexible and able to

Left top and bottom: **The Substation has earned the reputation of being a crucible for creative thinking and artistic development.**

Below: **The regeneration of the building is a metaphor for the energy of the artistic community and the perseverance of its private benefactors.**

collaborate with artists in their work, discussing ideas with them, trying to understand their needs and finding the best ways to present their work." "This," she goes on, "entails being constantly aware of new artistic practices, how they impact on the socio-political process and to be able to channel artists' ideas and energies into coherent expressions."

Watching a performance in The Substation is not a comfortable experience—the seats are hard and narrow—but there is a sense of intimacy and frequently of inventiveness within the space. The regeneration of the building is a metaphor for the energy of the artistic community and the perseverance of its private benefactors.

The Asian Civilisations Museum is situated within the restored Tao Nan School along Armenian Street. It forms the first wing to the Asian Civilisations Museum, which focuses mainly on Chinese culture and civilisation. Temporary exhibition galleries feature exhibitions on other Asian civilisations. The second wing, to be housed in Empress Place, will provide a more complete picture of Asia's rich cultural heritage.

ASIAN CIVILISATIONS MUSEUM

PWD Consultants Pte Ltd
1996

BY TAN BOON THOR

Below, left and right:
The design of the display shelves, in particular the showcases in the ceramic section, show an effort to give precedence to the artefacts.

The original Tao Nan school was designed with a neo-classical eclectic style, which was then the prevailing architectural idiom. The symmetry of the building and the fluted pilasters alluded to classical architecture. The layout of the building was influenced by the Straits Settlement bungalows, with rooms arranged around a central hall/atrium and the service spaces outside the principal building. The balconies fronting the façade were similar to residential verandahs.

The Asian Civilisations Museum is flanked by an open-air car park and conserved three-storey shophouses housing The Substation (an alternative art space) and the Museum shop.

The state of the building, which was abandoned after Tao Nan Primary School relocated to Marine Parade, and "the strict conservation guidelines laid down by the Preservation of Monuments Board, stipulating the original façade and interior shall be as closely preserved as possible" were some of the initial problems the architect had to address.

Apart from these constraints, provisions had to be made for reinforcing the existing structures to cater for the change of use from a school to a museum. The existing canteen and the toilets at the back were demolished to make way for the erection of a three-storey addition, with a basement to house the annex galleries and the necessary machinery, storage spaces and air-conditioning systems for the change of use.

To design gallery spaces in a building that was originally an educational facility and to introduce new services, a state-of-the art climate control system, ducts and a lighting system in an unobtrusive manner demanded great sensibility

from the designers.

Adaptive reuse of heritage buildings brings the architect in close contact with history. The conceptual attitude adopted by the architect may be to create a dialectical relationship between the existing built fabric with the new functional elements or to subtly design in order to create a continuity between the old and the new. Because of the strict guidelines in this project, much of the existing fabric was left untouched. The programme also called for introverted spaces and for most of the artefacts to be kept away from natural lighting.

The architects retained the parti of the original building and cleverly utilised the original layout to house the new galleries. The galleries are individual spaces, each with its own theme. They form non-linear and self-referential cells with the ability to exist alone or to be viewed as a string of gallery spaces.

The added upper and lower annexes, which house temporary exhibitions, form a continuous volumetric space in contrast to the conserved spaces of the original building. The design of some of the display shelves, in particular the showcases in the ceramic section, show a discerning effort to make the internal shelves "light", such that the artefacts take precedence. In areas where the display cases are angled or have low lighting, such as in galleries 3 and 4, the reflection of the light sources compromises the appreciation of the artefacts on display.

What is perhaps a missed opportunity is the lack of integration of the atrium space into the design of the whole museum. The atrium space therefore cannot be appreciated except as a circulation space. The exterior of the new addition subtly differentiates itself from the restored front portion through the use of colour and materials, but at the same time, the new addition replicates the proportioning system of the existing building.

Top and above: **The original Tao Nan school has been adapted to create the first wing of the Asian Civilisations Museum.**

chapter 3

ORCHARD ROAD

Originally named for its anchor tenant, Lane Crawford, the upmarket Hong Kong retail store, Wheelock Place is situated on an awkward L-shaped site at the highly prominent Orchard Road/Scotts Road junction, right in the heart of the Orchard Road shopping and hotel district.

WHEELOCK PLACE

**Wong and Ouyang,
RSP Architects Planners
and Engineers**
Design Consultant:
**Kisho Kurokawa Architects
1994**

BY TAN HOCK BENG

Opposite and right: **The glass
cone at the Orchard Road
entrance provides a major
landmark. The steel-and-
glass structure acts as
a dramatic entrance to lure
crowds from Orchard Mall.
Its layered transparency is
one of the most delightful
qualities of the building.**

Page 62: **The Heeren**

Page 63: **62 Emerald Hill**

have concentrated their efforts on the entrances. A colonnaded pedestrian walkway is incorporated around the building to link it to the Orchard Road pedestrian mall. These covered walkways are framed by a double wall comprising an outer wall with punched openings and finished in salmon-pink granite to provide a shaded promenade consistent with the tropical environment. The inner wall is a full-height transparent glass curtain wall that leans over the colonnaded walkway to provide visibility to the shopping activities within the podium. The resulting space is thus experienced by both shoppers and pedestrians. An underpass links the building to the MRT station and other major complexes and forms part of the Orchard Road underground pedestrian network.

The 16-storey tower component of the development, which faces Orchard Boulevard, consists of offices capped by an aluminium cone. The lower part of the tower is finished with polished granite to maintain continuity with the podium. The upper portion is a double-glazed curtain wall to provide contrast to the stone cladding below. The outer skin is blue-

Japanese architect Kisho Kurokawa has introduced one of the many conical structures found in his oeuvre into the Wheelock Place project. The seven-storey steel-and-glass structure at Wheelock Place acts as a dramatic entrance to lure crowds off Orchard Mall into the shopping centre.

Other entrances to Wheelock Place are located off Paterson Road and behind Liat Towers. As the main bulk of the L-shaped podium block is hidden by Liat Towers, the designers

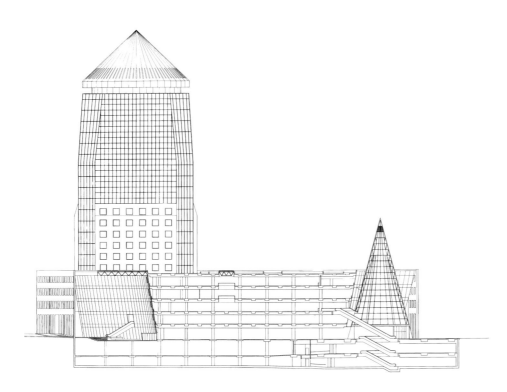

Above: **Section through the podium.**

Right: **The lower part of the 16-storey tower is finished with polished granite to maintain continuity with the podium. The upper part is blue-tinted glass.**

tinted glass, whilst the inner layer is a sloping glass wall leaning outwards to reduce the air-conditioning load.

There are five levels of shopping and two basement levels containing car parking and more shopping. A retail downturn in late 1996 led to the original anchor tenant Lane Crawford terminating its lease. The building owner then embarked on a substantial redesign of the podium. The 5,500-square-metre (59,201-square-foot) floor space was divided into smaller units, now occupied by a hugely successful tenant mix of giant Borders Bookshop from the United States,

Dome Café from Australia, upmarket noodle bar Nooch, the city club of the Singapore Armed Forces Reservist Association (SAFRA) and Marks and Spencers from the United Kingdom.

The glass cone at the Orchard Road entrance provides an attractive landmark and serves as a covered plaza leading into the complex. Extensive landscaping is provided around the building and podium roof to create a tropical garden environment consistent with Singapore's "Garden City" image. The building's overall simplicity and elegance mark a welcome change in retail design.

Left: A colonnaded pedestrian walkway is incorporated around the building. The inner wall is a full-height transparent glass curtain wall that leans over the colonnaded verandah.

Below: Facing Wheelock Place across Paterson Road is a wide expanse of landscaped park, which attracts large crowds of foreign domestic workers on Sundays. It adds to the vitality of Orchard Road.

The cinema is already a paradoxical space that mediates the ephemerality of film with the physicality of place. Yet today, the cinema business has begun to locate itself in the more compelling context of "media entertainment". This new catchword carries the weight of a new type of environment that reads "interactive, transient and global".

CINELEISURE ORCHARD

Architects 61
Design Consultant:
Mitchell Giurgola and Thorp Associates
1997

BY CHEE LI LIAN

68

Each escalator is aligned at a subtly different angle from another, thus generating a series of paths that cross but do not meet.

Opening its doors in November 1997, the new media-entertainment complex of Cineleisure at Grange Road by Architects 61 faces these and other tall orders. For one, it is scion of the famous Orchard Cinema, which was as much a cultural institution as it was a social and commercial one since raising its curtains in 1965 to a series of firsts: Singapore's first escalator and bowling alley and the only "supercinerama" screen in the country. For another, it is pressed to objectify the intangible electronic media phenomenon that prides itself on connecting every point on the globe through the "magic" of optic fibres and soundbites.

Herein lies the confrontation of two very poignant scenarios, the former calling forth a profound regard for continuity and the latter requiring drastic intervention. At the seam of memory and amnesia, the architecture negotiates difficult terrain: "We come here to remember and yet to forget." Has Cineleisure managed to address the duality of these issues?

Cineleisure's visual language appears to be a collage of forms that lock into each other—a skewed structural frame clad in glass that aligns itself to Grange Road and clings emphatically onto a backdrop of orthogonal solids that continue the grid of Orchard Road. Such a relationship disturbs the static conception of the external form with the skewed entity, defiantly asserting the presence of Grange Road as its major entry, violating the Orchard Road monopoly. A bright new red mast, in the spirit of Orchard Cinema's Art Deco façade, triumphantly signposts this building to the Orchard Road crowd and a blue panel mounted high beside the post awaits a new video display. The architects allude this vibrant parade of forms and colours to the roots of playful cinematic devices, the most important one being the screen. To this, the great glazed plane pays homage. It is undoubtedly the tour de force of the building's external form.

There is a refreshingly democratic air about Cineleisure. Somewhat exhibitionistic in character, it offers the outside world a peek into the looking glass. "All the world's a stage", as the architects elevate the spectacle of cinema-going to the level of the show itself.

Behind the screen, a series of escalators appears to criss-cross the space in random order. It is within this intersection of movement and display that one finds the most fertile space in Cineleisure. Far from being a neutral circulation zone, it is also a performance space. Here, an all-important kinetic element animates the space: the human body. The whole façade glows with a life not perceivable on paper. Some incredible possibilities have also cropped up as a result of this juxtaposition between the architectural elements and the cinemagoer. Each escalator is aligned at a subtly different angle from another, thus generating a series of paths that cross but do not meet. An apparent chaos challenges the audience's perception and the user's logic, making this interstitial space a true product of media-entertainment's hunger for the unexpected.

Architecture has the power to relate the past, through the present, to the future. In this case, the archi-

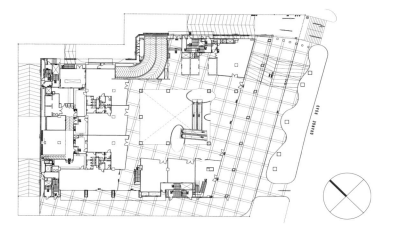

Below: **Cineleisure's visual language is a collage of forms that lock into each other. Cineleisure elevates the spectacle of cinema-going to the level of the show itself.**

tects have valiantly attempted to capture the playful spirit of the original Orchard Cinema, from reinterpreting elements like the original Art Deco post to what is now the red mast, to according abstract importance to the escalators and the screen which were sensations in their heyday.

Yet, Cineleisure is very much a building of its own time. As Diana Agrest succinctly puts it, "Design implies the transformation of sense, of memory of the known. It is not only memory, but amnesia". (1) To repeat the old Orchard would be tantamount to a pale caricature of the original. As such, the recomposition of elements is crucial to suggest their new significance to a contemporary audience.

On many counts, this is a heroic attempt to create an architecture that struggles to meet the demands of the "global". It is indeed a good opening sequence into the new millennium.

Notes

1. Diana Agrest, "On Practice, 1979" in *Agrest and Gandelsonas: Works*, (New York: Princeton Architectural Press, 1995), p. 292.

Nassim Jade condominium sits on the site of the demolished Jade House—Tiger Balm King Aw Boon Haw's villa that later became a jade museum. As a token of memory, the architects of Nassim Jade have planted a replica of the villa's cupola on a pavilion in the central courtyard. But the architects did not attempt to make any other historical references. They started largely with a clean slate.

NASSIM JADE

Chan Sau Yan
CSYA Architects
1997

BY VINCENT LIM

Right: **A system of adjustable louvred folding/sliding timber panels is used as a "permeable" skin. The louvred panels arranged in an orderly grid create a strong visual statement for the building.**

Below: **Section**

Typically, the developer called for the maximisation of land usage. CSYA achieved this to the tune of a 1.73 plot ratio and 10,000 square metres (107,639 square feet) of gross floor area (GFA) on a site of over 5,700 square metres (61,354 square feet). Thirty-nine units were apportioned from the 10,000-square-metre (107,639-square-foot) GFA, together with recreational facilities (swimming pool, gymnasium, spa and function room). While serving the developer's bottomline expectations, however, CSYA Architects also explored a range of design innovations.

Nassim Jade comprises seven blocks that follow the deflections of the site boundary. They define the

Far left: **The swimming pool evokes visions of a resort. It projects above the pool deck, a sandstone expanse, like a shimmering slab. Water flows over the extruded edges into concealed gutters.**

Left: **Entry into the central courtyard is via a spatial funnel bursting forth with dramatic flair—an assemblage of a pitched glass shard "stabbing" through the first storey slab, a pivoted mammoth green "butterfly" and hovering metal ribs.**

Bottom: **Section**

irregularly-shaped central courtyard. The swimming pool, which asserts its own skewed geometry, is the centrepiece of the courtyard. Scattered in the courtyard are palms that rise from planters in the basement through specially designed grilles.

Architecturally, the most notable contribution of the project comes from the roof design. The developer requested that the architects use copper roofing. It is tempting to cross-reference the green jade with the green copper roof. However, the roof form devised is anything but inspired by the roof of the Jade House. The shapes of the copper vault roofs are of a different set of geometric impulses; they are formed with two different roof-pitch angles joined together with an arc. The resulting figure is then

extruded along the horizontal datum.

These roof forms are no mere formal contrivances but are alternative ways of gaining attractive attic space, while complying with roof planning guidelines. By extending the rules, the architects managed to gain exhilarating internal spaces without falling back into Tudor-style roof pitches.

It is a device with parametric potential. With the use of arcs and tangents, it is possible to invent a family of quirky roof shapes based on permutations of angle, length and curvature. Each permutation may be tailored to meet specific needs; each situation dependent on the spatial requirement below the roof. Not least, the device provides a geometric way of pulling form, function and space into agreement. Some parts of the roof mass are

carved out to create roof terraces.

Another notable architectural feature is the system of adjustable louvred folding/sliding timber panels devised as a "permeable" skin. Porous, and delicate, the panels (along with the perforated screens for the service stacks) create a lively contrast to the concrete boxes. More importantly, they filter the sun's glare and provide privacy for the occupants.

"Abelia Apartments is a restrained and controlled version of architect Tang Guan Bee's repertoire. Forms are not merely autonomous. The relationship between form and function has been much more tightly interwoven, resulting in a self-assured building that is almost contemptuous of its pretentious, elaborately dressed-up post-Mod neighbours. It is more to do with principles than pastiche."

— *Tan Hock Beng*

ABELIA APARTMENTS

Tangguanbee Architects
1992

Right: **Section**

Below: **Voids and double-volume garden terraces connect levels spatially, while a concrete pergola adds another layer to the uppermost unit.**

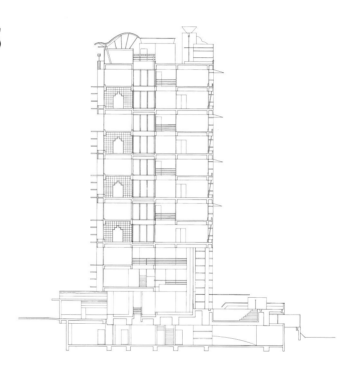

Located in the upmarket residential district of Ardmore Park, Abelia Apartments is a small development in comparison to its towering neighbours. Consisting of five maisonettes, the 12-storey building attempts to address the issue of tropicality through a modernist idiom.

The main intention in the design was to reinterpret the traditional responses to the tropical climate in a manner compatible with high-rise living. The result is an architecture of layers, realised both on plan and in the fenestration. For the latter, screens shade glazed openings and recessed planes and curves play against the main building surfaces while planter boxes create yet another layer in the elevations. On plan, voids and double-volume garden terraces connect levels spatially while a concrete pergola adds another layer to the uppermost unit.

The idea of layering is not new. It is part of the local vernacular in Southeast Asia. What Tang Guan Bee has attempted to do is to update these ideas employing modern materials, forms and textures.

The effort to craft a unique tower that responds to the tropical climate is commendable. Cross-ventilation is an important determinant of design, resulting in the units having interconnected voids and double-height garden terraces. These garden terraces provide a delightful realm that mediates the inside and outside. Dining spaces look into these terraces. Glass façades are also set back to achieve

well shaded internal spaces. Light casts patterned shadows at different times of the day. Lattice screens and sun-shading pergolas act as vertical landscape features, allowing climbing plants to provide greenery and form an additional layer of shading.

The design approach helped the architect to reconcile modern high-rise living with the need to respond to the tropical climate. The extensive use of glass to capture panoramic views—

Left: **The five maisonettes at Abelia Apartments are broken up to create three types of dwellings, each with its own intrinsic identity.**

Above: **This is an architecture of layers, realised both on plan and in the fenestration. Screens shade glazed openings and recessed planes and curves play against the main building surfaces.**

with a "base", "body" and "capital". Carrying the idea of differentiation further, each elevation is treated differently, reflecting the internal arrangement within each dwelling. Some are playful, others restrained. Together, they offer alternatives to the conventional treatment of high-rise buildings as uniform slab-blocks.

The garden terraces within each apartment are planted with palm trees. Abundant planting fills the planter boxes at each level and the ground level is heavily landscaped. The landscaping in this project is an indispensable element in the attempt to realise a truly tropical high-rise. "This, together with the architecture of layers and lyrical treatment of the façades", says Tang Guan Bee, "presents a contemporary solution to the current quest for a viable high-rise architecture with a tropical identity."

a norm in high-rise design—had to be tempered with the need for shade and shelter from the elements. Layering offered the opportunity to accommodate what at first appeared to be conflicting and unresolvable demands.

On a subtler level, the project also provided Tang Guan Bee with an opportunity to question some entrenched attitudes concerning the styling of high-rise architecture. Instead of a uniform treatment for all

the units, the five maisonettes were broken up to create three types of dwellings, each with its own intrinsic identity. Thus the units are physically seen as individual entities, supporting the architect's belief that each home should be seen as an individual domain. And yet, as a result of their common vocabulary, they also form part of a cohesive whole.

The result is a building of parts in proportion to each other—in effect,

The telegenic quality of The Heeren allows it to compete for attention with the decorative pyramids of Ngee Ann City and the glass cone of Wheelock Place, among others. It is about one-upmanship with image when all else architecturally is nearly equal.

THE HEEREN

Architects 61 Pte Ltd
1996

BY VINCENT LIM

Below: **Section**

Right: **A series of subtractive geometric operations are performed on the square-plan tower.**

In designing a commercial office tower, the primary requirement for a flexible open plan is the lowest common denominator. It is generic. What do you say after your 80 percent floor plan efficiency is achieved, the layout efficacy of the mechanical services solved thoroughly and the structure flogged to effectively span more width?

The office tower design of The Heeren follows much of that model. It is a frame structure that frees columns from the lettable spaces. The service core, predictably, is located in the centre. It is Cartesian logic, pure and simple—a square plan with five bays of 6.6 metres (21.7 feet) on each side. But it has an aesthetic agenda.

The project is strongly characterised by its subtracted form. The corners of the tower are chamfered such that the shape of the building changes as it ascends. At roughly the mid-height of the tower, the square is cut at one corner, subsequently reduced to a hexagon and finally transformed to a cruciform at the top two storeys. A skeleton is extracted from the underlying Cartesian grid to form a cage around the transformed mass. The result of this geometrical play is a building that is not just a banal extruded plan.

The image of the building by night is enchanting. Uplighters delineate the bottom flanges of the skeletal frame and wash the surfaces of the

tower. The clever lighting emphasises vividly the depth and space between cage and subtracted mass to create a luminous spectacle. Light and shadow take naturally to the carved out voids.

The Heeren development comprises also a shopping component. It employs the standard solution of the shopping-in-podium and office-in-tower model. Like other malls along Orchard Road, shops in The Heeren face a central atrium, characteristically topped with a skylight. Unlike other Orchard Road malls, however, The Heeren's atrium is circular and is fed, uncharacteristically, by diagonal corridors. The diagonal corridors feed off the two corner entrances facing Orchard Road. The diagonal corridor is possibly more effective in channelling pedestrians into the building by going with the directional flow of the mall. For the pedestrian, it is a slight shift in angle, instead of a 90-degree turn to filter in and out of the building.

Except for this innovative circulation route and the geometric treatment of the tower, much of the architecture of The Heeren follows formula, to optimise real estate yields. The efficient office tower design achieves the maximum floor area. The same bottom-line design mindset was applied to the shopping podium, as

evidenced by the literal echoing of the curved Cairnhill Road boundary for the building's setback limit along that edge. This echo may be pragmatic but it causes a break between the architectural language of podium and tower. The subtraction of a regular polygon game for the tower is not operated on the podium design. The latter, with its curved edge, speaks more of a plastic language, especially with the weighty granite cladding.

That plastic quality, together with its proportions, gives the podium, experienced at street level, an overwhelming presence. Neither the overlapping pattern on the façade nor the aluminium pergola (that helps dissolve the podium roofline) has any substantial mitigating effect. The breaking of the building's corner at Orchard/Cairnhill Roads for a glass box to pop out has some success in reducing the heaviness of the podium.

The Heeren is an urbane offering, though. Appended to the side next to Yen San Building is a metal and glass pavilion that houses an alfresco cafe. It draws activity out to the exterior onto what is a mere setback strip between buildings. The café is an attractive space for that much needed respite from the busy pedestrian mall.

Above: **At roughly the mid-height of the tower, the square plan is cut at one corner, subsequently reduced to a hexagon and finally transformed to a cruciform at the top two storeys.**

Left: **A skeleton is extracted from the underlying Cartesian grid to form a cage around the transformed mass.**

The Goei House involves the rebuilding of a terrace house in the Emerald Hill Conservation Area. Architect Chan Soo Khian chose not to retain the existing façade or indeed any of the interior. Everything is first erased and memory is then evoked to recreate a new house that embodies the spirit of the past and yet is not a literal copy.

GOEI HOUSE

**Chan Soo Khian .
SCDA Architects
1997**

SINGAPORE: ARCHITECTURE OF A GLOBAL CITY

76

Top: **Section**

Right: **The focus of 95 Emerald Hill is a huge central atrium with two mature trees at the centre and a limestone platform surrounded by a green tiled pool.**

Below: **Roof plan**

Bottom: **Second storey plan**

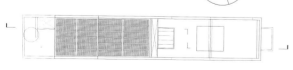

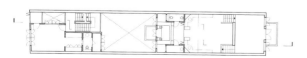

The entrance to the house has a hierarchy of privacy that draws precedence from the traditional shophouse form. It was most often the case that one entered a reception room or a first-storey shop and directly ahead would be a wall. Progress to the rear of the dwelling would not be along a central axis. Instead one would move either to right or left. Facing the entrance would be a wall which would delay the view of the interior and satisfy basic *feng shui* requirements.

Chan Soo Khian similarly delays the experience of the interior. From the lobby, one either moves to the right to ascend to the reception room or to the left to descend to a basement studio/office.

The focus of 95 Emerald Hill is a huge central atrium, far larger than the traditional air-well. It is like a public space, with two mature trees at the centre and a limestone platform surrounded by a green

tiled pool with a weir introducing the sound of water. The space could accommodate a small pavement cafeteria. It could be a space for a party under the stars, a stage, a theatre, a playground... It is as if the house has been turned inside out and a public space introduced indoors—a sort of inversion. Such ambiguities in the purpose of space have always existed in the shophouse form. The relationship of inside and outside and the interchangeability of the two is very much part of the design of an urban house in the tropics.

The house is divided into front and rear by the central atrium. The front of the house follows the profile of the gable roofs along the street and the interior makes references to the traditional shophouse with the insertion of stonework and timber fanlights above the living room doorways. The rear block assumes a more contemporary language, with the introduction of open steel and wood staircases and flat trellised roofs. The front half has, above the basement studio and princi-

Left: The three bedrooms have attached dressing rooms and bathrooms overlooking the central space. One can bathe and simultaneously have a view of the atrium activities.

Below: The atrium of the house is covered by a steel and timber pergola, which filters sunlight and casts shadows on the party walls. Above the pergola is a retractable glazed roof.

Bottom: The Goei House viewed from the entrance at dusk.

pal reception room, a double-height master bedroom suite with walk-in closets and a large jacuzzi set amid indoor landscaping and a second, smaller bedroom. The rear half has a kitchen and a servant quarters and two self-contained guest suites at second and third storey levels overlooking a second smaller airwell.

The external naturally-ventilated staircase at the rear ascends to a roof garden. This roof terrace maximises the potential of space in the inner city. Climbing to the roof in the evening, one has dramatic views of the city skyline and the distant hum of the commercial life accompanied by evening breezes.

The principal rooms look into the atrium and the three bedrooms have attached dressing rooms and bathrooms overlooking the central space. Behind fixed timber slate and sandblasted glass, one can bathe and yet simultaneously have a view of the atrium activities. The ambiguity of such in-between spaces is a recurring theme in Asian architecture.

The house at 77 Emerald Hill was built for towkay Low Koon Yee in 1925. The architect was R.T. Rajoo, who practised in Singapore between 1913 and 1920. Low Koon Yee belonged to a well-established Teochew Straits Chinese family. His father, Low Ah Jit, who was born in China, came to Singapore at the age of thirty and built a substantial business empire.

77 EMERALD HILL

Gilbert Osuga
KKS Consultants and
Designers Pte Ltd
1994

On the front elevation of the first storey, ceramic tiles depict pheasants in flight. Original canvas awnings operated by ropes and pulleys have been restored above the second-storey windows.

The house on 77 Emerald Hill was one of a terrace block comprising numbers 71 to 85 designed by Rajoo for Low Koon Yee. In all, Low owned seventeen houses, from numbers 53 to 85.

No. 77 was at one time linked by doors in the party walls to numbers 79 and 75. One explanation is that the original owner had a number of wives, as was common at the turn of century, and he accommodated them in adjoining houses. No. 77 is said to have been the house of his second wife. Chinese calligraphy painted on the original doors read "Fragrant breezes flowing into the Golden House" and indeed, the house does enjoy most pleasant cooling winds. It is at the very top of Emerald Hill and the large jasmine tree in the garden is probably as old as the house itself.

Low Koon Yee and his brother, Low Cheang Yee, carried on their father's business until 1923, when Low Koon Yee became sole proprietor. His son, Low Peng Soy, later managed the company (Lee 1984). He went on to become a successful cinema owner and operated the Roxy Theatre in East Coast Road in 1924.

The present owner of 77 Emerald Hill is Richard Helfer, the executive director of Raffles Hotel International & Resorts, who acquired the house in 1990. The house has been restored with loving care. It is not as deep as some houses in the street and it does not have the lightwell typical of most shophouses. At the rear is a partly-covered yard. To compensate for the

Left: **No. 77 Emerald Hill has been restored with great care and regard for historical accuracy.**

Below: **A cast-iron balustrade depicting hunting scenes is displayed in the rear patio.**

lack of depth, this house and numbers 79 to 81 are approximately 500 millimetres (20 inches) wider than other shophouses on Emerald Hill.

The original marble floor in the front reception area was retained, as were all the floor tiles in the rear and private part of the first storey. A tiled dado, which runs around the walls to a height of about 900 millimetres (36 inches), has also been faithfully restored. Original electrical fuse boxes made by Verity's Ltd, London, were likewise retained.

On the front elevation of the first storey, ceramic tiles depict pheasants in flight. Original canvas awnings, operated by ropes and pulleys, have been restored above the windows on the second storey.

Sensitive adaptations have been incorporated in the house by the present owner. Two windows that did not adequately light the rear of the house have been replaced by folding timber panelled doors which open onto a rear yard paved with Cantonese terracotta tiles. A breakfast area and kitchen open directly to this yard, with bamboo "chick blinds" forming the walls.

The scale of this patio is wonderful; a private court has been created for breakfast alfresco, a barbecue or pre-dinner drinks under the stars. Along one side of this patio is an *objet trouvé*, a cast-iron balustrade depicting hunting scenes fabricated by Walter MacFarlane and Co. of Glasgow.

At second-storey level, the cellular plan has been retained with the integration of stained glass screens from Beijing, which allow filtered light to penetrate the interior, adding to the layered quality of light and shade. The restoration of 77 Emerald Hill has enhanced this layered quality, which is the hallmark of traditional shophouse architecture.

The 158 Emerald Hill project, comprising three storeys and a basement, was an exercise in conserving a traditional terrace house on Emerald Hill Road. The owners were drawn to the area for its distinctive ambience. The purchase was also prompted by a hint of nostalgia, one of the owners having Peranakan roots and Emerald Hill Road being synonymous with Peranakan culture.

158 EMERALD HILL

Han Yip Lee Associates
1998

BY CHEW I-JIN

The terrace house at 158 Emerald Hill is located at the "top" end of Emerald Hill Road. It is characterised by an open verandah fronting the street and a steeply sloping site so that while the front façade is two storeys high, the rear accommodates basement level rooms, a utility area and a yard which acts as a buffer to the noise generated by traffic along the Central Expressway. The lot is 5.5-metre (18-foot) wide and is approximately 35 metres (115 feet) long. The original house, built in 1925 and designed by architects Lim and Seah, was neither wide enough nor deep enough to incorporate an internal courtyard, which is characteristic of so many shophouses on this street.

The new programme, which involved increasing the floor area by over one and a half times the original floor area, called for an inventive solution and one that did not involve strict adherence to its original plan. In contrast to projects that conscientiously preserve the mouldings, details and traditional spatial arrangements of the old shophouse, the circulation pattern, services and architectural language of 158 Emerald Hill were altered. To purists, there was not much to the internal character of the exist-

ing house to be preserved. It lacked the otherwise characteristic deep plan, traditional courtyard and spatial arrangements and had already undergone some ad hoc changes and makeshift partitions to suit the needs of the previous occupants.

The architects, Han Yip Lee Associates, were basically left with the task of reconfiguring the spaces between the two party walls while leaving the front façade intact. The solution involved reconstructing everything from the front façade inwards, although the ceiling heights, floor levels and roof of the original house were reinstated. A three-storey rear extension was incorporated to provide a service core and additional

rooms. This effectively doubled the footprint of the house while preserving a 1.5-metre (4.9-foot) wide slot at the rear of the house between the new extension and one of the party walls. This distinctly "modern" glass and reinforced concrete intervention is topped by a flat roof.

Despite the fact that this terrace house is one of a series in a block with the same elevational treatment, it asserts its own identity through its rich golden yellow painted façade, in contrast to the white or pastel hues of its neighbours.

The intimate verandah affords the house rare privacy and allows the front doors and casements to be open when the house is occupied. One can view

the gate from the kitchen deep in the house. Similarly, a view of the interior unfolds from the verandah, especially at night, when the glow of lights from within floods the exterior.

The formality and symmetry of the front façade has been addressed by mirroring it in the symmetrically planned forecourt and the wall that defines the interior end of the living room. The internal "screen" wall which confronts one on entry, is on axis with the entrance and marks the transition from street level to the raised heart of the building. It also serves as a screen for privacy and contains the less formal elements behind. This is a modern statement which boldly stretches the envelope of "conservation".

Above: **The architects' intention was to start with a simple structural layout and to achieve poetic results without losing sight of practicality. The variety and richness attained is no small achievement when working within the constraints of a 5.5-metre (18-foot) wide lot.**

Opposite left: **Walking along Emerald Hill Road, one barely has a glimpse of the interior worlds behind the preserved and untouched façades. This is characteristic of the place and cultures which have inhabited it: inward-looking and conservative. The forms are now being tested, within the constraints of conservation, to see if they can be adapted to contemporary living.**

Opposite right: **One entering the house is struck by the rich colours and the layering of spaces visible behind the screen wall that defines the edge of the living room.**

At 62 Emerald Hill, Wong Mun Summ and Richard Hassell of WoHa Designs have entirely stripped the interior of the terraced shophouse, leaving two parallel walls within which they have choreographed a lifestyle for the client, uninhibited by the forms or spatial qualities of the past.

62 EMERALD HILL

WoHa Designs and WH Architects
1998

There is a dramatic contrast in scale between the interior and exterior of the terraced shophouse.

Wong Mun Summ graduated from the School of Architecture at the National University of Singapore in 1989. In his pre-final year, he won a student prize in a national competition for the design of City 2000, which showed his concern for the "unsentimental analysis of the existing city fabric" and "a preference for clearly expressed formal solutions". Both of these concerns are addressed in his later works.

For a brief period in his "year-out" from architectural school, Wong was an intern at William Lim Associates and later, with Kerry Hill Architects (KHA). Upon graduation, he returned to Kerry Hill's practice and worked on several of the Aman resorts designed by KHA in the early 1990s, including the Datai in Langkawi and the Serai Resort in Bali.

Australian Richard Hassell, a graduate of the University of Western Australia, joined KHA at the same time. In 1994, Wong and Hassell left KHA and set up WoHa Designs, a regional design consultancy to explore all aspects of environmental design. In 1998, they established WH

Architects, a Singapore registered architectural practice.

"I don't believe in conservation!", says Wong Mun Summ. "I think it often inhibits creativity. The Urban Redevelopment Authority (URA) establishes guidelines and many architects simply adhere to these without any attempt to radically rethink the purpose or the internal arrangements of a building. It is so boring."

WoHa Designs has done some radical rethinking at 62 Emerald Hill, where a "stage" is created at the centre of the house, detached from the walls. Above is the master bedroom and one floor above that is an internal "roof terrace" looking into a triple height void above the dining area—much like a gallery in the upper stalls of a theatre. Beyond this is an outdoor courtyard with a swimming pool and further to the rear of the site is the kitchen and a guest annex.

When one steps through the entrance, there is a silence and remoteness from the city that is at first unnerving. As one enters from the street, there is a dramatic change of scale. The interior is theatrical; it is like a small urban setting within the

house which invites performances of familiar daily rituals, breakfast on the terrace and dinner under the stars, overlooked by the windows of the rear annex. The lighting further enhances the drama of the interior, with numerous combinations of uplighters and downlighters.

"We purposefully direct the attention of urban houses inwards", says Hassell. "If you look outside your window in any Asian city, the view is going to change frequently and usually not for the better. It's chaotic out there, a beautiful vista that has determined the orientation of a house might be blocked by a monstrous tower block a year later. We believe you can do so little to influence what goes on outside the house that it is important to create an interior over which the owner has complete control. So our houses look inward."

As both admit, however, this is not something that will necessarily be a permanent feature of their work. "But one thing that we both focused upon when working on resort hotels", says Wong, "is the way a special character is created. Similarly, with urban houses, there is a need to give them privacy and a special ambience."

Top: **There is a silence and remoteness from the city as one enters from the street.**

Centre: **The interior of the terraced shophouse has been stripped, leaving parallel walls within which the architects have devised a plan uninhibited by the former internal structure.**

Bottom: **A "stage" is created at the centre of the house, detached from the party wall. Lighting enhances the theatrical ambience.**

The emphasis on the verticality of major structural elements gives Scotts 28 condominium a slender appearance. In contrast, window transoms, which function as shading elements, are expressed as lighter horizontal elements.

SCOTTS 28

Architects 61
1998

Architects 61's (A61) contribution to mega projects in Singapore has meant an accumulation of knowledge and experience. Now the practice has its own definable product and the firm can lay claim to expertise in various spheres, including "performance wall" design and high-rise luxury condominiums. In the design of residential projects, the firm recognises the balance between the developer-clients'

requirement to maximise saleable floor areas and the end-users' demand for an increasingly sophisticated and gracious living environment.

A61 has developed a niche market in the design of what might be termed "the super condo"—a residential development of extraordinary exclusivity and luxury, utilising carefully selected materials of a very high quality, generously proportioned interiors and resort-like landscaping. Scotts 28 is in this category. It exhibits a consistent modern architectural language guided by function and technology.

Completed in December 1998,

Scotts 28 is a 30-storey condominium in the very heart of the Scotts Road residential area close to the principal retail artery of the island. A swimming pool, gymnasium and indoor tennis court are dovetailed into the confined urban space adjacent to the tower. Scotts 28 has its main entrance at Scotts Road and a secondary exit/entrance off Cairnhill Road.

The tower plan has a high level of fragmentation, with a dog-leg configuration in response to the sharply tapering site. This results in three units on each floor facing Scotts Road and two units set at right angles,

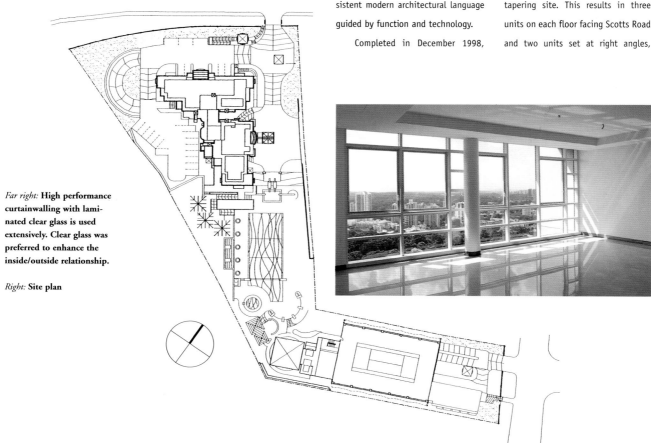

Far right: **High performance curtainwalling with laminated clear glass is used extensively. Clear glass was preferred to enhance the inside/outside relationship.**

Right: **Site plan**

Above: **The tower has a high level of fragmentation in response to the site configuration. This results in three units on each floor facing Scotts Road and two units set at right angles, with the stair and lift core forming a linking element.**

Left: **Scotts 28 is a 30-storey condominium in the very heart of the Scotts Road residential area close to Orchard Road.**

with the stair and lift core forming a linking element. Above the 27th storey are larger units and at the 30th storey are two penthouse suites with access to private roof gardens. The design employs a highly articulated plan arrangement with a coherent expression on the façades of the functional elements.

A61's director and principal designer on the project, Michael Ngu, has worked with I.M. Pei and Kohn Pederson Fox (KPF) in New York. He has specific experience on the design, design development and architectural/technical detailing of exterior cladding. This is particularly relevant in the case of the design of the Scotts 28 tower, which utilises an elegant modern language, with careful atten-

tion given to the proportion of the architectural elements of the façades.

High performance curtainwalling with laminated clear glass is used extensively for all the living spaces. Clear glass was preferred in order to give transparency and to enhance the inside/outside relationship in this unique "wooded" setting in the city centre.

There are certain themes at work in this design that I identified in an earlier project by Mok Wei Wei for the Lem House (pages 206–207). Paterson Edge explores the tension of living in the city, the desire for recognition and yet to be anonymous, the need for concealment and the simultaneous wish for exposure, to be remote and yet accessible.

PATERSON EDGE

Mok Wei Wei.
William Lim Associates
1999

A roof top lap-pool is literally pushed to the limit, with a glass wall at the end of the pool giving swimmers a view of the city twelve storeys below.

Paterson Road is connected at right angles to Singapore's principal shopping artery, Orchard Road, where millions of locals and tourists flock to consume contemporary fashion. The wide promenades which flank both sides of Orchard Road are thronged with pedestrians.

Considering its proximity to this activity, Paterson Road has a significantly different ambience. Traffic engineers have contrived to relegate it to a link road: a fast six-lane, dual carriageway connector, which slices through an area of low rise bungalows edged by a narrow sidewalk.

Paterson Edge is located along this road. The site of the apartment block has an extremely narrow rectangular configuration—100 metres (328 feet) long by 8 metres (26 feet) wide—running parallel to the highway. And it occurs at the intersection of two very different urban morphologies. It is this difference which Mok has exploited in the plan form.

The architectural language of the two principal elevations reinforces this duality. Facing east, a transparent fili-gree of glass reveals the lifestyle of the inhabitants to the gaze of passing commuters, yet they are simultaneously remote and inaccessible. The notion of "edge" is suggested by this curtain wall, stretched taut along the boundary and viewed through a screen of mature rain trees.

The west facing elevation overlooks the established low-rise residential area of One Tree Hill. Here, the architectural response is altogether more planar and appropriately layered, with the additional attribute of shielding the building from the setting sun and accommodating service ducts.

There are certain themes at work in this design that I identified in an earlier project by Mok for the Lem House (see pages 206–207 and *The Urban Asian House*, Powell, 1998). The tension of living in the city is explored, as well as the desire for recognition and yet to be anonymous, the need for concealment and the simul-taneous wish for exposure, to be remote and yet accessible. We see it in the way celebrities court public-ity and yet complain of intrusion into their privacy, how they resent invasion by the paparazzi and yet desire to be in the spotlight.

The roof design dramatically, almost dangerously, expresses the adrenalin-pumping pleasure of "life at the edge". A roof top lap-pool is literally "pushed to the limit", with water cascading over the parapet and a glass wall at the end of the pool giving swimmers a view of the city 12 storeys below.

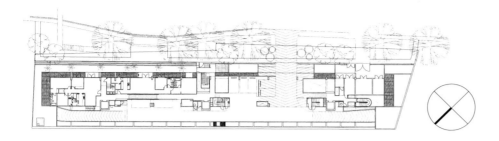

Left: **First storey plan**

Bottom left: **Facing east, a transparent filigree of glass reveals the lifestyle of the inhabitants to the gaze of passing commuters.**

Bottom right: **The west facing elevation overlooks the low-rise residential area of One Tree Hill. Here, the architectural response is altogether more planar and appropriately layered.**

chapter 4

HOLLAND ROAD
AND
GRANGE ROAD

The Morley Road House is, conceptually, a group of pavilions. A sequence of movement is choreographed along a processional path working from a formal reception space to a formal dining space and eventually to a private entertainment space. All of these pavilions are arranged around a courtyard.

MORLEY ROAD HOUSE

Mok Wei Wei .
William Lim Associates
1998

Opposite: **The underlying ideas in the Morley Road House are derived from the movement and the framing of views within a Chinese garden in Suchow.**

Right: **First storey plan**

Page 88: **Eu House I**

Page 89: **Crescent Girls School**

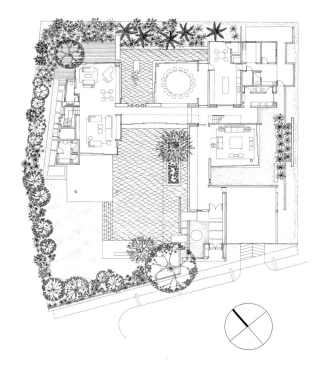

articulating the sequence of spaces.

The architectural language used to convey the ensuing narrative is distinctly modern: white planar surfaces are juxtaposed alongside grey granite walls and aluminium framed, clear glazed fenestration. Flat concrete roofs, supported on slender circular reinforced concrete columns, project beyond the walls of the house. Interior floors are off-white marble.

The architecture is experienced as choreographed and edited episodes of compression and expansion, of light and shade, of linear spaces and soaring volumes. There are thresholds of privacy and a structured sequence of spaces with framed views and a continuous narrative capable of multiple interpretations.

The entrance is a tightly constructed space—a door opening from the public road leads directly to a small open-to-sky courtyard. A second door gives access to the lobby but one's view is restricted by a transverse wall. Two steps to the left and a long, narrow gallery is revealed, terminating in a distant framed view of the garden.

The device of moving around the edge, I would suggest, has its origin in the southern Chinese courtyard house typology. Morley Road House follows closely that typology, with its entrance placed in the southern corner of the roughly square site.

Mok Wei Wei agrees, but argues that the underlying ideas in the Morley Road House are more specifically derived from the movement and the framing of views within a Chinese garden, in particular a garden with which he is familiar in Suchow. In the Morley Road House, Mok builds upon these ideas, working with landscape architect Martin Palleros. The stone walls which define the garden become part of the architecture, assisting in

Above left and right:
The ingress of sunlight announces a two-storey-high reception space—a square pavilion with full-height glazing on its eastern and southern facades. This well-proportioned pavilion is furnished with classical Chinese chairs and a low marble table.

A linear roof light bathes the left wall and a low marble bench runs the full length of the gallery, accentuating the single-point perspective.

Advancing along this axis, the visitor first encounters a vertical slot of glazing on the right, which gives a glimpse of a bamboo garden with a cool grey pebble floor. Almost immediately, the ingress of sunlight announces a two-storey-high reception space—a square pavilion with full-height glazing on its eastern and southern façades. This well-proportioned pavilion is furnished with classical Chinese chairs and a low marble table. A horizontal painting by Chen Kezhan dominates one high wall. The space, with a muted palette of white, russet brown and olive, leaves a lasting impression of calm and tranquillity. The interior space flows out into the garden, where a stone seat is carefully placed to permit a place for contemplation.

Turning left at the end of the gallery, a new spatial experience is revealed: another gallery—on this occasion, a two-storey-high linear space—overlooked by a balcony, culminates in a horizontally striated grey stone wall. Here, there is a moment of indecision, for the spatial sequence can be interrupted and a deviation made to the dining pavilion, a second high, square space with a central roof light. This pavilion also has glazed walls and is flanked by cool, dark fish ponds and a small fountain. A long horizontal aperture in one wall reorientates the narrative back to the primary route.

The interest now focuses on the garden. The calm blue-grey water of the pool in the central courtyard and a willow tree become part of the carefully constructed narrative. A vista unfolds, but for the present, it is tan-

Above left: **The living room opens on the south side of the house to a splendid double-height pavilion open on three sides, overlooking the garden.**

Above right: **A lasting memory of the house is of a compressed space focusing upon the willow tree overhanging the pool.**

talisingly held at a distance by the pool in the foreground. One crosses a threshold into the private domain of the house—the book-lined walls of the library and the living area. The muted palette of colours employed thus far has given continuity to the unfolding narrative. Now, primary colours are sparingly introduced.

The living room opens on the south side of the house to a splendid double-height pavilion open on three sides that overlook the garden. But once again, the narrative can be interrupted and its culmination delayed by diverting to a quiet timber deck outside the library and encompassed by foliage, where there is a momentary feeling of solitude.

It now remains to complete the journey. Stepping out to a turfed area beyond the living room and skirting the pool, one turns to contemplate for the first time, a panoramic view of the south facing façade of the house. This is a dramatic and exhilarating climax, for the whole architectural composition is revealed in the reflective surface of the pool. A stone seat is almost casually located at this very spot—a place to sit at the end of the day.

Retracing this route is to experience a reverse reading of this spatial sequence or alternatively, one can return directly via an opening in the grey granite wall to the starting point of the journey, the entrance court. The final image is of compressed space focusing upon the willow tree overhanging the pool.

In the Morley Road House, there is a convergence of memories and connections to cultural roots in a residence, which simultaneously advances the modernist paradigm.

Richard Meier's work is instantly recognisable by its trademark white panels and the systematic grid which covers elevations and plans. It is remarkable how every element in the design is made to conform to this geometry and the precision of structural joints and material finishes is flawless.

  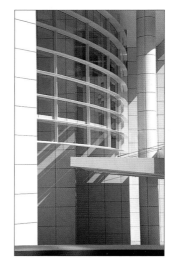 

94

CAMDEN MEDICAL CENTRE

DP Architects Pte Ltd
Design Consultant:
Richard Meier Architect
1999

Top from left to right: **The control that Meier exerts over every component, the meticulous intersection of construction joints, the layering of planes and the limited palette of materials are all present here.**

Opposite: **The entrance area of the Camden Medical Centre has tall open spaces and a handicapped access ramp is used sculpturally.**

The Camden Medical Centre, developed by Pontiac Land Pte Ltd, is an elegant 18-storey cylindrical building surrounded by tropical landscaping. Designed by American architect Richard Meier, the centre offers tenants from selected areas of medical specialisation an opportunity to establish their operations in a landmark building at the intersection of Orchard Boulevard and Grange Road, on the western edge of the city. The local architect for the project was DP Architects Pte Ltd, one of Singapore's largest multi-discipli-

nary practices and winner of numerous SIA and CIDB Awards.

Richard Meier is widely recognised as one of the major architects of the latter part of the 20th century. He was a member of the famed "New York Five", which also included Peter Eisenman, Michael Graves, John Hedjuk and Charles Gwathmey, who were credited with the revival of modern architecture in the United States in the 1960s. Their early work was disseminated by Kenneth Frampton and Colin Rowe in *Five Architects*, an influential book pub-

lished in 1972. Meier went on to win the Pritzker Prize for Architecture.

The Camden Medical Centre was conceived in 1990. The circular form of the tower strongly resembles earlier Meier designs, most notably the Madison Square Garden Redevelopment proposal of 1987 and an office building for a site in Frankfurt in 1989. When first submitted, the Camden Medical Centre provoked objections from surrounding residents; I was one of the Planning Appeal Inspectors who rejected their appeal. Nevertheless, the plans did go through

several modifications before it commenced on site and the tower, as built, is far more refined than the original.

Richard Meier's work is instantly recognisable by its trademark white panels and the systematic grid which covers elevations and plans. It is remarkable how every element in the design is made to conform to this geometry and the precision of structural joints and material finishes is quite flawless. This characteristic of Meier's architecture has not always been greeted with affection; indeed, it has been said that it displays a lack of concern for the inhabitants. But this is not true of the Camden Medical Centre, where the architecture conveys a restful and calm ambience appropriate for its purpose as a hospital.

The entrance area of the tower has tall open spaces and a handicapped access ramp is used sculpturally. Both are elements which are familiar in Meier's vocabulary. The control that Meier exerts over every component, the meticulous intersection of construction joints, the layering of planes and the limited palette of materials are all present here, giving physical expression to Meier's guiding principles "that the responsibility of an architect is really to create a sense of order, a sense of place, a sense of relationships".

Crescent Girls School in Tanglin Road was completed in 1993. The design marked the beginning of a new phase in the architecture of government schools and the advent of "single session" secondary schools. It was constructed shortly after the publication of a new Concept Plan for the island and *Living the Next Lap*, a book which articulated the vision of the second-generation political leaders in post-independent Singapore.

CRESCENT GIRLS SCHOOL

PWD Consultants Pte Ltd
1993

Below: **First storey plan**

Right: **A duality exists between the outside walls, which express protection, and the inside façades, which express openness, exuberance and delight.**

In 2000, the Crescent Girls School campus acquired a feeling of permanence and nurtured its established traditions. The landscape has matured and everywhere, there are signs of personalisation. The school has a distinct identity, from the mature garden beyond the entrance foyer to the pottery exhibits located at various nodes to the hydroponics laboratory adjacent to the science block. The message is transmitted strongly of a school which is building upon tradition while embracing change.

The framework for this sense of identity was firmly established in the original layout which took advantage of the sloping topography of the site. The experience of moving through the school is carefully orchestrated. The architect has choreographed a series of spatial experiences. The project has

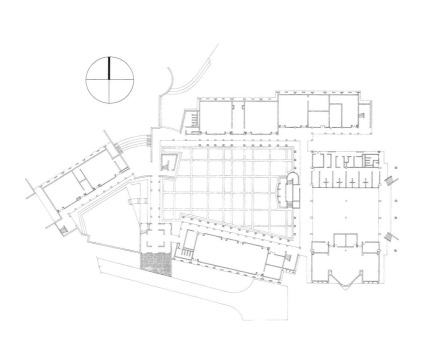

the imagery of a small town with an interplay of solid and void, street and square, paths and gateways, landmarks and nodes.

The school is compactly designed, with the main assembly space in the form of a paved "plaza" well shaded by four-storey blocks on two sides and the multi-purpose hall on a third side. Sufficient voids in these perimeter blocks enable gentle breezes to penetrate the main square.

A consistent language of form is found throughout, reinforced by a carefully selected palette of colours. A duality exists between the outside walls, which express protection, and the inside façades, which express openness, exuberance and delight. The architecture of the parade square has the feeling of a civic space as well as a hint of grandeur, with its tall circular red columns and the flat arched entry from the administration block.

Some elements in the architectural language appear to have been inspired by the work of Italian architect Aldo Rossi. A Rossi-like drum is used as a vertical circulation element; it becomes a "tower of the winds", inducing an upward movement of air. Its form works admirably as a hinge when two or more blocks are brought together. This element was to find its way into several schools designed in the 1990s.

The school works well with the existing topography which slopes gently from the north to the south. Ramps and stairs go beyond mere utility and assist in giving variety to the spatial experiences. The interplay of levels is one of the positive aspects of the design and can be seen as a forerunner of several "single session" secondary school designs.

When it was completed in 1993, Crescent Girls School created a new benchmark in terms of environmental quality. Numerous features within the building have found their way into the PWD repertoire of architectural strategies.

Above and below: **The architecture of the parade square has the feeling of a civic space and a hint of grandeur with its tall circular red columns.**

Left: **Some elements in the architectural language appear to have been inspired by the work of Italian architect Aldo Rossi.**

Stamford Raffles established a small experimental Botanic Gardens on the lower slopes of Government Hill in 1822–23, in which the commercial possibilities of agricultural products were tested. The garden fell into disuse in 1829 but was resurrected in 1836–46.

BURKILL HALL

PWD Consultants Pte Ltd
1992

Above: **This upper verandah, open on three sides, formed the main living area of the house and enjoys natural cross-ventilation.**

Below: **Section**

In 1859, the Botanic Gardens was relocated to the present site, off Cluny Road. From then until 1875, Lawrence Niven supervised the layout of botanical specimens. In 1877, rubber plants were imported from Kew Gardens in Britain and in 1888, Henry Nicholas Ridley pioneered the rubber industry in Malaya and devised a method of tapping the tree without damaging it (Turnbull 1977).

Burkill Hall was built in 1866. It was home for several of the gardens' directors, including Nathaniel Cantley (1882–87), Henry N. Ridley (1888–1912), I.H. Burkill (1913–25) and his son H.M. Burkill (1957–69), after whom the house is named (Edwards and Keys 1988). The build-

ing was named a Preservation of Monuments Board Historical Landmark on 3 October 1992.

The house was constructed in a simple and elegant style, with a high-hipped roof with a short ridge, deep overhanging eaves, a broad verandah under the extended eaves and living spaces with lofty ceilings. This was typical of early bungalows in Singapore.

Houses built during this period were influenced by the English tradition but were varied to suit the tropical climate. Typically, the houses were square and compact, with plain plastered walls.

Burkill Hall has these very same features. The plan view of the house

was symmetrical and divided into three bays, with the front entrance on the central axis. Following the English custom, the drawing room and bedrooms were on the first floor. Before the introduction of piped water and modern sanitation, bathrooms were located on the ground floor, accessible from the bedrooms or nursery by separate stairs. Later, bathrooms were added on the second storey and the first-storey bathroom was enclosed and converted to store rooms.

The original ground floor was an open space, with a staircase, two bathrooms and a store room occupying the four corners. In later years, the ground floor was enclosed and used as a dining area. The second

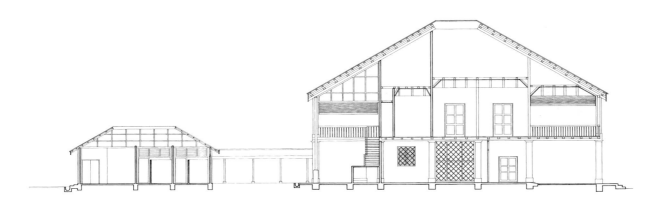

The second-storey timber verandah, in the centre of the elevation facing the park, is tucked under the large roof and is carried on two plain Doric columns resting on square brick plinths.

storey consisted of two bedrooms, a dressing room and a nursery with two large verandahs, one serving as a drawing room, facing the front and rear of the house.

The house is delightful, more so for the simplicity of its design. The roof is supported on two-storey-high timber columns which appear remarkably slender. The second-storey timber verandah, in the centre of the elevation facing the park, is tucked under the large roof and is carried on two plain Doric columns resting on square brick plinths. This upper verandah, open on three sides, forms the main living area of the house and enjoys natural cross-ventilation.

The high roof is also ideal for the tropics, providing both insulation and air movement.

A *porte-cochere* provided access for carriages in the monsoon season, whilst the stables and the servants quarters, connected by a covered way, were in separate accommodation at the rear.

In 1972, Burkill Hall was adapted to house a School of Horticulture to meet the demand for horticulturists. It was used for this purpose for the next two decades.

Further conservation works on Burkill Hall began in June 1991, the intention of the National Parks Board being to adapt it once again to create

a reception hall. The outhouse has been converted to toilets and service rooms housing electrical equipment and pumping gear.

The work has been elegantly executed and is a reminder of a way of life before air-conditioning. When one had to build with regard to the climate in order to have comfortable living conditions, the indigenous architecture provided all the exemplars.

Burkill Hall should be studied by architectural students before they embark on their careers and periodically by professionals in mid-career to remind themselves of the basic principles of a house in the tropics.

The plan form of the Reuter House is a rough approximation of the large "black and white" mansions of the colonial period. A squarish front block is connected to a rectangular rear block via a covered walkway or corridor. In a past era, the front block would have been the family residence of the owner, whilst the rear block would have housed kitchens and servants' quarters.

REUTER HOUSE

William Lim Associates
1990

Supporting the pyramidal roof of the front block of the house are ten huge circular balau timber columns.

In the Reuter House, the architect almost reverses these functions—the rear block becomes the private family domain, separated by an open court and swimming pool from the reception rooms, dining area and the more public domain of the house. The kitchen/utility and servants' quarters are contained in a separate service block at an angle to the main block.

Supporting the pyramidal roof of the front block of the house are ten huge circular timber columns. These are made of red balau tree trunks, surmounted by black-painted steel capitals which support the main roof trusses. The association that some

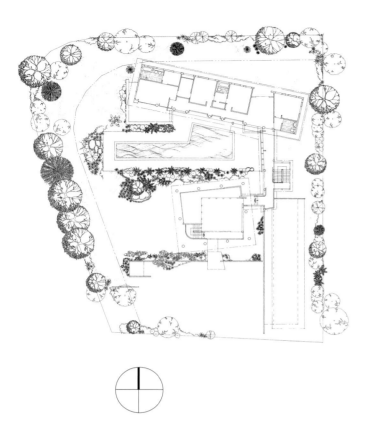

Above left: **Second storey plan**

Above right: **Traditional timber details are juxtaposed with steel balustrades and column capitals.**

Below: **The rear block is a single-storey structure containing the private domain of the house.**

people draw from this is with Chinese temples or old houses in China. Other observers associate these same columns with the classical porticoes of colonial buildings.

The expression of the brief on plan is as subtly related but clearly articulated separate blocks. The front block of the house is simple at a first reading but is actually much more complex. The main pyramidal roof, supported on the two-storey-high timber columns, projects beyond the core of the house. It floats like a pavilion, in the manner of the best vernacular tropical architecture. It sheds rain directly to storm drains on the ground.

Set within the perimeter columns is an inner concrete structure, articu-lated in a modernist language. Within this is yet a third layer—a lightly framed, square timber element with glazed walls that can be opened to allow cross-ventilation. This square is rotated within the main rectangle. The geometry of the inner square sets up the alignment for the connecting corridor to the rear block.

Traditional horizontal timber louvres contrast with steel balustrades and column capitals. The use of modern and traditional materials has some similarity to the work of the Venetian architect Carlo Scarpa.

Reuter House goes some way towards fusing a universal language of architecture with local/vernacular traditions and creating a regional modern architecture.

Geoffrey Eu's house consists of a group of four pavilions around a pool, in a U-shaped configuration. The house has a clearly defined gradient of privacy. It is a memorable house for its tactile qualities, the earthy and voluptuous colours used sparingly alongside natural materials, the orchestration of internal views, the processional route and the changes of mood. It is a house with a strong focus and which contains a harmonious fusion of cultures.

EU HOUSE I

Ernesto Bedmar .
Bedmar and Shi Pte Ltd
1993

Top: **Section**

Right: **Looking across the pool towards the guest pavilion, the house exudes immense tranquillity and calm.**

Opposite top: **The house is entered through a carved Chinese door with filigree panels that give a glimpse of the interior.**

Opposite bottom: **The third pavilion houses the living room, the library and a high-ceilinged bedroom.**

One enters Geoffrey Eu's house through a carved Chinese door with filigree panels that give a glimpse into the interior.

Crossing the threshold, one is confronted by a granite wall, in which a rectangular, arched opening is fashioned, visually connecting the vestibule with the inner space.

To the right is a two-storey guest pavilion. Moving to the left of the granite wall, a verandah leads to the private domain. A single-storey kitchen and dining pavilion overlooks the black-tiled pool. A slight drop in level, responding to the topography, leads one to the third pavilion which houses the living room, the library and a high-ceilinged bedroom. The last of the four pavilions is the study,

which is elevated above the garden and accessed from the bedroom by a short, covered verandah.

The influences on the designer are elusive, but there are unquestionable references to Chinese culture in the entrance arrangement, the hierarchy of privacy and the grouping of the pavilions around a courtyard. Balinese influences are also evident. To some visitors, the open volumes of the rooms evoke the bungalows of India and the Thai *sala*. Other commentators read its patterns as being derived from Melakan *kampung* houses. All these have some cultural relevance in Singapore, which is a multicultural society of migrants from many parts of Asia. The architect has successfully integrated the various cultural influences in an unselfconscious manner.

But the house is much more than an assemblage of cultural inferences, more than a delightful play of scale between the four pavilions set in the landscape; it is a deliciously sensitive and poetic experience. The shift of light, the reflections on the water and the breezes are enchanting.

Eu House II is the second house that Ernesto Bedmar has designed for Geoffrey Eu. The first was the widely acclaimed house in Belmont Road (Eu House I, pages 102–103). This later house indicates a gradual shift in Bedmar's architectural language from a literal interpretation of the vernacular in his early work to a modern aesthetic.

EU HOUSE II

Ernesto Bedmar
Bedmar and Shi Pte Ltd
in association with
B+S+T Architects
1997

Top: **Section**

Below: **Section**

Opposite bottom: **From the dining area, the pool is revealed in its entirety and attention shifts to another space beyond the pool, a timber deck contained by a pierced concrete wall which draws a veil across the intrusive windows of a neighbouring house.**

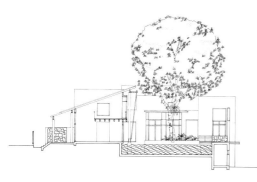

Singapore Building Regulations insist upon 3-metre (9.8-foot) set-backs from the boundary on the sides of a plot and a 4.5-metre (14.8-foot) set-back on the rear boundary. This is a remnant of British building by-laws but it has the effect of perpetuating endless (sub)urban solutions. The designer has, with great ingenuity, produced an internally orientated solution which defies this suburban bias.

The parti for the house is a series of rectangular blocks in a ziggurat formation stepping along the hypotenuse of the triangular site and in the process, gradually opening up an open space at the centre of the site. In this central space is a huge Angsana tree which has, with some difficulty, been retained by the architect and which is the focus of the courtyard, along with a swimming pool.

The elevation to the street is almost entirely blank, with a single small rectangular window. The entrance, with its granite slabs set in dark grey sea washed pebbles, conveys a quietness and sense of retreat that permeates the whole house.

One can appreciate this house at several levels. The landscape works with the building, which is neither deferential nor overwhelming. There is an overall simplicity in the detailing. Bedmar has made a major departure in this project from the technology employed in earlier houses designed by his practice. Well seasoned timber is becoming harder to acquire and very expensive to maintain. In this house, natural anodised aluminium is used. Although it lacks the warmth and tactile qualities of timber, it has its own appeal in terms of the crisp modernist aesthetic and the sense of transparency it conveys.

The house is utterly Asian yet simultaneously universal, completely modern and yet ancient. With its flat and 20-degree mono-pitch roofs, this project takes Bedmar beyond the literal interpretations of the vernacular

that one encountered in his earliest houses to an architecture that removes entirely the paradox that Paul Ricouer saw between being modern and yet being rooted in one's culture. (Ricouer, 1963)

Entwined within the primary circulation route are a number of diversions and secondary routes. Activities are overlaid: there are spaces for relaxation, for solitude, for conducting business, for formality and for exuberant play. Indeed, the house lends itself to use as an extended family dwelling, with enormous flexibility within the layout to accommodate changing family lifestyles.

In contrast to the central courtyard, with its shimmering blue swimming pool and gentle fountain, is a smaller rear courtyard, a place of seclusion and solitude, shaded by a screen of *kayu manis*, *salam*, oil palm, *kelay layu* and *leban* trees along the rear boundary. The space has the serenity of a Japanese shrine.

Far left: Steel columns, with diameters of 200 millimetres (8 inches), support the roof and secondary sun-shading devices at the southwest façade of the living room.

Centre: Early morning sunlight streams through a screen wall and dances on the floor.

Left: Partially obscured behind a lattice screen wall is a water spout that issues into a pond.

The architectural language that Ernesto Bedmar employs in the Victoria Park House shows a return to modernism. The vernacular connections are still there but the technology employed, such as anodised aluminium window frames and steel "I" beams, the precision of details and the "stripped down" aesthetic is altogether different from his earliest work. There is also a "lightness" now that was less evident in the houses of the 1980s.

VICTORIA PARK HOUSE

**Ernesto Bedmar .
Bedmar and Shi Pte Ltd
in association with
B+S+T Architects
2000**

The transformation of Bedmar's work was not achieved without a struggle. Many new clients are initially attracted by his earlier works and some insist upon traditional features. But the transition has now been made and the Victoria Park House, completed in 2000, is indicative of the extent of the shift.

The site of the house is roughly rectangular, narrowing slightly at the northern end, where tall mature trees stand. Trees also stand along the east and west boundaries. One enters the site from the south. The topography consists of a flat plateau with a 3-metre (9.8-foot) drop from the centre to a lower flat area. The architect has chosen to place the house on higher ground to exploit the view to the north. The accommodation is split into two parallel wings running north to south, facing each other across a central landscaped courtyard.

The threshold to the house is via a simple rectangular projecting porch through a granite screen wall and thence across a bridge over fish ponds. This layering of space ensures privacy and builds up anticipation. The porch leads to an open verandah which links the two "wings" of the house.

There is poetry in the house. A narrow vertical window at the base of the staircase "squeezes" light into the stairwell, contrasting sharply with the external landscape which tumbles

casually and effortlessly down the slope. The change in level of the garden is emphasised by the manner in which a stone faced wall alongside a cascade of granite stairs is permitted to "float" above the ground.

The house plan suggests a casual and relaxed environment without the distinct order that often results from the programmatic separation of functions. Emphasis has been put on the integration of landscape and architecture so that there is an almost seamless continuum between interior and exterior, although this can never be achieved in the way that a rural house interacts with its environment. Nevertheless, the design encourages air movement, passive cooling and a harmony between nature and the built environment.

Traditional Southeast Asian pavilion architecture is still the source of inspiration for his residential work, but in the Victoria Park House, Ernesto Bedmar confirms a significant realignment of his architecture in terms of tectonics, construction materials and aesthetic.

Above: Houses designed by Bedmar invariably contain a variety of water features.

Left and opposite: The living room has an exterior extension enclosed by timber louvred walls that give permanent yet adjustable natural ventilation and simultaneously provide security and privacy. When the louvred screens are thrown open, this space connects directly with the garden and the pool. An external timber deck projects out into the surrounding trees.

Bottom left: The focus of the house is the garden; all the rooms have a view of the trees at the rear of the site or into the central space, where there is a lawn alongside the swimming pool and a 2-metre (6.6-foot) high waterfall.

Bottom right: A two-storey-high, two-level flat-roofed verandah links the two wings of the house.

No. 178 Coronation Road West is a private residence located in a quiet tree-lined cul-de-sac just off Bukit Timah Road. The clients initially envisioned a Balinese-style home, complete with all the associated architectural motifs. The approach adopted by the architect from the outset, however, was not to mimic the traditional archetypes or imagery associated with "Balinese style", but rather, to draw out the essence of the client's perceptions and expectations.

CORONATION ROAD WEST HOUSE

Chan Soo Khian
SCDA Architects
2000

BY CAMPBELL IAIN CUMMING

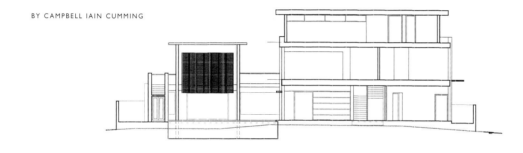

The house on Coronation Road West is composed of two boxes—a heavyweight box firmly attached to the ground (the three-storey main house) and a small lightweight box (the pavilion) which floats delicately over a single-storey wall that connects the two and completes the composition. The main house is organised around a simple, highly functional plan layout and is enclosed in a generic box form. While the plan is highly resolved, it is the architect's expression and articulation of the external envelope of the box that creates the dynamism evident in the final design.

The design is an exercise in breaking the box apart. Walls are treated as a composition of planes that slide past each other, overlapping and intersecting where necessary to let in light, to allow cross-ventilation and to control views and privacy. For this project, emphasis was placed on the importance of integrating the

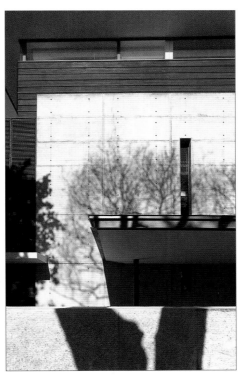

Opposite top: **Section**

Opposite bottom: **Off-form concrete used on the front façade imparts an air of permanence to the structural wall planes (a departure from the more conventional practice of concrete framed construction with plastered brick in-fill).**

Far left: **The lightweight steel frame structure of the pavilion is clearly expressed. Raised up above the swimming pool on steel posts, the pavilion is clad on all sides with a slatted timber screen that further emphasises its generic box form.**

Left: **A simple palette of materials has been employed by the architects to accentuate the reductionist qualities of the design.**

structure and the overall form of the house. Careful articulation of openings, coupled with the introduction of timber screens at the second-storey master bathroom and stained plywood cladding at the third storey, helps to temper and break down the scale of an otherwise imposing front façade.

The progression from the public frontage of the street to the more private spaces at the back of the house can be characterised by the hierarchical expression of their defining walls, which change from fairly solid at the front to full-height glass screens at the back. Instead of completely excluding the weather and

isolating the building's occupants from the external environment, the architect has maximised the interface between the inside spaces of the building and the sanctuary of the coconut grove behind by transforming the external envelope of the house into a series of full-height sliding doors, sliding windows and pivoting screens. A slatted timber screen, amounting to half the width of the rear elevation, acts as a veil to the more private master bedroom and study area located on the second storey of the main house. The use of slatted timber screens throughout the project enables subtle modification of

light and shadow, but it is only at night, when both the main house and the pavilion are lit up like lanterns from within, that the subtle differentiation between the solid and transparent building elements becomes evident.

It is the sensitive modulation of the threshold between the inside and the outside spaces that raise this project to a level beyond simply an exercise in the modulation of the local climate. Rather, the architect has used the climate as a springboard from which to explore the less tangible yet more sensual and poetic qualities that add up to a vital tropical architecture.

chapter 5

BUKIT TIMAH ROAD

The body is in harmony when all its separate systems function as an integrated whole. So, too, for a building—the whole being greater than the sum of its parts and all functioning seamlessly as one entity. In practical terms, this would relate to aspects of arrangement, efficiency and comprehensiveness.

KANDANG KERBAU HOSPITAL

Akitek Tenggara II
Principal Consultant:
PWD Consultants Pte Ltd
1997

BY HEE LIMIN

The Kandang Kerbau Hospital (KK), located on a 4.8-hectare (11.9-acre) site at the junction of Kampong Java Road and Bukit Timah Road, is certainly planned around the concept of efficiency. The idea of grouping the common Diagnostic and Treatment (D&T) facilities at the centre of the plan, with separate women's and children's lift lobbies at the fringe, results in a comprehensive and efficient cir-

culation system. The natural position of siting the nurses' stations to overlook both sides of the "race-track" ward corridors allow good supervision of the comings and goings within the wards. The "race-track" ward corridors also allows for the use of Automated Guided Vehicles (AGVs), or robotic transporters.

Some health researchers have recommended that the proportions of a healthcare building should reflect

the proportions of a healthy person. KK's parti is one of sleek curved blocks projected at the ends and anchored by robust round columns onto a heavier concrete podium. The tripartite arrangement is congruent with a classical scheme of design and the overall image is one of strength and stability. The articulation of the façade elements—the thin sleek metal sunshading fins for the towers and the taut-edged concrete fins of the podi-

Opposite: **KK's parti is one of sleek blocks with curved projections at the ends, anchored by robust round columns onto a heavier concrete podium. The overall image is one of strength and stability.**

Right: **The building meets the eye always at an angle which changes with movement, revealing and unfolding as one moves along the driveway. The symmetry of the building is more of a subliminal experience than a real one.**

Page 110: **Gentle Road House**

Page 111: **Cluny Hill House**

From left to right:
The façade's sunshading elements combine to give a strong horizontal emphasis to the tower blocks.

um—emphasises the horizontal and root the building to the land. Ideas of shelter, strength and security are embodied in the architecture of mass and durability.

While the interior environment of KK still lies very much in the domain of institutionalised healthcare, it scores well in the generous provision of window areas in the ward towers, which, with the double L-shaped ward plan, allows sweeping vistas of the urbanscape from all bed areas.

The legibility of the plan form and clear vertical segregation of functions help the visitor have a clear sense of navigation. The separate entrance levels for ambulant and non-ambulant patients are linked visually by a water feature and read clearly as the entrance to the building, being located at the nodal intersection of the two interlocking squares of the podium. The expansion of spatial volumes at the more accessible public

areas contrast well with the more intimately scaled private areas of the wards and specialist clinics.

From the architects' point of view, the "ensouling" of a building occurs when a building, having been completed, "takes on a life of its own". The quality of aliveness is when a building delights and touches human emotions. This design approach aims to create a bridge to transport the imagination from here to there—the past, the present or the world of wonder. Architecture is choreographed to alter the perceptions of the viewer as a further dimension of input to static design strategies. In other words, the juxtaposition of different and often opposing design ideas create a tangible delight for the user, opening up avenues of possibilities and other worlds of perceptions.

The core concept of the design to group the common D&T facilities in the centre of the plan with separate

women's and children's lift lobbies at the fringe forms the underlying ordering instrument. The basic organisation of the building is further determined through the vertical arrangement of having the common treatment facilities within the tiered podium block, while the women's and children's wards are housed within the sleek L-shaped towers.

Ancient Chinese philosophers and physicians believed that occurrences in the universe were mirrored by the principles governing the body and where there was a harmonious relationship, the *chi* (energy flow) between the environment and the body flows evenly. If one believes in this theory, the principles of balanced values between the healing process and the optimum conditions of the designed environment to facilitate this process are essential to the idea of wholeness, of architecture and life.

Below: **Elevation**

Bottom: **An important architectural decision was made to taper the tiered podium edge.**

Genesis is the backdrop to a stunning coconut grove, a rare urban "oasis" surrounded by single-storey government-owned housing and private terrace houses. Both the front and rear façades of the building are covered with a "veil" of balau timber to screen traffic noise, sun and rain, while maximising filtered light and giving a measure of visual privacy.

GENESIS

**Kerry Hill Architects
1997**

BY CHEW I-JIN

Immediately to the rear of
Genesis, a rare coconut
grove survives.

Marketed as the ultimate office environment, Genesis, a five-storey mixed-use development, promises something different in the workplace. On the street front, it is flanked by a row of traditional shop-houses and a petrol station. It replaces four shophouses and takes advantage of the increased plot ratio for this area. The narrow vertical spaces previously occupied by the old shophouses are replaced by horizontal layers of commercial and office space, topped by apartments.

Driving along this busy stretch of Bukit Timah Road, one could easily miss the building. The unconventional use of fine timber slats, which cover the main building mass, softens the impact of an abstract composition of pure, rectilinear forms. The building has a discreet quality about it, but once noticed, it is hard to ignore. This reticence is also due to the lack of obvious reference to scale and function. Apart from its inscrutable nature, the building has an uncommon crafted quality.

Having complied with the necessary set-backs and maximisation of floor area, the architects had to consider the aesthetic impact of an essentially rectilinear building and how to overcome the problems of traffic noise, a deep block and lack of privacy. The use of a detached timber veil in front of a plate glass façade is a perfect solution—glass is an ideal acoustic barrier which allows light into the building while the screen provides the necessary privacy and protection from direct sun and rain. Between the two skins is an intermediate space which is only inhabited where it is transformed into a verandah for the apartments.

The timber veil is a bold move and the architects and owners alike accept that the balau timber will, in time, weather and turn its characteristic silver-grey colour.

The development consists of a showroom on the first storey, two open-plan offices on the second and third storeys and two apartments each on the fourth and fifth storeys.

As with the traditional shop-house, the 16-metre (52-foot) deep block is punctuated by lightwells, which allow for each room to receive natural light and ventilation. Unlike traditional shophouses, however, the entire outer skin of the building is "transparent", but this is screened for privacy. As such, the interior spaces never acquire the sense of introverted darkness characteristic of a shop-house. Within the circulation core is a

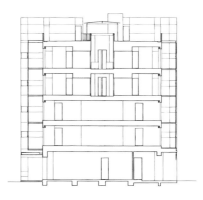

lightwell connecting each floor with the sky above and the dark reflecting pool below. Between the apartments, the interconnected levels of the entrance lobbies are also suffused with light filtered from a glazed but ventilated lightwell above. This is a luminous space in the heart of the building, which remains cool, quiet and serene.

The architects have reinterpreted the traditional shophouse to create a mixed-use building that satisfies the contemporary needs of their clients, as well as achieving a building with spatial qualities which are just as captivating as those found in traditional shophouses.

In their classic formulation, "Tropical Architecture in the Humid Zone", Maxwell Fry and Jane Drew propose that "the key to aesthetics in the tropics appears to be a dramatic accent on the definite and artificial; the creation of order". This originates from a perception of "rampant nature" in the tropics. In the context of contemporary Singapore, although we are largely surrounded by an urban environment that incorporates extensive roadside planting, one cannot help but feel that the sense of what is truly "natural" has been lost. In rare pockets such as Makepeace Road, the grove and the surrounding buildings have stood in natural juxtaposition with each other for decades—they complement each other. Genesis, likewise, suitably handles the transformation of the shophouses into a larger scale building in a manner that sustains this dialogue.

Far left: **A detached timber veil allows light to penetrate into the building while simultaneously providing privacy and protection from direct sun and rain.**

Top right: **Section**

Above left and right: **Because of the delicacy of the façade, the building has a refinement and beauty normally associated with a smaller scale object—one can compare it to a piece of furniture consisting of timber set within precisely engineered steel parts.**

Dominique Perrault was appointed to carry out the conceptual design of the Alliance Française de Singapour. The building, on a rectangular site in Sarkies Road, is situated on the fringe of the Orchard Road shopping and condominium belt and within walking distance of the Newton MRT station.

ALLIANCE FRANÇAISE DE SINGAPOUR

Point Architects
Design Consultant:
Dominique Perrault
1995

Entrance to the Alliance Française is via a glazed atrium at the western end of the building.

Development in the immediate vicinity of Alliance Française de Singapour, a centre for the promotion of French culture and art, consists mainly of medium-rise condominium projects which are steadily replacing low-rise housing and non-conforming developments along the Bukit Timah residential corridor. The architects' response to the context is extremely pragmatic. It consists of a compact, beautifully fashioned, five-storey rectangular box set-back within a perimeter access drive.

The "box" is entered via a glazed atrium at the western end. The side and rear elevations of the box are clad in polished dark-red granite, with a carefully controlled fenestration rhythm. The building is, in some ways, like a many times enlarged package containing an expensive French perfume. The analogy may not be altogether inappropriate, for once inside the building, its many delights are revealed.

A steel staircase that ascends to the cafeteria on the third level is detailed with extreme restraint and yet brings a sense of drama to any cultural event with sartorially elegant people becoming part of the spectacle. The warm glow of timber panelling contrasts well with the neutral texture of the cement screeded floor. Kreon of Belgium is responsible for the fittings used in the creative lighting of the interiors. The Gallery on the fourth level is a particularly successful venue. The Gallery was a late addition during construction, when the Alliance Française decided to omit the originally planned roof garden.

The 250-seat auditorium on the ground floor, with wall panels that can be adjusted to suit different events, has a delightfully informal air. Its narrow entrance, tucked in a cor-

Left: **A steel staircase that ascends to the cafeteria on the third level imparts a sense of drama to the foyer. Visitors to the Alliance Française become part of the cultural events.**

Bottom: **Section**

ner, is always congested immediately before and after a performance. Perhaps that was intentional.

Like its compatriot, the French Embassy (page 130), also located in Bukit Timah Road, the Alliance Française is undeniably elegant. At night, the 8-millimetre-thick, green-tinted glass at the northwest façade glows like a television monitor, becoming a dramatic five-storey high screen and the visitors to the cultural events become "actors" on a stage.

Indeed, the visitors become the cultural event. Of course, the large amount of glazing on the northwest facing elevation can be uncomfortable in the late afternoon and early evening when visitors gather for performances. The lack of a projecting canopy can also be inconvenient in the event of heavy rain. These climatic determinants of architecture in the tropics appear to have been given secondary importance to the fashioning of a beautiful object.

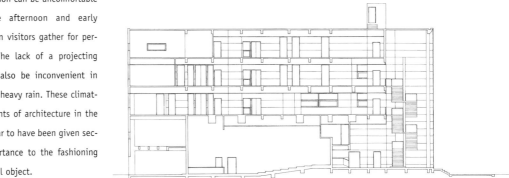

The plan of Check House II approximates the configuration of a muscular shoulder attached to an upper arm, hinged at the elbow and with a forearm embracing an open space. It is designed for a three-generation family, with the plan reflecting the spatial separation and the tissues binding the different generations.

**Tan Teck Kiam and Tan Kay Ngee
KNTA Architects
1999**

The architectural language of Check House II suggests an early modernist influence, such as the work of Mendelsohn and the 1927 Weissenhof Siedlung, Stuttgart.

CHECK HOUSE II

It is difficult to pin down the architectural precedents for Check House II. KNTA initially gave a plausible explanation that the form is derived from the site but the house has an enigmatic quality found in other works by the practice.

The circular windows that feature in several projects by the practice suggest an early modernist influence—the work of Mendelsohn and the 1927 Weissenhof Siedlung, Stuttgart. There is also a faintly nautical air about the project, with its circular windows and suggestions of a ship's hull in dry-dock hovering above the pool deck. KNTA denies this reading emphatically.

The partners are initially reluctant to discuss the conceptual ideas behind the built form. Pressed further, however, they reveal that it is derived not from architectural precedence but from art and sculptural form and an interest shared by both partners in "human movement". The plan does indeed appear to open and close like a claw or a prosthetic device.

To the visitor, the house reveals itself coyly at first. At the end of the long private driveway, a corner of the building beckons tantalisingly, leading

the eye to the right. The drive abruptly swivels in this direction and ascends steeply to the entrance portico and carport, while the building gently curves away to the left. There is a glimpse of a swimming pool and a garden in a lower courtyard and then one ascends five steps to the second storey lobby overlooking the lower garden court.

This is a large house. To the left of the entrance is a self-contained suite for the owner's parents. Immediately ahead is a top-lit family room, a master bedroom suite and two bedrooms with en-suite bathrooms and dressing rooms. A "grand" curved staircase descends from the entrance foyer, hugging the external wall, and reveals a vista across the swimming pool and the sun deck beneath the piloti, which supports the master bedroom. The house finally embraces the site, protecting the family and detaching itself from the outside world.

Stepping out onto the sun deck, the idea of "movement" becomes more comprehensible. In the seclusion of the garden at the end of the driveway, the house elegantly pirouettes and turns like a ballerina, throwing out a

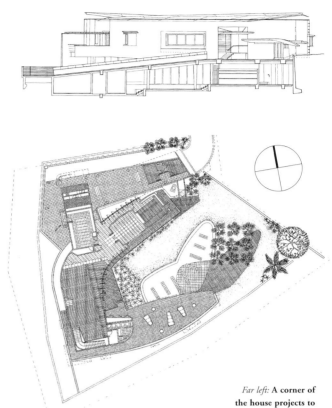

Far left: **A corner of the house projects to greet the visitor.**

Top: **Section**

Above: **First storey plan**

Below left and right: **In the seclusion of the garden, the house elegantly pirouettes and turns. Undulating glazed planes refract and reflect multiple images.**

pointed toe, dipping and is momentarily frozen. Undulating glazed planes refract and reflect multiple images. As in an earlier house for the same client, a secondary roof is added above the primary structure, with an air gap between the roofs. The purpose is to protect the main roof from excessive solar heat gain. The roof appears to be spinning off like a boomerang on a tangential trajectory.

In Check House II, there is no attempt to bring the landscape into the building or to plant in a picturesque manner. Indeed, the pool, the pool deck and the trees are treated as geometric elements related to the built form. Although almost all the windows are capable of opening to provide natural ventilation, "tropicality" is not the primary agenda pursued by KNTA Architects. Their houses accept the seeming inevitability of air-conditioning being required in Asia's burgeoning cities. The forms of their houses are derived from art and sculpture, particularly an interest in the sculpturing of space from the outside and a preoccupation with how light enters a building.

The Bukit Timah Nature Reserve contains the last vestiges of Singapore's natural forest heritage. Amazingly the reserve contains more species of trees than can be found in the whole of North America! The forest is a source for scientific education and many schools use the area to acquaint students with natural history and ecology. It is also a place where one can gain respite from the stress of city life.

BUKIT TIMAH NATURE RESERVE INTERPRETATION CENTRE

PWD Consultants Pte Ltd
1992

The architectural detailing of the Centre is appropriately low-tech, with wide, overhanging pitched roofs and shaded verandahs.

The Bukit Timah Nature Reserve Interpretation Centre is located at the Hindhede Drive entrance to the Reserve. For many years, other than a car park, the only facility at the reserve was a small warden's hut. This has been replaced by a two-storey rectangular building with a single-storey off-shoot at the rear. The plan form is reminiscent of a large colonial bungalow.

The architecture is of an appropriately low-tech design. Natural ventilation is supplemented by ceiling

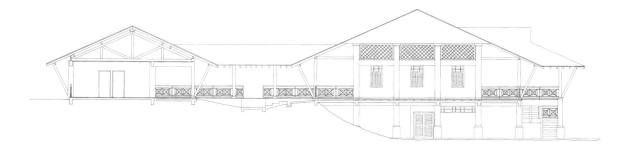

fans. The generous roof overhang shades the external walls of the building, making it cool even on the hottest of days. Water is shed from the roof without the use of gutters.

The Interpretation Centre is located on the edge of the primary forest and is sensitively built into the gently sloping site, with the giant Dipterocarpaceae and Seraya trees forming a magnificent background. The site was formerly a small *kampong* (village). The resettling of the kampong folks initially relieved the pres-

sure on the Nature Reserve and created a buffer zone between it and Upper Bukit Timah Road, but new condominiums in the area are putting the reserve under severe pressure and threatening its viability.

The Urban Redevelopment Authority's Design Guide Plan (DGP) for the area is remarkable for its lack of sensitivity to the fragile ecology. A new road linking Dairy Farm Road to the BKE has put further pressure on the reserve. The construction of easily accessible cycling tracks around the

perimeter of the reserve is gradually eroding the forest.

The most important attribute of the Interpretation Centre for a nation fast losing its links with the natural environment is the modest but informative exhibition space that occupies the entire second storey of the main building. It displays most of the common insects, butterflies, moths and small mammals of the reserve, with notes on their rarity and vulnerability.

Kerry Hill Architects brings to this house on Cluny Hill two and a half decades of experience of building in Tropical Asia. Hill has produced a modern interpretation of a planter's bungalow with a huge second-storey living room, which has views of the Botanic Gardens from its elevated location. The precedence for this form might be traced to the architecture of European dwellings in Singapore built in the late nineteenth century and early twentieth century.

CLUNY HILL HOUSE

Kerry Hill Architects
1998

Above: **The living room overlooks the pool terrace. At the opposite end is a minimalist bath house.**

Right: **Section**

The plan form for Cluny Hill House is undeniably modern. The parti consists of two rectangular blocks—one single-storey high, the other a double-storey structure—placed at right angles to the lower block and joined by a bridge across a reflecting pool.

One enters the house via the lower of the two blocks through a simple rectangular portico projecting from a heavy masonry wall. The wall is a screen, conveyed by the fact that it is pierced with random rectangular apertures. The wall serves as a veil, concealing from direct view large window openings to the dining room and study.

The entrance lobby serves as an orientation point—to the left is the study and a guest suite; to the right is the dining room and a large en-suite kitchen overlooking the pool deck. Directly ahead, on passing through the lobby, is a bridge that links the lower of the two blocks and the two-

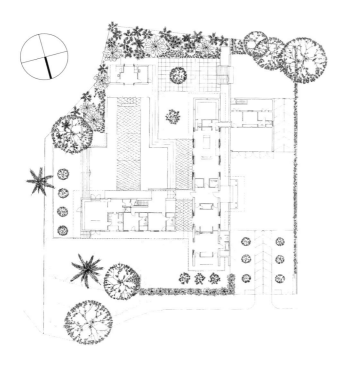

Above: **The entrance to the house is through a rectangular portico projecting from a masonry wall.**

Left: **First storey plan**

Below: **The dining room overlooks the pool terrace. External sliding timber screens provide shade.**

storey block. The bridge passes over dark, still water and demarcates the transition from the public areas of the house (guest suite, reception and dining room) to the private areas (bedrooms, bathrooms and living room). The demarcation is not so rigid, however, for the upper storey of the two-storey block is a huge living room intended for entertaining on a grand scale. Boundaries are hence more fluid than those in a traditional black-and-white house.

The external walls of the second-storey living room are designed with large sliding glazed panels that allow air-conditioning or if desired, natural ventilation. Top hung timber louvres are mounted outside the glass with hydraulic hinges. The living room has a sunken long-bar and a balcony overlooking the pool terrace.

The pool itself has many of the qualities of the resorts that Kerry Hill Architects is acclaimed for. Placed at right angles to the living room, the grey-blue surface reflects the mature trees that surround the site. At the opposite end of the pool is a minimalist bath house. There is a sense of uncluttered calm. In the evening, the poolside becomes a magical place surrounded by stepped terraces. The whole design is a celebration of life at the interface of the constructed and the natural world.

Most importantly, Hill brings to the design of Cluny Hill House a sense of bravado, an ability to boldly tackle a large house without permitting it to become grandiose. It is a critical response to the many post-modern classical monstrosities springing up all over Southeast Asia.

King Albert Park House was an opportunity to explore "modern tropicality". It relies on the juxtaposition of pure form against water and vegetation to create an image and an experience of the tropics. Openness and transparency and constantly changing vistas and light are calculated to engage the imagination. A client who was sympathetic to architectural intentions and a superb site gave Akitek Tenggara the opportunity to define a tropical lifestyle.

KING ALBERT PARK HOUSE

Akitek Tenggara II
1994

Top: Section.

Right: The house is a rigorous investigation of the art of designing a modern house in the tropics.

This modern tropical house is a poetic statement in the language of "line, edge and shade". King Albert Park House has all the attributes of a well designed house in the tropics—major living spaces that are "open-to-sky", orientation to catch the prevailing breezes, openness in the plan arrangement to encourage cross-ventilation, extensive use of water and planting, a structured hierarchy in its plan arrangement, wide overhanging eaves, the opportunity to adjust the penetration of sunlight through the use of manually operated blinds, secondary shading devices and the restriction of air-conditioning only to rooms where it is strictly necessary.

One enters King Albert Park House by a modest gateway which betrays little of the open lifestyle that the owner enjoys. The gate opens to

Above left and right: **The architectural language employed is uncompromisingly modern. A language of thin projecting concrete slab edges; of secondary horizontal shading elements; of louvres and light diffusing screens, the modern equivalent of the traditional chick blind; of raised undercrofts, green algae-tinted ponds and a lifestyle that works with rather than against the natural world.**

reveal a short drive to the car porch and entrance vestibule. The rough stone wall that surrounds the car porch has a fortress-like quality which conceals the openness of the house beyond. One enters through a small opening in this wall into a circular pavilion. The visitor then proceeds along a causeway that crosses a carp pond to the living room; family members and close friends turn a sharp right and, skirting the pond, make their way directly to the more casual day areas adjoining the kitchen.

The day areas are open on all sides—a void deck if you like, a unique Singaporean feature of sheltered open living spaces. It could also be read as a derivation of the space beneath the Malay *kampong* house.

The house is a kaleidoscope of different moods. The entrance court is formal and quiet, a place for contemplation, for formal greetings, for walking with a measured tread. The pool court is different. It is a place for laughter, for fun and games, the brilliant blue of the pool conveying the ambience of a tropical resort. Penetrate further into the house and the ambience changes. The two-storey-high undercroft, with its tall circular columns and palm trees, is the equivalent of a tropical rain forest, shaded and cool.

The site drops away to the east and on a lower plateau is an eco-pond. All these habitats are linked by a meandering pathway which follows the natural contours of the land and the house is experienced as a series of changing vistas and patterns of light and shade.

It has become alarmingly easy to find badly proportioned and outlandish additions and alterations to houses. Often, proud house owners brandish their wealth in a bid to outdo, outshine and most importantly, outbuild their neighbours. Once in a while, however, one encounters an example of how the shell of a modest building can hold potential for better things.

GENTLE ROAD HOUSE

Tan Hock Beng
MAPS Design Studio
2000

BY PETER SIM

The staircase and pool form the visual focus of the house and is accentuated by a frosted glass butterfly roof that filters diffused light through the recesses of the house.

When Maps Design Studio embarked on this house at Gentle Road, the first and most challenging factor it faced was the constraints of the existing structure. The original house, a semi-detached unit, was linked structurally and integrally to its neighbour and the architect was left with little option but to retain the existing structure, down to each column and beam. This perceived quandary, however, has turned out to be an interesting excursion into the hidden possibilities that lie within the shell of the old house.

The requirement to accommodate the owners' modestly sized family as well as a substantial private art collection determined the need to provide appropriate natural light not only for gracious living but for art appreciation. In order to create a visual linkage between the internal spaces, as well as between inside and outside, the architects made two fundamental changes. The first was to knock down the myriad of walls that had created cell-like enclosures out of the spaces. Secondly, two courtyards were intro-

duced to bring light deep into the house and to serve as a space for the display of sculpture.

The resultant plan is simple: it consists essentially of three segments divided by two courtyards. The first courtyard is interiorised, being more like an atrium space, and features a newly inserted staircase and reflective pool. This atrium separates the living and dining areas on the ground floor. The admission of natural light through a glass roof creates an ambiguity in the demarcation of interior and exterior, imbuing an effortless flow between spaces.

On the second floor, two bedrooms are located towards the anterior of the house while the master suite is located towards the posterior. An open platform that overlooks the central atrium and delineates the common family area unites these rooms. Through careful calculation, an additional floor was gingerly inserted into the existing structure above the master bedroom. This serves as a private study and is accessible via a spiral stair hanging in the rear court.

The owner's collection of paintings gave rise to the significance of how a large wall area can serve beyond its architectonic role, acting now as a dramatic backdrop not unlike the case of a gallery wall. The wall between the house and its neighbour is given prominence by the astute pulling away of the upper floors from it. Essentially, this gesture creates a large vertical

surface, at times three storeys in height and bathed in light, that has been appropriated as a worthy plane for art. The main circulation route is also along this axis, accentuating the importance of this wall both as a feature in itself and also as a visual and structural datum stringing together the different parts of the house.

With sleight of hand, the design capitalises upon the most valuable assets in this residence at Gentle Road with a single stroke, bringing the sensibilities of space with the appreciation of beauty into a unanimous entity. One enters the house at this gallery, navigates along it, and appreciates the art in it.

In the context of the urban environment, Gentle Road House illustrates the possibility of an evolving and progressive urban fabric without the need for visually jarring tears and fissures.

Below: **More than a good home for its occupants, Gentle Road House is indicative of the spatial and architectural potential that remains possible even with a simple shell.**

Bottom: **It speaks both of the value in being responsive to pragmatic requirements and of how this can allow a way of living that can be raised beyond the banal and the mundane.**

Nestled between a block of restored shophouses and a four-storey apartment block near the junction of Cluny Park Road and Bukit Timah Road, the French Embassy building sits in such quiet repose that an unfamiliar visitor would surely miss it. It was the winning scheme in a competition held in 1993 by the French Ministry of Foreign Affairs for the design of a new building to unite the French Embassy and Consulate offices.

THE FRENCH EMBASSY IN SINGAPORE

**Dubus-Richez (Paris) and
TSP Architects + Planners Pte Ltd
(Singapore)
1999**

BY HEE LIMIN

The French Embassy faces north and overlooks the Botanic Gardens.

The French Embassy building can be discerned as two unaligned rectilinear volumes, interlocked by a third implied steel-framed volume capped by a sail-over flat canopy, which demarcates the entrance. The narrow frontage of the building is punctuated by a small gate-house—a sculptured white volume of concrete and glass. Proceeding inside, an elongated flat slice of canopy, defying gravity, hints the way to the main entrance doors, which are cradled at the intersection of the two building masses. The entrance is slightly elevated from the ground, imparting a subtle sense of hierarchy to the entrance, also allowing for the basement to be slightly raised.

The atrium lobby, deliciously carved out of the two volumes, is bathed in a light and ambience that could only be described as Mediterranean. The clever use of small diameter timber rods, each about 1 metre (3.3 feet) in length, interspersed in a grid below the glass sky-

light, cuts out a warm and cheerful piece of blue sky as the centrepiece of the atrium space. The light from the improvised timber "chandelier" bathes the vertical feature of the steel and glass lift ensemble, compositionally an extension of the skylight, to transmit the light further down into the space.

The honey-hued interior exudes warmth and showcases the palette of *au naturel* materials favoured by the architects. The corridors that fringe the space are rendered lightweight and insubstantial by the clever use of satin-finished steel edging, glass balustrades and tube-steel handrails. The effect is further dramatised by the use of wall-wash lighting at the edge, which (un)defines the meeting of horizontal and vertical planes. Walls and doors are deliberately kept indistinct and flushed to continue the theme of clean lines and simple planes that define the central space.

High-ceilinged visa halls, confer-ence rooms and public offices on the first storey are followed by more intimate administration offices on the second and third storeys, while the fourth storey, which is the Chancellery, is more formal and solemn. The soft-filtered light, which streams through the windows, is moderated on the east façade by frit glass sun-shading, while metal-finned *brise-soleil* shade the windows on the side elevations.

If some spaces are defined by light, then the offices facing north, which overlook the expanse of the Botanic Gardens and the nearby National Institute of Education campus, must indeed be defined by the view. From the fourth storey window, the view skims over the canopies of vast rain-trees and appropriates the space beyond to extend the realm of the interior.

Through the use of simple volumes, elegant materials and space definition through the play of light, the architects seem to have captured the essence of things. The containment of clutter within the crisp defining planes and volumes allows the visitor to experience the delight of pure space and the exquisite materiality of form and textures. Yet, it would be too convenient to label this piece of architecture as minimalist, as the enjoyment of space is not merely on an abstract level, but at the level of the tactile and of a humane quality. The assemblage of light, space and materials does not intimidate but engage one's sense of participation in the space. The building does not exert its tectonic quality (the columns are embedded in partitions as far as possible) but asks to be appreciated as the space to be within. The visitor's memory of the building would surely be the initial promise, by the flat raised canopy roof at the entrance, of a bit of "French sky" against the tropical glare and then just that strip of blue sky within, with a dream of somewhere far away.

chapter 6

THE
SOUTH AND WEST
OF THE ISLAND

Thanks to the Amans and the Four Seasons in Bali, the academic argument about critical regionalism in architecture, under the umbrella of placemaking, is brought down stylishly from its intellectual perch to sensual fetish level. The Institute of Southeast Asian Studies (ISEAS) building, conceptually underpinned by Southeast Asian architectural precedents, has taken the Aman-esque trail. Its façade echoes a style that has been largely hijacked by seriously expensive tropical-style bungalows and resorts.

THE INSTITUTE OF SOUTHEAST ASIAN STUDIES

| PWD Consultants Pte Ltd
| 1998

BY VINCENT LIM

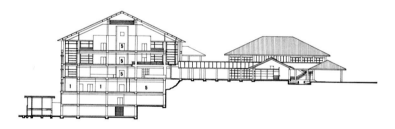

Above: **Section**

Opposite: **Entry to the ISEAS is across a bridge spanning a pool. The reception area encodes various Southeast Asian architectural precedents.**

Page 132: **The SAFTI Military Institute**

Page 133: **Henderson Community Club and the Bukit Merah West Neighbourhood Police Centre**

At the ISEAS, you enter via a doorway punched through a rough-hewn granite wall and onto a bridge laid over a pond. A pitched roof shelters this short route into the reception pavilion. The open pavilion, decked out with ethnic-style furniture, surrounded by plants and refreshed with the aural treat of gurgling water, facilitates moments of peace. In another place, you would expect to be served a welcome drink. The sanctuary-like setting of the ISEAS is to be applauded—the think-tank building could have been conceived and designed in the manner of those faceless and aircon dependent NUS buildings.

The ISEAS complex comprises four blocks pinwheeled compositionally around a central courtyard. The seminar block and the administration blocks are located east and west of the entry foyer. Interlocking "walkway" arms connect the entry foyer to the massive pyramidal-roofed six-storey library block and the five-storey research block organised around its own courtyard.

From Heng Mui Keng Terrace, the ISEAS complex appears to be at most three storeys tall, until you cross at entry level into the internal court of the research block. Here, the ground falls to reveal four floors (with another two levels below that). Only then does the architecture clue you in to the three-storey slope of the 1.3-hectare (3.2-acre) site the building sits on. The site has apparently been cut and filled, but to visually maintain the entry-level datum, the architects clad the parts of the building below that datum line with granite to effect massive podiums. This is a literal quotation from the tectonic standards of vernacular Southeast Asian architecture—the tripartite composition of base (or podium), superstructure (post and beam timber construction) and roof (pitched and with generous eaves).

In fact, in their answer to the identity conundrum, PWD Consultants architects have relied heavily on this tectonic model. The superstructures of the research and library blocks rising from the granite podiums are designed to be seemingly analogous to tradi-

Above left: **The architects clad the parts of the building below the entry-level datum line with granite to effect massive podiums.**

Above, right: **Bali-based landscape designer Made Wijaya was brought in to design the courtyards and gardens of the ISEAS.**

Right: **Roof plan**

Opposite top: **The bridge over the pond at the entrance leads to an open pavilion surrounded by plants.**

Opposite bottom: **The architectural language is that of vernacular Southeast Asia— a tripartite composition of base (or podium), super-structure (post and beam timber construction) and roof (pitched and with generous eaves).**

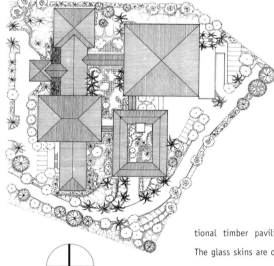

tional timber pavilion construction. The glass skins are detached from the structure to emphasise the skeletal reinforced concrete (RC) frame so as to evoke references to traditional post and beam construction. Yet another example of evoking the pavilion form: rooms in the administration block are configured with free-standing walls, all sheltered by an encompassing trop-ical "umbrella" roof.

The tectonic game is but one of the precedents the architects have extracted from history. They, of course, did not forget the sacrosanct-under-the-traditional-Southeast-Asian-architecture rubric courtyard.

The courtyard takes up two key posi-tions at the ISEAS. The smaller of the two is the ordering void for the research block while the bigger central courtyard holds the four blocks of the ISEAS together.

According to the project archi-tect, the form of the central courtyard is inspired by the in-between spaces found within a traditional Balinese compound house. Unfortunately, the ISEAS version, intruded upon by the corners of the administration, library and research blocks, is a seemingly residual mesh of rectangles that has not acquired a strong shape to give it the figural presence of a focal point.

The strategy of extracting a set of general defining characteristics of tra-ditional Southeast Asian architecture without bracketing the search into particular types makes sense for the ISEAS project. For the ISEAS is about Southeast Asia, a political "frame" for a culturally heterogeneous region. Forms, spaces, silhouettes, materials and tectonics, borrowed as a set of generalised conventions, are enough to give that Southeast Asian buzz.

In an urban landscape increasingly transformed by the forces of global capital flows, the shophouse has re-emerged as a viable and versatile type which is able to accommodate a wide variety of spatial densities and programmes.

28 ENG HOON STREET

LOOK Architects
1998

BY LEONG TENG WUI

Weak party wall structures of adjacent shophouses and the proximity of the MRT underground tunnel led LOOK Architects to use a steel structure frame when rebuilding this shophouse.

Shophouse living is back in vogue as an alternative to high-rise apartment living and the stand-alone house. However, the predominant image of the shophouse still tends towards the conservation variety, which is not surprising given the large scale conservation efforts by the planning authority. The remaining stock in traditional shophouse districts, such as Emerald Hill and Chinatown, has largely been gazetted. But beyond the bourgeois appeal of living in a conservation shophouse, the shophouse type still represents a significant form of workspace for many small-to-medium businesses and service industries. No. 28 Eng Hoon Street in Tiong Bahru defies easy categorisation, but it is instructive to see how the shophouse typology can be interpreted anew.

The shophouse was the earliest form of high density living in Singapore. Introduced during Raffles' colonial administration, the building typology was a specific and innovative response to the socio-economic needs of the fledgling entrepôt economy, given the available building technology, climatic factors and the growing

density in the city. By rationalising and compartmentalising work on the first storey and living spaces for the upper floors, the shophouse was a highly efficient machine for habitation, production and capital accumulation for the emerging entrepreneurial class. The simple party wall construction and narrow-but-deep parti allowed the shophouse to be replicated en masse economically and quickly, thus addressing the problems of large numbers of immigrants and the needs of commerce.

In the latter half of the 20th century, with a globalising economy and the increasing rationalisation of modern life, the activities of working and living became increasingly differentiated and segregated. As a result, many shophouses in the central area were demolished in the 1960s and 1970s to make way for high-rise office and commercial blocks.

Fortunately, it was not a complete tabula rasa for the shophouse districts. As Rem Koolhaas wryly pointed out: "When it became clear that the upward curve of tourism was about to intersect the downward graph of historical presence", the

active conservation of and adaptive re-use of the remaining stock took on an added urgency.

Interestingly, Eng Hoon Street is not in a designated conservation area. The architect was therefore able to innovate a modern approach to the shophouse typology. The juxtaposition of No. 28 and its immediate neighbours is a fascinating gallery of the various possible interpretations of the shophouse type. Looking from the front and starting on the left of No. 28, a somewhat dilapidated two-storey shophouse represents the "original" shophouse, or what most of the shophouses along Eng Hoon Street used to look like. On the right of No. 28 is the mimicry option—a slavish and uncritical reproduction of a typical three-storey conservation shophouse.

As an important counterpoint to both the mimicry and dumb-box options, No. 28 offers an innovative take on the reinterpretation of the shophouse type. Beyond its striking mien, what is particularly significant is how the interpretive strategy shows up a new modern consciousness that is not ahistorical or reductive.

The site was beset with several constraints: an essentially small infill situation, weak party wall structures of adjacent shophouses and the need to minimise the vibration caused by the MRT underground tunnel. In response, LOOK Architects opted to insert a steel structural frame into the site. Thereafter they adopted a consistent "industrial aesthetic" in the material palette and details.

In the final analysis, No. 28 Eng Hoon Street offers important lessons on a contemporary design ethos that can be modern and inventive but without the hubris and naiveté often associated with high modernism.

The architecture of No. 28 Eng Hoon Street is a significant redemption of the unfinished modern project, giving new meaning to the much maligned modernist maxim, "form follows function".

UE Square is a development of connections, of rich integrated relationships. The nature of its connectivity is diverse and firmly disciplined, ranging from internal to external linkages, from monumental to intimate scale, executed both formally and spatially. Selected connections are direct, while others remain implicit, articulated with subtlety. Through these connections, UE Square proposes an expanded role for architecture in our communication and information society.

UE SQUARE

Architects 61 Pte Ltd
Concept and Master Planner:
Kenzo Tange Associates
1997

BY ANN GERONDELIS

U E Square proposes an emphasis on architecture's relational implications, both inside and outside of its given boundaries. It offers its users a sophisticated experience of multiple connections in dialogue.

The 3.2-hectare (7.9-acre) site of UE Square is part of Robertson Quay, the growing riverfront entertainment, living, and shopping district. UE Square is one of Singapore's largest mixed-use developments, with an 18-storey office tower, 130 service apartments on a retail podium and 345 residential apartments, all above three levels of underground parking.

Kenzo Tange's theories of structuralism—which call for increased emphasis on the connections between individual elements to structure the whole—appear to richly influence the

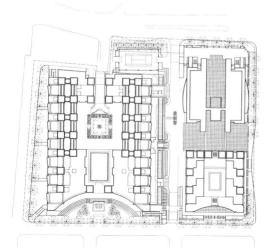

Left and opposite top: **The architectural expression of UE Square is dominated by the language of the gridded frame, intended to provide the compositional unity and balance offset by the different scales of uses.**

Above: **The design of the formal components strongly support the spatial expression of urban and internal connections through the disciplined design of parts in relation to multiple contexts.**

Opposite bottom left: **First storey plan**

Opposite bottom right: **UE Square has established itself as a landmark, sited at the intersection of Clemenceau Road and River Valley Road.**

design of UE Square. (These theories were generated in contrast to functionalism's concern for the mere enabling of each individual functional element.) Responses to structuralist concepts are particularly evident in the systematic connections developed within the project and the implicit connections to the urban environment beyond. An articulate observer of overall systems of order beyond individual components, Tange argues that it is not the individual buildings but the environment created by their placement that gives character. (Tange, 1996)

Massing strategies build connectivity with UE Square's immediate diverse neighbours and the larger urban fabric. Adjacent perimeter masses are often "mimicked" within UE Square, thus "weaving" the project into its surrounding context and establishing new orders in the adjacent urban street spaces. The retail podium, for example, addresses the shophouses on Mohamed Sultan Road, while the stepped profile of the complex addresses the river.

UE Square is marketed as The Intelligent City, designed to accommodate the latest in information technology. Tange believes that the more progress made by such indirect communication, the more direct communication becomes necessary. Through the connective strategies of UE Square, the environment of the intelligent city is articulated as an environment of visible communication.

The large monumental spaces of the project serve as mediators between urban and architectural scales, and between internal and external environments. They are highly ordered, axial and symmetrical, drawing direct relationships to adjacent urban orders.

Intimate spaces also promote diverse connections and communications. The architectonic nature of the grid allows for variation in detail and scale, while maintaining overall cohesion. Handled with discipline, each façade appears to possess subtle echoes of the others, creating an environment of active, sophisticated discourse. The tectonic expressions of the smaller components of UE Square, such as the mullion systems, balcony railings, façade details, light fixtures and canopies, further celebrate the joining of part to the whole. They effectively mediate the monumental scale of the project to a human scale.

Few architectural works in Singapore achieve such a level of integrative complexity and articulate connectivity. From the intimate to the urban, its forms and spaces connect and communicate. The dialogue is indeed refreshing.

Buildings that articulate societies and culture and bring the individual designer in touch with the values of the community have preoccupied architects throughout the ages. The designer who wants to respond to communal needs is forced to define a community. A society that is fluid, mobile and unpredictable is best accommodated by design solutions that afford maximum flexibility and minimum functional specialisation.

AYER RAJAH COMMUNITY CLUB

Akitek Tenggara
1997

BY HEE LIMIN

The Ayer Rajah Community Club acts as a basis for life and culture and does not make any prescription for an identity that should be adopted for the community.

The new Community Club (CC) has to underpin a good and caring society, with a total involvement of the community, allowing the able and the disabled, the young and the old, to interact, appreciate and understand one another's needs and problems. This is the mainstay of Akitek Tenggara's design—making a building that will grow and change with the community, instead of turning to any formulaic solution. The role of the architect here is no longer that of "formgiver", but rather that of the responsive agent. The task they have set for themselves is one of creating a framework that will be enlivened by people and activ-ities and will take on its patina from the communal presence.

The old Ayer Rajah Community Centre was partially demolished to accommodate the new L-shaped extension. This is the first Community Club to include extensive day-care facilities for pre-schoolers and the aged, so that activities are generated

Above right: **The architects' intention of dematerialising the wall is clear, with one wing entirely screened by a horizontal lattice of timber rods mounted on steel frames.**

Below: **The transparent layering around the courtyard creates an expectation of liveliness that people will infuse into the community club.**

143

throughout the day in a virtual "social condenser". Beyond the rather blockish early 80's double-storey badminton hall, the only clue to the new extension is a tenuous entrance vault which leads one through an intimate sky-lit foyer traversed by unassuming bridges linking the old and new constructions. This opens out to the courtyard and one is presented with an ensemble of forms not generated by plan, but by the premises of design that derive from the intentions to create shade, shelter, shadow and profile.

The architects' intention of dematerialising the wall is clear, with one wing entirely screened by a horizontal lattice of timber rods mounted on steel frames. These overhang from the second storey and extend beyond the roof to form an airy transition with the sky. The lattice wall is in turn punctuated by bridges leading to three geometrically shaped pavilions which project into the courtyard and act as viewing platforms to the courtyard.

Movement and activity will be the embellishment of the architectural canvas. The transparent layering and the siting of the circulation corridors, vertical lift and stair core and the pavilions around the courtyard create

an expectation of the liveliness that people will infuse to the building. The building is a backdrop to communal life.

The use of materials in the Ayer Rajah Community Club is refreshing, as one is reminded that architecture can be evaluated by an entirely different set of criteria other than merely visual ones. That involves the appreciation of craft and an expressive emphasis on what Kenneth Frampton terms, its tectonic and tactile dimension. The use of naturally finished materials—milled steel, timber, bare concrete and bricks—allows the gaze to penetrate the manifestation of form into the realm of craft and the intrinsic veracity of materials. The patina of wear will enrich the experience of the passing of time and allow the elements to leave their mark. The image is one of calmness, suffused with an innate vitality.

In the context of Community Centre buildings in Singapore, where many attempts have been made to find the right imagery, the Ayer Rajah Community Club circumscribes culture and defies time, a strategy that will sustain its immediacy and relevance to the community at large.

The Beaufort was Singapore's first resort style hotel and is located on Sentosa, a leisure isle off the mainland. Designed in the mode of idyllic beach resorts found in popular travel destinations such as Bali and Phuket, The Beaufort differs significantly in its treatment of architectural imagery, which is done in a non-pastiche manner.

THE BEAUFORT SENTOSA

Kerry Hill Architects
1991

BY TAN HOCK BENG

The Beaufort Sentosa
appears to draw subtle
references from the old
British military buildings
on the island.

S et on a sprawling 11-hectare (27-acre) site, the low-rise development of The Beaufort is broken up into separate masses that respect the topography and draw subtle lessons from the old British military buildings and barracks that exist on the isle. A symmetrical and cross-axial composition is imposed rather rigidly and forcefully onto the site.

Based on the notion of framing views, rhythmic sequence of columns capture frames that include picturesque tropical forests, harbour scenes and unruffled expanse of reflecting pools.

Designed as a complex of understated buildings with a maximum height of five storeys, The Beaufort has six guestroom blocks housing 214 rooms, five separate blocks housing

the public spaces and four super luxurious private villas that have individual swimming pools. These villas face a quiet meandering road that brings guests right to the lobby. Delightful use of verdigris finish and mirror tiles at the lobby heighten the sense of grandeur in a non-ostentatious manner. Long axial walkways lead guests to the Pavilion lobby lounge, a huge

building open on all sides. Roll chick blinds modulate the amount of light streaming in from all sides.

The open spaces between the buildings are filled with a vast expanse of reflecting pools. The calm of the main swimming pool is unruffled and, lined with iridescent blue-black tiles, it has a deep sense of quietude. This most appropriately captures the pervading mood of the understated resort, whose serenity has not really been appreciated by many Singaporeans.

The equally understated, albeit more tactile, interiors are designed by Ed Tuttle of Design Realisation. Their rich interplay of materials and muted tones provide a good complement to the simple blocks that are proportioned and detailed with minimalist rigour. However, the most obvious architectural triumph is the building's lack of stylistic clichés so pervasive in Southeast Asian resorts.

Above: **Spaces between the buildings are filled with reflecting green pools.**

Top left: **The architect uses a variety of devices to frame views and create shaded axial walkways.**

Bottom left: **A symmetrical and cross axial composition is imposed on the hilly site.**

There is probably no other institution that is more grounded in tradition than the military. Wide in its scope but unlike any other, military tradition is born completely out of necessity, for at the heart of it all, tradition here is directed towards a single purpose—the committed and dedicated defence of the nation. Given the magnitude and brevity of the task, it is understandable that one specific military tradition, that of the training necessary to be ready for a contingency in any crisis, has always been a wholly closed-door affair.

THE SAFTI MILITARY INSTITUTE

DP Architects Pte Ltd
Design Consultant:
Mitchell Giurgola and Thorp
1995

BY ANAND KRISHNAN

At the SAFTI Military Institute, four major axes have been generated. They provide the complex with a formal order by which the various buildings are placed on plan.

With the new SAFTI Military Institute, this particular tradition has been adjusted to respond to a changing world. Without compromising on security, the new complex has been designed more like a public facility than a military one. Precise demarcated militarised space is now softer-edged and open. The complex has no security checkpoint as we know it; neither is it located on a remote site or have any visible barbed-wire fencing along the boundary. It is next to a university campus and adjacent to HDB housing. Above all, the public is openly encouraged to visit the complex, to drive through it and have picnics or even jog on the landscaped lawns fronting its new lake. In a bold gesture which only heightens the demilitarised perception of the complex, a very accessible (and very public) Discovery Centre is located on the grounds right next to the lake—in fact, right next to a public-use outdoor performance stage. It says a lot about how, through design, a specific institutional facility can be sited on an increasingly urban piece of land in

Above left: **The most prominent landmark on the site is the triangular SAFTI tower.**

Above right: **To suggest the notion of progression, MGT breaks away from the formality of the orthogonal, axial plan when it introduces the only major curve in the complex for the main building of the Command Staff College.**

land-scarce Singapore.

The project called for a hierarchy of functions, a number of tenants and a dual user base—that is, private and public areas were needed. The overall plan is formal (though not rigid) and highly axial and utilises the landform to great effect. Individual buildings are sited according to function, hierarchy and meaning and they are interconnected by covered verandahs and walkways. The overall result is a plan that embodies a reasoned, intellectual approach to place-making.

Four major axes have been generated. Two are obvious and are referred to as the first and second axes but it becomes clear, upon reading the plan, that another two axes are present. All four provide the complex with a formal order by which the various buildings are placed on plan.

Overall, it is discernible that the entire series of buildings is located with a close appreciation of the land. Up close, the architecture is, like the site planning, hierarchical and formal. The achievement of this balance (or harmony) between built form and natural form has been acknowledged by Mitchell Giurgola and Thorp (MGT) to be the result of a collaborative effort with landscape architects Aspinwall Clouston.

The SAFTI Military Institute is a superbly orchestrated complex of many parts brought together with a fine understanding of the whole. Despite the machinations innate in both programme and process, as can be expected in a project of this kind and of this size, MGT have managed to imbue the place with a refined grace and a sense of order amidst the formality. Against the animation that the cadets and other trainees bring to the

place as a matter of course, the complex sits regal and elegant on its natural perch. If the former is the expression of the serious disciplined character of military training, the latter can only be the product of a skillful definition of cultural and architectural traditions. While the complex may have been designed to appear as if it "wanted to be there" on the hilly terraces, the fact is it certainly looks that way. On the whole then, while it has been said that the concept for the SAFTI Military Institute was to be evocative of the notions of itinerary and ritual, this is perhaps a subtext. What is clearly evident is a complex evocative of the notions of pride and place, the complementary notions that best befit a very new, national military institution.

The architecture of the Singapore Discovery Centre (SDC) is essentially a container with a darkened interior for holding a dazzling display of light and sound. It is programmed as an interactive museum that exploits the heat generated by popular entertainment methods for the purpose of educating the masses on issues of military and national defence and stirring patriotic Singaporean sentiments.

SINGAPORE DISCOVERY CENTRE

DP Architects Pte Ltd
Design Consultant:
Mitchell Giurgola and Thorp Associates
1996

BY VINCENT LIM

Above and right: **The architects have exercised good taste and restraint to create a subtle piece of work that boxes up the functions imaginatively.**

Given the transparency of the programme, you would think that the architects would attempt to load some kind of symbolism onto the image of the building. But they would rather not, it seems. A prudent decision perhaps. A programme like this, if taken to its literal and logical conclusion, could easily lead to kitsch. Mitchell, Giurgola and Thorp Associates (MGT), in association with DP Architects Pte Ltd, has exercised its characteristic good taste and restraint to create a subtle piece of work that boxes up the functions imaginatively.

The building (located at the corner of the vast SAFTI Military Institute site) cannot be seen from the main road. Vehicles have to be relinquished at the parking lot by the main road so that however the visitor arrives, one way of approaching the building, the way the architects have determined, will be experienced by all.

The SDC is reached after a short trek uphill along a covered path. At a strategic point, the path twists to the right to create a transition which reveals a commanding vista of SAFTI Lake (with a lone fountain) on the left and the SDC up ahead. It is also revealed at this point that the museum is a large metal slice wedged on the side of the lake. The architects have raised an earth berm around the lake so that from the SDC, the ground datum largely excludes views of the

nondescript industrial buildings surrounding it. The enclosing device gives the illusion of seclusion.

Up ahead, the SDC beckons, but its presence is somewhat diluted by the triangular SAFTI Tower which looms in the background like an elegant needle—another vista incidence intended by MGT. It will become apparent as the route is traversed, that not only have the architects planted a series of choreographed vistas, they have also threaded a sequence that balances the allure of artificially induced sensations with the restorative charm of nature.

It is ironic that the SDC should somewhat resemble the grey industrial buildings it is trying to exclude from

view. The first impression of this interactive museum is that of a reticent metal wedge set against a verdant backdrop. The usual expectation of the front façades of museums is conspicuously missing. Whatever the reason for downplaying the architecture, the reticence successfully builds up to the surprise which the architects intend to spring upon the visitor.

At the entry plaza, merriment is provided by a clutter of boxes which contain the three ancillary facilities—the smallest is painted in yellow, the next (housing the hospitality area) is coloured red while the largest (containing the Iwerks Theatre where a three-dimensional wire-frame chilli crab performs its virtual action) is fin-

ished in white. The boxes are collaged against the main body of the building, an imposing triangular mass with a mono-pitched roof. The strong shape begets the question: "Why a triangular shape?" Could the triangle have been chosen for its three faces, which like the SAFTI Tower, are supposed to symbolise the triumvirate of army, air force and navy?

Once past the main door, in the parallelogram-shaped lobby, a ramp ascends to a large picture window where the architects offer another view of SAFTI Lake. It is the last glimpse of nature before the visitor is squeezed through a small doorway into a journey of technologically manufactured sights and sounds.

The museum is a large metal slice wedged on the side of the lake.

Above: **The ramp between the "Promise of Peace" exhibit and the lower galleries opens out to a courtyard festooned with military hardware.**

Right top: **Section**

Right centre: **Elevation**

Below: **First storey plan**

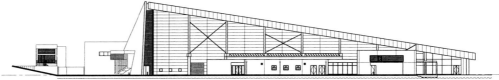

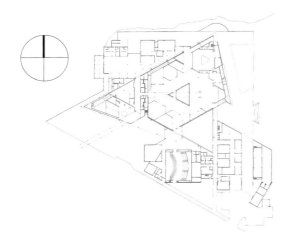

The short history of Singapore, from the days of colonial yore to the horror of the Japanese occupation, from the pre- and post-Independence traumas to the present day, is collapsed into a brief walkthrough in this section. For a yet unknown reason, the floor continues up a ramp along the entire route in this section—christened "Milestones"—going past dioramas (e.g. a near full-scale mockup of a HDB flat complete with washing on bamboo poles) and interactive displays (e.g. mini video monitors tucked into HDB-style letter boxes revealed only when the flaps are lifted).

The reason for the ramp is unveiled with dramatic flair just past the threshold into the next section, known as "Singapore Today". Low-key experience switches to a superlative mode here, and a cavernous space opens up without warning. It's a blockbuster effect.

It becomes apparent that the ramping up is calculated to sweep the visitor off his feet at that strategic threshold—the elevated platform from where the many digital treats and thrills that fill the triangular hall are held out to entice. This is a Hollywood-style impact. But there is also a pragmatic reason for the ramping up—it clears a space at ground level for tucking in service areas in a cleverly compact way.

To this point and for the next few exhibits, the experience of the museum is in the possession of the architect and the curator, so to speak. The visitor, after having adjusted to the big surprise, is trundled along on the axial bridge (not unlike the one that used to span across the atrium of Raffles City) to a video wall terminus. Here is the "Promise of Peace" exhibit, an imaginative piece of illusion making. Four canted panels of mirrors flank the bank of video screens to create an illusion of a spherical video wall with edges that recede into virtual infinity.

The prescribed and ceremonial route to the video wall slices through the heart of the museum, a triangular pavilion nestled within the triangular main body. The surfaces are lined with a grid of sleek black mirrors. This pavilion is perhaps the tightest attempt at interfacing technology and

Left: **The interactive museum exploits the heat generated by popular entertainment methods for the purpose of educating the masses on issues of military and national defence and stirring patriotic Singaporean sentiments.**

Below: **The visitor crosses an axial bridge to a video wall terminus. Four canted panels of mirrors flank the bank of video screens to create an illusion of a spherical video wall with edges that recede into virtual infinity.**

151

architecture in the SDC. The walls of the pavilion are multi-tasked, serving as enclosure as well as screens. Technology is grafted onto the skin. At the call of buttons, each tagged with a simple question on Singapore, panels flash to show popular local icons—such as a grinning Ah Meng.

How the exhibits should be seen is written out for the visitor like a storyboard. There isn't much room for one to assemble one's own narrative of exhibits and sequence as one submits to a curriculum of activities. That prescribed route, however, breaks down and dissipates once past the video wall exhibit.

The circuitous route is dissolved in the lower hall by locating the exhibits freely within the triangular space. The visitor is able to roam randomly among the exhibits and interactive displays, which include advance versions of Nintendo games that let

one parachute or slay villains virtually. Less high-tech attractions include a simulation of a jungle at night.

It is to the credit of MGT that it has integrated the siting and the programme to achieve much needed moments of reconnecting with nature. The ramp between the "Promise of Peace" exhibit and the lower galleries opens out to a courtyard festooned with military hardware (planes, tanks, guns, etc.) set against a green backdrop. It is a welcome break, the burst of natural light providing a much needed respite from the surfeit of blinking lights and images. At the end of the sequence is a café, which also has a little outdoor extension, a deck shaded by a membrane canopy that hangs over the water. With these attractive interfaces, MGT has demonstrated that the blind-box is not an inevitability for a digital media-type interactive museum.

Just as at the start of the sequence, the café at the end returns the visitor to the view of SAFTI Lake with its lone fountain. The return to the key vista gives a sense of closure to the Singapore Discovery Centre journey.

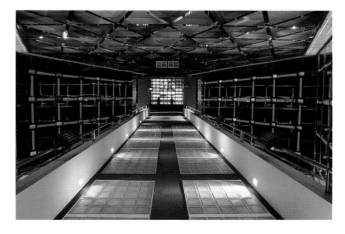

Another revolution has taken place, albeit a quiet one, at the corner of Bukit Merah View. In what has been called its first co-location project, the People's Association's (PA) brief for the new Henderson Community Club involved its integration with the Bukit Merah West Neighbourhood Police Centre. While it is not a new concept to combine community clubs with other facilities, the amalgamation with the police centre would certainly raise some eyebrows, even evoking the days of riots and political strife.

HENDERSON CC & THE BUKIT MERAH WEST NEIGHBOURHOOD POLICE CENTRE

Forum Architects
2000

BY HEE LIMIN

The juxtaposition of the two functions of a community club (CC) and a police centre brings to mind Foucault's idea of heterotopia—a place that has the power of juxtaposing, in a single real place, different spaces that are incompatible with each other. The architectural problematic of creating a marriage of the institutionalised form of discipline and the law and that of a veritable "social condenser" had to be met by understanding the issues involved in the combination of such binary opposites, and not merely providing the styling of the container. The architects' strategy was to "try to ameliorate the differences and to focus on the common points of the

brief. Instead of creating a fortress or castle, an elegant solution in the form of an articulated mesh screen was used to create a neat and structured façade.

As one approaches the community club, the building grows out of the hillock site, unveiling first, a two-storey-high curved glass block that turns round to reveal the curved articulation screen wall, and finally, the more solid form of the police centre. The screen offers tantalising glimpses of what may be behind it, while a jaunty canopy, uplifted by flamboyant yellow struts, invites the visitor entering from the street. With just a little anxiety as to what to expect by entering via the stairs or lift, one is pleas-

HENDERSON
COMMUNITY CLUB

antly surprised to discover the sudden opening out of the space into an upper level courtyard. Here, the organisation of the massing and space becomes clear, with the community club and foyer on your right and the police block on your left.

The mesh screen offers clear views of the surrounding blocks opposite the street. Circulation elements, such as stairs, a bubble-lift and corridors linking the two facilities, are found behind the mesh screen—defining itself as a three-dimensional façade. Bright primary colours, such as red, blue and yellow, are employed as highlights to project the fun and recreational function of the community club against the more neutral and serious front for the police centre. Colour is also extended to the floor finishes to emphasise circulation nodes. The neutrality of the articulated mesh screen gives the building

an air of quiet reserve, but at night, the screen magically transforms the building into a luminous lantern animated by the bustling goings-on behind its façade.

A characteristic of heterotopia is that, in relation to the rest of space, it creates a sense of illusion that reveals how real space is more illusory. Anyone can enter the heterotopia, but in reality, this itself is an illusion. One thinks that one has entered but by entering, one is really excluded. Here, binary opposites are played out: the porosity of the mesh façade versus the solidity of the police centre; the shared courtyard space which is, in reality, the "other" from the point of view of the police centre—a space only to watch but not to partake in;

the seemingly well-linked complex is ironically really separated by the linkway, which has separate flights of stairs for each facility; the connectedness of the blocks is illusory—in fact there is no through way due to the high security required by the police centre.

Given the diametrically opposite requirements of the CC and the police centre, the PA may want to review if such a marriage is indeed tenable or simply an act of convenience that cannot be consummated. Only through a process of community participation, of negotiation and even contestation of space can a synergy and pride of place occur in such an institutionalised construct of a place for the people.

Left: **At night, a curved mesh screen wall is magically transformed into a luminous lantern animated by the bustling goings-on behind its façade.**

Above: **Elevation**

Below left to right: **Circulation elements, such as stairs, a bubble-lift and corridors, are found behind the mesh screen.**

Opposite: **The seemingly well-linked complex is ironically really separated by the "linkway".**

Enigmatic from the exterior, Gallery Evason Hotel was conceptualised as a HIP (Highly Individual Places) Hotel. This "class" of hotel was classified/identified by Herbert YPMA through two publications, *HIP Hotels City* and *Escape*. Associated with "big-name" designers, the likes of Starck, Conran and Hempel, these hotels are defined by YPMA as an "exciting, stylish alternative to the dreary sameness of chain hotels and the stuffy pomposity of traditional 'grand' hotels".

GALLERY EVASON

**William Lim Associates
and Tangguanbee
Architects
2000**

BY PETER SIM

A twisted cuboidal form,
with seemingly random and
multicoloured windows,
stands like a massive pop-art
signpost at the Mohamed
Sultan Road end of the site.

The developers and architects of Gallery Evason Hotel sought to place it in the HIP class of designer hotels that intentionally fall outside the staid star rating system. The purpose was to create a specific lifestyle for the design-conscious jet-setter who looks for a twist of the extraordinary.

Gallery Evason reads like a puzzle and consists of several seemingly disjointed, perhaps even unrelated, building forms, collaged together. Planted on a newly cleared urban sector previously colonised by warehouses, the site itself is an experimental and temporal space-in-transition.

The combination of architects involved is almost as interesting as the building forms themselves. William Lim and Teh Joo Heng (who now heads his own practice) from WLA and Tang Guan Bee from Tangguanbee Architects all give one another equal credit for the design. Known for their strong design language and individualistic flair, both firms have an impressive *oeuvre* of work. Three generations of the local architectural fraternity are represented between them and embodied in this quirky piece.

Consisting of a main building mass divided into three distinct parts, with a series of smaller volumes interspersed around it, the formal composition is hardly simple. However, this complexity feels entirely appropriate for the site and programme at hand, as well as for the agenda of the designers.

The transparency and interaction

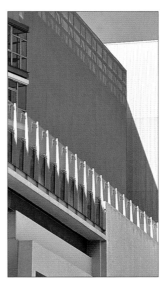

Far left: **Gallery Evason collages together a variety of forms.**

Centre: **The complex array of forms feels entirely appropriate for the site.**

Left: **A central rectilinear block is veiled by a perforated steel screen, meant to serve as a climatic filter as well as a projector for images.**

Bottom: **In sharp contrast to the elevation along Mohamed Sultan Road, the façade facing the Singapore River is almost industrial in appearance.**

between the interior and exterior are symptomatic of many parts of the design. The architects wanted to reverse the conventional, inward-looking and hermetically sealed atriums of establishment hotels. And in doing so, encourage a greater sense of activity with the urban environment and streetscape.

Secondary facilities, such as restaurants and a health club, are located in several small building forms not contained within the main mass but surrounding and attaching themselves like bodily prosthetics to the parent hotel block. These "minor" parts contain several witty elements—the more obvious ones being a cantilevered glass swimming pool and a tongue-in-cheek pseudo warehouse form recalling a less-than-ten-

tative allegiance to its roots.

Beyond the visual titillation and spatial excitement, the designers insist that there is a strong underlying theoretical basis for the design. William Lim enthuses that the design is about the present urban condition in a post-modern era, one of plurality and difference. What's refreshing to note here is the fact that the architects are moving beyond the catch-phrase of "tropical architecture" and are trying to address larger issues pertaining to the condition of living in a millennial metropolis. After all, is architecture not as much (or arguably more) a cultural construct as it is a physical one?

It can be a little difficult to remain objective about the Gallery Evason Hotel, but this involuntary

subjectivity may already be a measure of its success it provokes and challenges. It dares to be.

HIP or not, the idea is to make essentially a hotel that can replace the experience of the place of travel. When Gallery Evason succeeds in becoming the destination, the end itself: a sight and an experience worth the extra mention, not second fiddle to the other kitsch, campy tourist class hotels in Singapore, then, HIP it shall be. However, as far as architecture can go, the architects have managed to create an eye-catching, unconventional and provocative piece of work. At the end of the day it must be asked how one actually quantifies a notion as cryptic as "HIP"? Indeed where does style end and substance begin?

chapter 7

BEACH ROAD,
KALLANG
AND EAST COAST

The concept of community has, in recent years, become problematic. Community can no longer be tied simply to the place where one lives. With increased social mobility, we have become members of "other" communities—the community of the workplace, the fitness club or the church. Many people across a wide age range belong to the "community of the Internet". People often spend more time at work or in their leisure pursuits than in their home location. Marine Parade Community Centre (MPCC) seemingly sets out, explicitly or otherwise, to tap into these other pursuits.

MARINE PARADE COMMUNITY CENTRE

William Lim Associates
2000

Opposite: **The community centre is clad in a huge wall mural, a commissioned work of art by Thai artist Surachai Yeamsiri.**

Right: **Adjacent to a HDB estate but no longer embedded within it, the new community centre can be seen as an attempt to engage the wider community.**

Page 156: **The Gateway**

Page 157: **Sennett House.**

Marine Parade Community Centre's multiple programme includes a branch library, a Starbucks Café, a "black box" theatre occupied by The Necessary Stage (a juxtaposition that would have been unthinkable in the not-too-distant past) and the community centre itself, with its diverse range of pursuits.

The siting of the building is important. Adjacent to the HDB housing, but no longer embedded in it, the new CC can be seen as an attempt to engage the wider community. The activities of the complex are planned to overlap and to coalesce: the MPCC becomes a one-stop destination for the entire family—at least that is the theory. The barriers to access seem-

ingly disappear altogether with public routes directly through the complex.

This potentially rich congruence of programmes is expressed architecturally as a collage of diverse elements. The library is predominantly glass, with horizontal fins and a transparency which belies the usual idea of a library as an inward orientated pursuit. Starbucks Café has a street

Above left: **T.K. Sabapathy, the art critic, describes the wall mural in terms of its "dynamic, symbolic content, the whole coming together, either recessing or projecting".**

Above right: **The roof form of the CC can be read as a metaphor for the leaves of the palm tree.**

frontage and the potential to spread into the shared forecourt. It, too, is transparent and open and its activities are likely to be exteriorised, given the current penchant for alfresco coffee drinking. The Necessary Stage entrance is downplayed as a result of the late introduction of this activity into the programme but perhaps that can be turned to an advantage—after all, you do not need neon lights to advertise an avant garde theatre. The building looks as if it is the product of several designers within William Lim Architects (as indeed it is) and this

again can be considered a strength, as the earlier CC's often expressed an improbable homogeneity. William Lim promotes a pluralist approach, expressed through a multiplicity of materials and forms.

The CC itself is clothed, embellished or clad in a huge wall mural, a commissioned work of art by Surachai Yeamsiri, which effectively "hides" the activities within. The paradox here is evident: the library that ought, one might think, to look in, looks out, while the CC, which one would have thought should look out and engage

with the community, looks in.

The wall mural thus has to perform several functions simultaneously, perhaps more than was initially envisaged. It has to convey heterogeneity, pluralism, a coming together of diverse interests and groups. The art critic T.K. Sabapathy does not subscribe to my view that it also "conceals" the overt political nature of a CC. He describes the work in terms of its "dynamic, symbolic content, the whole coming together, either recessing or projecting". He argues that the work of art has "to frame the commu-

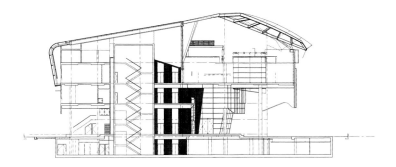

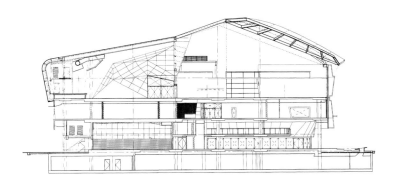

Above: **The rich congruence of programmes is expressed as a collage of diverse elements.**

Left top to bottom: **Three sections depicting the community centre's diverse programmes.**

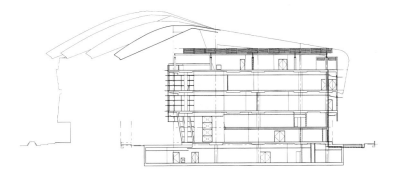

nity" and yet simultaneously "disengage" itself from the activities within the CC. Marine Parade CC is undoubtedly an aesthetically pleasing piece of public artwork, sufficiently bold to create an impact at a distance, while inviting closer scrutiny. This is an important attribute and it is a huge achievement by the artist to have transcended these two scales.

The "crowning glory" of the CC is its roof form, which can be read as a metaphor for the leaves of a palm tree. The roof floats above the rooftop basketball court. This, too, is a departure from the norm; in other CCs, the basketball court occupies space at ground level. At another level, the form of the building can be interpreted as a "dragon" with the roof as a

crest and the the artwork as the eye of the dragon. The horizontal louvres on the library block can be seen as the tail fins of the auspicious beast.

In response to the brief, the architects and the team of consultants have produced a design which makes a substantial leap forward in expressing the new "concept of community" in the Singapore context.

Stretched taut in the sunlight, the glittering profile of the Singapore Indoor Stadium's roof is a dazzling sight. The rising, curved roof, seen most dramatically from the Benjamin Sheares Bridge, seems to possess an almost ethereal, floating quality. Like the framed expressive structures we have come to associate with many modern stadiums built by contemporary Japanese architects, the Singapore Indoor Stadium is a sculptural object that gives form to the internal space. The manner in which the roof of such building types is conceived is instrumental to the character of the building.

SINGAPORE INDOOR STADIUM

**RSP Architects Planners
and Engineers
in association with Kenzo Tange
1990**

BY TAN HOCK BENG

The metal-clad surface of
the luminous roof contrasts
strongly with the monu-
mental concrete steps to
give an ambivalent sense
of lightness combined
with mass.

A need for a world-class indoor stadium to replace the antiquated indoor sports complex at Geylang was fulfilled when the Singapore Indoor Stadium was officially declared opened on New Year's Eve, 1990. At Kallang, the unrepentant modernist, Kenzo Tange, a master of the bold gesture, continued his quest for pure and universally beautiful forms. He sought to recapture the crisp elegance of his Tokyo Olympic Swimming Pool, a favourite among architectural *cognoscenti* and widely acclaimed as Tange's most outstanding building.

The crowning feature of the Singapore Indoor Stadium is definitely not as dramatic and complex as the Tokyo Olympic Pool. In fact, many of Tange's critics feel that his recent projects, though proving the continuing relevance of modern architectural schemata, have not demonstrated any innovation nor discovered new expressive territories. Yet he continues to be an immensely popular architect in Singapore.

Tange's stadium yields all kinds of images, depending on who is look-

Above left: **The stadium is a variation on a monochromatic theme.**

Above right: **On reaching the bottom of the broad flight of steps, the building disappears from view, only to unfold slowly as one moves up. This architectural device adds a sense of ceremonial drama.**

Left: **Plan at concourse level**

ing at it. Because such a conspicuously visible symbol of technology exists somewhere between abstraction and representation, it inevitably evokes subliminal associations, ranging from a hat to a Chinese temple to Mount Fuji. The metal-clad curved surface of the luminous roof contrasts strongly with the monumental concrete steps at the front entrance to give an ambivalent sense of lightness combined with mass.

Situated on an axis with the approach route, the silver-grey sheen of the symmetrical complex beckons the visitor with the promise of soaring space. But on reaching the bottom of the broad flight of steps, the building disappears from view, only to unfold

slowly as one walks up. This architectural gesture works well and adds a sense of ceremonial drama. The controlled variation on a monochromatic theme also gives the stadium a potentially monumental rhetoric. Shaped like a diamond on plan, the great vault of the roof has an unsupported span of a staggering 100 metres (328 feet) and rises magnificently to a peak of 40 metres (131 feet).

Inside the large arena of the stadium, the taut curve of the roof is accentuated by swathes of light from the skylights which follow the contours of the roof membrane. The result is a virtuoso display of spatial and experiential richness.

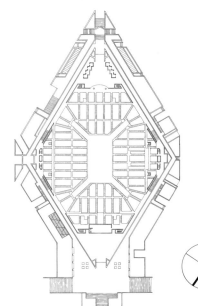

The Gateway is a handsome, well-engineered development. Its identical parallelogram tower blocks, clad with smooth aluminium and butt-jointed tinted glass, have a powerful sculptural quality. The precision of the sharp corners allied to the reflective images gives the towers a unique identity. This is one quality of a gateway.

THE GATEWAY

Chua Ka Seng & Partners
Design Consultant
I.M. Pei and Partners
1991

Above: **The simple geometric building forms have a dynamic relationship to each other and to the observer. The angle of the sun plays a role in this relationship so that in certain conditions the towers sparkle like cut diamonds.**

Right: **First storey plan**

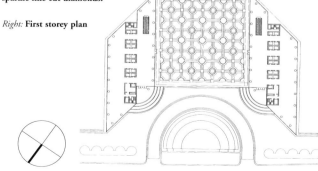

The 37-storey Gateway twin office towers are located at a key vehicular entry point to the city from the eastern suburbs of the island. The axis between the two towers appears to be related to a notional line extended to the mouth of the Singapore River. Each 150-metre (492-foot) high building is a pure parallelogram with its apex transformed into a sharp point at a 45-degree angle. A triangular notch running up one of the narrow sides of each building creates a multi-faceted façade as well as additional corner office space.

The cast-in-place reinforced concrete structures are sheathed with alternating bands of clear anodised aluminium spandrels and fixed panels of lightly-reflective tinted glass. An aluminium string course separates the fixed glass vision panels from a 450-

millimetre (18-inch) strip of partly operable glass openings.

The simple geometric building forms have a dynamic relationship to each other and to the observer as one's angle of vision changes. The angle of the sun plays a role in this relationship—in certain conditions, the towers sparkle like cut diamonds.

It is arguable, however, that it has not totally achieved the impact intended by the developers who hyped it as "an aspiring, soaring building...symbolic of the nation which has achieved much and continues to strive for greatness". In reality, the two towers appear to be stunted in relation to the space between them. The "soaring" quality that was intended really demands that the two towers be at least another 15 storeys higher, thus reducing the apparent distance between them. This was not achiev-

able because of the height restrictions imposed in the Paya Lebar military airport flightpath.

Passers-by who admire the sculptural form of the towers may miss what is possibly the least known quality of the building—a beautifully landscaped plaza at the base of the towers. It is a remarkably cool haven with seats set among small fountains and dappled shade beneath a canopy of carefully placed trees. It is paved with granite that extends into the one-and-a-half storey lobby of each tower. On an island formed by the semi-circular drive at the major entrance, a large fountain falls into a semi-circular pool and separates the courtyard from the noisy highway. The design of this space won an award from the Italian Accademia Delle Belle Arti Carrara in 1992 for the combination of stone, water and greenery.

As with so many tower blocks in Singapore, the question arises whether The Gateway, with its sheer glass façade, is a suitable response to the tropical climate. Its form is more suited to Europe or North America.

Left: **The landscaped plaza at the base of the towers is a cool haven with seats set beneath a canopy of carefully placed trees.**

Below left and right: **The identical tower blocks, clad with smooth aluminium and butt-jointed tinted glass, have a powerful sculptural quality. The precision of the sharp corners allied to the reflective images gives the towers a unique identity.**

Paul Rudolph has designed two high-rise towers in Singapore, the Colonnade in Grange Road (1985) and the Concourse. Like the Wisma Dharmala Sakti in Jakarta, the highly articulated external façades of Rudolph's Singapore projects clearly reveal the internal accommodation arrangements.

THE CONCOURSE

Architects 61 Pte Ltd
Design Consultant:
Paul Rudolph Architect
1994

Right top: **Section**

Right bottom: **Approaching the city from the international airport, the tower stands out as a landmark for its distinctive silhouette when viewed across the Kallang River basin.**

The correlation between form and function in the Concourse is no accident and arises out of Rudolph's grounding in modern architecture, for he was taught by Walter Gropius at Harvard. But perhaps inadvertently, it also suggests an appropriate aesthetic for the Tropical Skyscraper. The use of solar shading, wide overhangs, communal gardens and external balconies has some similarities with the ideas advanced by Dr Ken Yeang for the Bioclimatic Skyscraper.

The site was acquired in competition in the 1979 URA (8th) Sale of Sites. The project commenced in 1981 as the Hong Fok Centre but construction stopped when the Singapore economy was hit by recession in the mid-1980s. Architects 61 and Paul Rudolph re-designed the complex in 1987, retaining what was already constructed but revamping the remainder in order to accommodate new programmatic requirements.

The mixed development comprises a 41-storey office tower, a three-level retail podium and nine storeys of serviced apartments. This again is an

Left: **The most obvious architectural feature is the aluminium curtainwall system incorporating inclined windows which form clusters of units.**

Bottom left: **The faceted façade of the serviced apartment units.**

Bottom right: **The use of solar shading, wide overhangs, communal gardens and external balconies suggest an appropriate aesthetic for the Tropical Skyscraper.**

interesting programme and it critically questions the single use zoning practice. The three distinct components, with their different usage, have separate entrances.

Approaching the city from Changi Airport, the tower stands out as a landmark because of its distinctive silhouette when viewed across the Kallang River basin. Its most obvious architectural feature is the aluminium curtainwall system incorporating inclined windows that form clusters of units. These interlocking clusters are stacked vertically (like dinner plates), one above the other, rotating around the building.

The tower is octagonal in plan (in Chinese culture, the number eight is associated with prosperity) and is supported by huge pilotii. This again is a feature of Rudolph's earlier buildings in the United States such as the Art and Architecture building at Yale (1964) and also of the Colonnade.

A five-storey atrium lobby greets visitors to the Concourse and 14 sky-atria within the tower form reception lobbies for multinational corporate organisations. The serviced apartment units in the lower block vary in size and facilities include a swimming pool, squash courts and a fitness centre. The apartments overlook Nicoll Highway and the Rochor River basin. Shops are arranged around another three-storey sky-lit atrium in the retail podium.

Kallang Airport was the first civil aviation terminal in Singapore. It was completed in 1937 to the designs of Frank Dorrington Ward, chief architect of the Public Works Department. The original airfield was circular, with the principal runway orientated roughly east-west, along the line of what is now Stadium Road. Sea planes landed in the Kallang River estuary and the present Police Coast Guard HQ is located here.

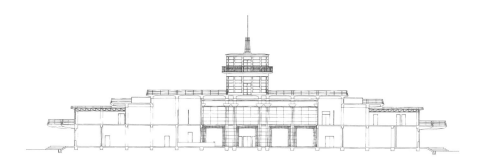

PEOPLE'S ASSOCIATION HQ
KALLANG AIRPORT TERMINAL

Architects 61 Pte Ltd
1993

Top: **Elevation**

Below: **The approach to the former terminal building is along a palm tree lined boulevard, flanked by buildings which once housed subsidiary airline offices.**

The modernist language of the former Kallang Airport terminal building, with its parallel concrete floor and roof slabs and a central cylindrical glass tower, has been interpreted as a metaphor for a biplane with an elevated cockpit. Many early modernist buildings had similar imagery, with references to machines and ocean liners.

The complex of buildings now serves as the headquarters of the People's Association (PA), an organisation with numerous roles but principally concerned with youth and community development. The PA took over the building in 1960. In 1993, the building was substantially renovated at a cost of S$4 million. Numerous appendages were removed and its elegant lines were once again revealed. The main entrance was moved back to its original position in the centre of the terminal, aligned with the principal axis road.

The approach to the former terminal building, along a palm tree lined boulevard, flanked by buildings which once housed subsidiary airline offices and the old Qantas hangar, is magnificent. Sadly, the setting of the building was compromised by the construction of Nicoll Highway, a semi-expressway which now cuts across what was formerly the airport taxiing and departure area. But one can still imagine the days of yore when DC3's and De Havilland Comets lined the tarmac and friends waved farewell to departing travellers from the roof and balconies of the terminal building.

Left: The modernist language of the former airport terminal building, with its parallel concrete floor and roof slabs and a central cylindrical glass control tower, has been interpreted as a metaphor for a biplane with an elevated cockpit.

Above: The People's Association (PA) now uses the former airline offices for their community-related projects.

The former president of LaSalle-SIA College of the Arts, sculptor Joseph McNally, sees the overall development plan as "contributing to a robust, carefree yet creative learning environment". The college is perceived to have an international laissez-faire style of administration, which is subtly conveyed in the juxtaposition of forms and the architectural language employed.

LASALLE-SIA COLLEGE OF THE ARTS

William Lim Associates
1995

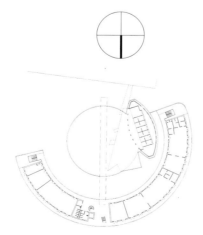

Above: **The strong curved form responds to the curvature of the Geylang River. It creates a potent image for the college when one approaches from the city.**

Right: **Plan of the Fine Arts/Design School. The Fine Arts/Design School is a semi-circular building.**

They did not have a clean canvas to work on and had to deal with an existing 1960s school building designed by the Public Works Department (PWD), which divided the campus into unequal and unbalanced portions. They adopted the approach of developing the campus in phases, when building funds become available. The architects see the project as an ongoing and dynamic process. The site-planning sought to provide positive open spaces, a clear circulation and orientation system, and the sub-division of the college into distinct parts. Complexity and diversity were achieved through the placement of buildings in relation to the spine. The existing school buildings were kept and utilised for a number of key functions, including administration and galleries such as the Earl Liu Gallery.

The first new facility on site was the Fine Arts/Design School, a semi-circular building completed in 1995. Its strong curved form responds to the curvature of the Geylang River. It creates a potent image for the college when one approaches from the city and it is first seen as a curved build-

In 1991, William Lim, Mok Wei Wei, Teh Joo Heng and project architect Ng Weng Pan devised an overall development strategy for LaSalle-SIA College of the Arts, which sought to break the campus into a series of courtyards enclosed by new building blocks and linked together with a two-storey high "spine-connector".

ing wrapped by a projected giant concrete sunscreen. This concrete sunscreen shields the building from the afternoon sun and behind it are smaller, scale-giving elements. The curved building has many merits in terms of its contextual response and its ability to enclose a space. It terminates the two-storey-high "spine-connector" that runs the entire length of the campus.

A single-storey canteen is cradled within the inner curve of the Fine Arts/Design building overlooking an outdoor amphitheatre. This building is conceived as a large-scale sculpture; an "assemblage of fragments" which provides visual interest and contrast to the curved block behind. The canteen is a catalyst for informal student/staff interaction. The soaring roof structures are a strong focus and a convivial social space directly related to the outdoor amphitheatre.

The second building completed, at the opposite end of the spine, within the overall master plan is the Drama/Dance School. Its inherent flexibility has been well received by its users. The south façade has a timber louvred screen intended to protect the building from direct afternoon sun. It can also be interpreted as a giant billboard, a suitably scaled sign to signify the front of the school.

The strategy of employing a spine-connector and a series of court-yards to mould the disparate parts into a cogent whole is masterly, as is the decision to sub-divide the major project into small, identifiable parts.

Above left and right: **The Drama/Dance School— a simple structure with "overtones of Aldo Rossi's rationalism". The south façade has a timber louvred screen which is intended to protect the building from the afternoon sun.**

Left: **Elevation of the Fine Arts/Design School**

The Khoo House is located in an established residential neighbourhood comprising bungalows and semi-detached houses in a variety of styles typical of middle-income estates. As land becomes an increasingly scarce commodity in Singapore, such sites are becoming much sought after. Existing houses are invariably demolished to make way for new residences with increased floor areas.

KHOO HOUSE

Ken Lou Architects
1995

The front façade is an inter-play of horizontal and verti-cal elements, characterised by a focal point corner bal-cony and an asymmetrical curved roof.

Curiously, the Khoo House does not look like a semi-detached house. Ken Lou set out to question the typology in which a house shares a common wall with its neighbour in a slightly defer-ential manner and usually looks out onto a front and a rear garden.

The parti for the Khoo House utilises and innovatively transforms a different typology—that of the Singapore urban shophouse which, in this context, becomes a 30-metre (98-foot) long, 7-metre (23-foot) wide rectangular extrusion with two inter-nal airwells (landscaped courtyards).

It is an ingenious ploy. The main entrance to the house is at the side and the geometry of the first storey is shifted so that it is angled at 2 degrees to the second storey, thus cre-ating a subtle tapering of rooms at the front of the site. A practical reason for this is it creates additional width at

Above left and right: **A strong sense of free-flowing space pervades the house. External spaces penetrate into the interior so that conventional constructs of "interior" and "exterior" are questioned and redefined.**

Bottom left: **Elevations to Dunbar Walk**

Bottom centre: **Section**

Bottom right: **Side elevation**

the side of the house to park two cars. It also sets up a related shift in the geometry of the front boundary way to deflect bad *feng shui* at an inauspicious "T" road junction.

Ken Lou describes his intentions in the following manner: "Each courtyard in the house plan has its own character and function. The front lawn is a split-level terrace for entertaining, the internal courtyards are miniature gardens for ventilation and contemplation and the rear courtyard is a utilitarian space for washing and drying clothes.

"In terms of architectural expression, the building is a composition of interlocking planes and voids. The reinforced concrete structure and flat roofs define a physical framework within which a strong visual sense of free-flowing space pervades the house. This is especially evident along the party wall, which at the ground level continues visually uninterrupted from front to back, throughout the entire length of the site."

"This ambiguity of boundary is a recurring pattern in Asian culture and here, it is incorporated into a house that is contemporary, utilising a "late modern" architectural language.

"Its simplicity represents a contemporary response to the notion of tropical design within an urban setting, without necessarily recalling the imagery of pitched roofs and colonnaded arcades."

The house responds to climatic considerations in several ways: with doors in the open-to-sky courtyard and in the north and south elevations, air movement is induced by the "venturi effect". The 3.5-metre (11.5-foot) floor to ceiling height provides air-mass to aid in natural cooling.

The Khoo House questions the definition of suburbia. In this instance, the adjoining semi-detached "twin" is dwarfed. The party wall, instead of expressing conjunction and similarity, becomes a device for expressing demarcation and difference. In the Singaporean context, it is a phenomenon that might be described as the "urbanisation of suburbia".

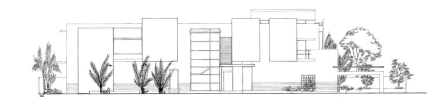

Educational institutions are highly complex architectural types, charged with many competing tendencies and ideological differences on how they should be planned, used and seen. Divergent priorities are manifested at different levels, such as the desire to project the sense of institutional continuity and tradition, yet at the same time wanting to appear "modern" and "progressive".

ITE BALESTIER

Architects Vista
1997

BY LEONG TENG WUI

The field is framed as a formal urban space.

Users of institutions are not passive subjects; they shape and particularise spaces in ways often not intended nor anticipated by those who design or plan institutions. These forces are encoded and represented through architecture in various ways throughout the historical transformation of its architectural type. From the traditional master/apprentice studio to the Foucaultian education machine for supervising, hierarchising and

rewarding, the architectural type does not exist *a priori* but is constantly reinterpreted in light of the ethos, aspirations and demands of its time. Such ethos often reflect the changing relations of the collective and the individual, the public and the private, and the object and the subject. To compound this further, modern educational institutions, which are in the care of public stewardship, have the added ethical responsibility to certain "public" interests and a budget often

involving public funds. Hence educational institutions have often been held as the public icons of their times in that they are seen as the material representation of collective values, social agendas and enduring qualities cherished by the particular "public".

Seen in this light, the Institute of Technical Education (ITE) in Balestier, located at the junction of Balestier Road, Jalan Kebun Limau and the Central Expressway, offers a conceptual lens for scrutinising ideas such

Far left: **The gridded wall frame is the dominant visual element in the design.**

Left: **An axial spine is the principal organising device.**

Above: **ITE Balestier is a coherent, disciplined and well executed project.**

Below: **Elevation**

as "publicness", identity and how the changing roles of modern institutions are translated (or not), negotiated and mediated through architecture. Three perspectives are offered as possible readings of the institution.

- The institution in the city as a specific form of public space—how the idea of the "public" is represented through the institution's spatial, visual and architectural relationship to the surrounding context and the city in which it is located.

- The institution as a type with all its received architectural conventions—how the interpretation of the architectural type invariably encodes and embodies certain assumptions about its history, the use and behaviour of the users, and the desired public

reception. Of interest here is how the type is re-interpreted in the light of modern ethos as well as the exigencies of its specific context and time.

- The institution as a contested space and how the project negotiates and mediates the complexity of competing or complementary issues surrounding that of the institution.

Although there are notable formal innovations and an admirable clarity and restraint in the control of form and space in ITE Balestier, the way the spaces are conceptualised is still based on the accepted conventional paradigm of education programming and use. This makes it fundamentally no different from the way the previous generation of schools were planned. While upgrading the

image of technical education is in itself an important first step, the basis for architectural invention is limited more to creative form-making rather than a radical and holistic re-thinking of educational spaces in tandem with modern social realities. While architects often objectify and idealise the ways architecture will shape society and its subjects, the subjects themselves invariably shape the buildings in their own ways and the project will invariably assume a complexity far greater than the sum of its architectural parts. Perhaps this is a timely reminder of the need to temper the profession's object-oriented rationality with a sobriety that actively seeks new ways to enable and accommodate social practices, and not to reduce or compartmentalise them.

In Singapore, the stunning success of public housing is laudable. With over 80 percent of the Singapore population housed in these contraptions, the state has outdone itself in providing "decent housing" for the masses. But as the Housing Development Board (HDB) celebrates its 40th year and as social demands, lifestyles and technological means change, the value of the home has shifted in the Singaporean's priorities.

CAMBRIDGE ROAD HOUSING

CESMA International Pte Ltd
1997

BY CHEE LI LIAN

New apartment blocks sprout in a facsimile manner across Singapore and the ones that do not are visually unmistakable. The Cambridge Road Housing, which consists of 291 apartment units, is of this genre.

As the euphoria of mass demand and mass supply is sated, questions of the extent to which the great housing experiment has matured must resurface. The initial manifesto was simply stated, though by no means easy to do: it was to accommodate the masses within the most economic means and to bring about improved social connections among the different ethnic and income groups. Now, newer issues take the spotlight, while the original concepts continue to apply, albeit fashioned by today's diversified demands.

Recent apartment blocks sprout in a facsimile manner and the ones that do not are visually unmistakable—Cambridge Road Housing, which consists of 291 apartment units, is of this genre. CESMA International Pte Ltd is a subsidiary of the HDB and specialises predominantly in overseas projects for the Southeast and East Asian regions. The flats were conceived as slim vertical markers and the architects were thoroughly conscious of the flats' high visibility. Having visually surprised many through its fresh vocabulary of architectural language, the project qualifies as suitable subject matter for this brief investigation into the social housing experiment.

Outwardly, the scheme manages to express an individuality that remains unrivalled in the suburban cocktail that forms its site. Social housing from an earlier period and private terrace houses reside along with the stuff that breathes life into Singapore's typical suburb—the community centre; the wet market, with its infamous hawker centre attachment; and the school, where the status quo is first introduced to young minds.

At first glance, you will be forgiven for thinking that this is a private condominium. And there are many reasons for this misconception. Even without a gated compound, the massing reads of exclusivity, with only four blocks sharing the plot. Also, the highly articulated blocks digress from the HDB norm of simple pre-cast construction. The re-thinking of this formal strategy has resulted in a series of energetic forms dressed in a lively

Far left: **Outwardly, the scheme manages to express an individuality that goes unrivalled in the suburban context.**

Above left: **A strong feature defines the point of entry.**

Above right: **The architects must be congratulated for their attempts to redefine the "skin" of public housing.**

ensemble of colours and materials.

Having met the basic physical requirements of public housing—i.e. high-density living at affordable unit prices supplied in quick time—the apartments at Cambridge Road are at least commendable in that they have achieved these exacting criteria without sacrificing individuality. Yet bold form-making to create an armature for daily life is not enough.

On closer inspection, it becomes apparent that the architecture constitutes no more than mere cosmetic treatment in elevational terms, probably executed with the expressed aim to reconcile them with the more "prestigious" condominiums. Disturbingly, there are no apparent signs of probing further into the fundamentals of shared living, no radical departure in the site layout nor the planning of the apartment units themselves. Whatever the reasons for this inertia, the results hint at some questions that are in need of urgent re-evaluation.

We speak of the new age, the impact of technology and the probability of working from home. Do these not faintly hint of a re-invention of what "home" may now mean? Changes in lifestyles (including choices of food and clothing), domestic habits and family patterns should be observed as closely as commercial trends. These are indeed clues for re-thinking the elements that constitute a "home".

The architects for the Cambridge Road Housing must be congratulated for their attempts to redefine the skin of public housing. That it is continually sought out for its striking appearance is a good start. More intense architectural thinking is needed to rejuvenate the soul of such social housing schemes, however. This is no easy task and will be met with resistance from various parties, not least a public still grappling with the second-rate label attached (by them) to public housing. Yet architecture may just be the prescription for fabricating a community that places great pride in its origins. The home unit remains an accessible and most basic component for nation building. Having measured up to many criteria, the Cambridge Road Housing will stand to be scrutinised against these specific demands.

Bugis Street is remembered by many as the infamous and boisterous haunt of transvestites who entertained visiting naval fleet during the post-war period. In the early 1990s, the old shophouses that housed the restaurants, bars and brothels in the area were acquired by the state.

178

An intelligent mix of a five-star hotel, a multiplex cinema, restaurants, bars, retail outlets and supermarkets contribute to a vibrant example of urban revival.

BUGIS JUNCTION

DP Architects Pte Ltd
1997

The Bugis Junction development site was formed by the amalgamation of three land parcels and the roads between the building blocks, namely Malay Street, Hylam Street, Malabar Street and Bugis Street, to form a single development parcel.

A planning requirement imposed upon the developer was that the pattern of existing streets, together with some of the old shophouses, were to be retained. In the past, these streets, although accessible to traffic, were pedestrianised in the evening and food stalls were set up in the manner of a traditional *pasar malam*, or night market, for dining in the street.

The increased plot ratios permitted for the site allowed two high-rise blocks to be located at the ends of the rectangular site, while the shophouses were retained in the central portion. In due course, development commenced and despite the best efforts of

the contractor, once excavation started for the contiguous underground car park which stretches the whole length of the site, it proved impossible to underpin the crumbling structures.

What the visitor sees today is a complete reconstruction to match the former buildings. To paraphrase Umberto Eco, "the entirely fake has become the new reality". The former streets are covered by glazed skylights, which create the surreal experience of a shophouse within an internalised environment.

For the purist, this experience of the shophouse in an air-conditioned street lacks authenticity, but there is no denying Bugis Junction's huge popularity and its reputation as the most successful shopping centre on the island in terms of numbers of visitors. This is, no doubt, in part a result of the location at one corner of the development of the Bugis MRT station, which permits direct access for shop-

Left: The streets in Bugis Junction are covered by glazed skylights which create the surreal experience of a shophouse within an internalised environment.

Above: The outdoor spaces at Bugis Junction are among the most successful constructed in recent years. An interactive water fountain is a huge attraction. It creates spontaneous "street theatre".

pers and commuters from all parts of the island. A multiplex cinema is also located in the complex.

The urban spaces are among the most successful constructed in recent years. An interactive water fountain is a huge attraction for children. It creates spontaneous "street theatre" and a large crowd often gathers to be entertained by the youngsters' efforts to avoid a soaking.

An intelligent mix of a five-star hotel, a multiplex cinema, restaurants, bars, retail outlets and supermarkets contribute to a vibrant urban experience which underlines the value of good urban design. It may not be the Bugis Street experience of old, which has resurfaced in a sanitised form in other "margins", but it is a successful urban place nonetheless.

Once conceived as objects surrounded by vast space, the first bungalows in Katong were private places—plantation country houses, seaside retreats (1) and dwellings for the numerous wives and mistresses of the rich Chinese *towkays* (tycoons) (2). From within, the inhabitants maintained a sense of privacy from "the other" while still enjoying a dialogic relationship with the natural environment enveloping them.

BOURNEMOUTH 8

**Chan Sau Yan Associates
1998**

BY ANN GERONDELIS

The bungalow plans are identical. Difference is created by the unique roof profiles capping the individual units—pitched, curved or barrel vaulted.

In 1998, Katong saw the emergence of a new housing type, the strata-bungalow, which transformed the traditional notion of bungalow. As a component in the strata-bungalow development, the house maintains its ground level datum, but exists as an integrated part of a small, high-density living community.

The inherent density of the strata-bungalow compound requires the bungalow's reconception not as an isolated object in space, but as a component of a composition balancing notions of privacy and openness, the individual and the community, articulated as much by spatial volume as by building mass.

The rectangular 3,468-square-metre (37,329-square-foot) site of Bournemouth 8 is organised by an internal linear street fronted by eight four-storey living units of approximately 450 square metres (4,844 square feet) each. The intimately scaled central spine space—defined by the eight bungalows, the spaces between them and their landscaping—becomes a dominant foreground architectural expression. The building mass interfaces with the street through an articulate asymmetrical façade language of highly modulated pure solids and voids. Throughout the strata-bungalow complex, form and space are richly intertwined to achieve a balanced composition of formal and spatial volumes.

The bungalow plans are identical, yet their masses bear subtle differences. Most notable are the unique roof profiles capping the individual units—pitched, curved or barrel vaulted. The visual impact of the roof forms remains subtle from within the complex due to the projecting façade volumes. The community formed by the combined individual unit masses articulates a cohesive whole while still creating a sense of identity for the individual bungalows beyond their mere location along the street.

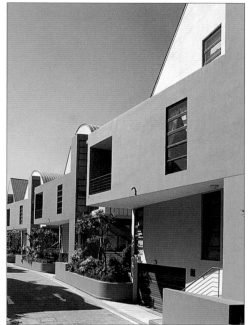

The notions of privacy and openness are complexly reinterpreted through the creation of interface layers of semi-public/semi-private zones. This is achieved most strategically in the design of the void between the units, which houses the private pool and landscaped garden. This semi-private/semi-public space is bounded by the living space of one unit and the solid end wall of the neighbouring bungalow. The view of this void is celebrated from within, actually forming the datum for the plan organisation. The adjacent living space is faced with operable glass panels opening directly to the pool garden, allowing for views and ventilation.

The pool and garden space interfaces delicately with the public realm. From the public street space, the activities of the pool and garden can be heard and seen in glimpses through the landscape screen. The reflected light from the pool surface can also be seen glimmering delicately on each bungalow's cantilevered soffit.

In the midst of the neighbouring private, walled bungalows of Bournemouth Road, whose grand scale façades call for a site far more vast than exists, the bungalows of Bournemouth 8 stand powerfully in harmony with their landscape, their open space and with each other.

Unlike the Katong bungalows of the past, the strata-bungalows are not places of great seclusion or of vast scenic views. Still, they effectively achieve a sense of privacy in the midst of community and enjoy a relationship with their natural surroundings, albeit on a smaller scale. The strata-bungalow housing type emerges, efficiently and powerfully reinterpreting modern community bungalow living.

Notes

1. Phua Yue Keng, Roy and Lily Kong, "Exploring Local Cultures: The Construction and Evolution of Meaning and Identity in Katong", *Portraits of Places: History, Community and Identity in Singapore, Singapore: Times Editions, 1995, p. 117.*
2. Edwards, Norman, The Singapore House and Residential Life, 1819–1939, *Singapore: Oxford University Press, 1990.*

Above left, top and bottom:
The bungalows of Bournemouth 8 are in harmony with their landscape, their open space and with each other.

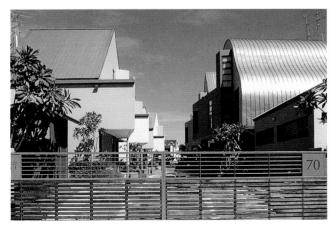

Private and public, once seen as distinct entities, have become increasingly blurred. Now, more and more dwellings are playing with the notion of transparency so that, to quote Winy Maas, "putting the inside, even your own, on display seems a very modern thing to do".

FORTREDALE

Tangguanbee Architects
1998

Fortredale exudes confidence and a defiance of convention. It struts its stuff along Tanjong Rhu while its neighbours look, by comparison, aesthetically geriatric.

Fortredale is certainly in this spirit, a growing tendency in the Singapore context. I have noted it, for example, in Paterson Edge and the Lem House by Mok Wei Wei (*The Urban Asian House*, 1998).

Fortredale is an eye-catching 19-storey tower block on a narrow rectangular site at the junction of Tanjong Rhu Road and Fort Road. Like earlier towers by Tang Guan Bee, the building stands apart for its strongly individualistic expression.

It can be seen as the fourth in a series of evolving ideas on the decoration of the "skin" of the building. No. 11 Institution Hill (1988) is a planar 11-storey concrete structure off River Valley Road. Its external wrapping is deconstructed into horizontal bands with diagonal cuts and a juggling of solid and void overlaid with multiple colours. A giant number *11* is etched into the stair tower.

Six years later, Tang Guan Bee was the conceptual designer for the 20-storey Balmoral Gate Condominium

(1994). The personalisation of the façade again involved the expression of difference rather than deference to the suburban context.

The 12-storey Abelia Apartments at Ardmore Park (1992), illustrated elsewhere in this book, carries the idea of differentiation further, with each elevation treated differently, reflecting the internal arrangement within each dwelling. Some are playful, others restrained. Together, they offer alternatives to the conventional treatment of high-rises as uniform

slab-blocks.

At Fortredale (1998), the decoration of the skin again takes priority, but here, Tang Guan Bee experiments with the degree of transparency. Three elevations of the 19-storey tower are clothed in glass. This is not his first venture into an aspect of the modern condition where "voyeurism intersects with exhibitionism" and where individuals in the city seek anonymity but also desire recognition. See, for example, Windsor Park House by Tang, also illustrated in this book.

But is architecture just about decorating the skin? Arguably yes, for when the developer's bottom line is to maximise floor area and to minimise the thickness of the external wall, much effort and ingenuity goes into creating a unique identity on a largely two-dimensional "canvas". Tang Guan Bee uses advanced glazing technology in the form of 6-millimetre Asahimas green tinted and 6-millimetre Asahimas blue tinted glass, together with 6-millimetre Ceragraphic Ceramic Frit Pattern glass with Lemon Drop Positive Dots of 3-millimetre diameter on clear tempered glass. Two glass-walled elevators ply the face of the building. In addition, two circular steel hoops project over the two penthouse apartments—which one wit has described to be "like a pair of Chanel sunglasses" pushed to the back of one's head—leave the apartment occupants squinting out towards the Straits of Malacca on the horizon.

The result is that Fortredale exudes confidence and defiance of convention. It struts its stuff along Tanjong Rhu Road, while its neighbours look, by comparison, aesthetically geriatric.

In terms of planning, the apartment units, like those of Tang's earlier towers (with the exception of Abelia), do not break new ground and the structure is that of a conventional slab block. But that is not the objective here. Tang Guan Bee succeeds in adding value and elevating a potentially mundane developer's package to a visually delightful artistic object.

Above: **Two circular steel hoops project over the two penthouse apartments. They have been likened to a pair of Chanel sunglasses.**

Far left and left bottom: **Much effort and ingenuity has gone into creating a unique identity on a largely two-dimensional "canvas".**

Left top: **The decoration of the skin takes priority. Tang Guan Bee experiments with the degree of transparency. Three elevations of the 19-storey tower are clothed in glass.**

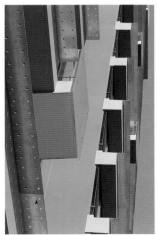

Sennett House is designed for a three-generation family. A married sister and brother, together with their spouses and children, share a compound with their mother. In the face of globalisation and the inexorable influence of the Western media, the "extended family" and "filial piety" are enduring Asian values.

SENNETT HOUSE

Chan Soo Khian
SCDA Architects
1990

Below: **The architect has devised a new typology, rethinking the semi-detached house form.**

Opposite top left: **The house looks inwards, in effect turning its back on the neighbours and on the city.**

Opposite top right: **The family area at the second level.**

Opposite bottom:
First storey plan

The client owned two semi-detached houses on the Sennett housing estate: these were not back-to-back (i.e. sharing a common party wall) but faced each other across a boundary fence. Architect Chan Soo Khian first demolished both houses, then he replaced them with two linear units, mirror images of each other, to be occupied by the siblings and their families, with a shared central courtyard. The existing party walls on both flanks were extended to the limit of the front and rear building-lines and presented formidably solid barriers to the neighbouring houses.

The two units are organised around a linear, central courtyard, which extends from the front of the site to the rear boundary. Its character changes as it relates to different activities within the adjoining houses. At the front of the site, it is a semi-public space. As one progresses further, its role changes to one of a private space, a shared recreation area related to the entrances to the houses. Towards the rear of the site, the central courtyard becomes a service yard, shielded from the gaze of visitors by a head height wall.

Thresholds along the way signal the transition from public to private space. Entering through either of the two entrance gates, one encounters a screen wall comprising horizontal slabs of grey granite which restrict the view of the family's private activities.

To the left and right of this screen wall is a landscaped forecourt which precedes a short flight of steps to the raised central courtyard, the principal external space related to the first-storey living areas. At the centre of the private domain is a dark blue reflecting pool.

The linear central courtyard is the principal organising element but the spaces within the two flanking dwellings are also carefully orchestrated. Having entered the private courtyard area, one turns either right or left. The main entrance to each "wing" is located in a fissure between the dining and living areas and opens into a central double-storey lightwell that forms the visual and circulatory focus of each house. The dining area sits within this double-storey volume at the first storey and the family rooms relate to it at the second storey. The two living spaces face each other across the central pool, revealing the daily lives of the two families yet maintaining a slight social distance.

The two halves of the dwelling are mirror images. At their closest point, they are just 5 metres (16 feet)

apart and a "bond" is forged between them. They "cling" to each other and yet preserve a finely balanced social distance that seems to capture the essence of the family relationship. The proximity of the two roofs reinforces the physical relationship.

The house looks inwards, in effect turning its back on its neighbours and on the city. This response to context is an inevitable result of the rapid growth of cities in Asia. Given the chaotic nature of our surroundings, which we are increasingly unable to influence, it is eminently sensible to look inwards. It might be said that the house exhibits a certain "unfriendliness", but the alternative, which is perhaps more objectionable, is to overlook one's neighbours and to visually intrude into their private space.

Chan Soo Khian has devised a startling new typology, rethinking the semi-detached house type and allowing the extended family to share many common areas. Working with a supportive client, the architect has rejected the deferential nature of the semi-detached house in favour of the expression of difference.

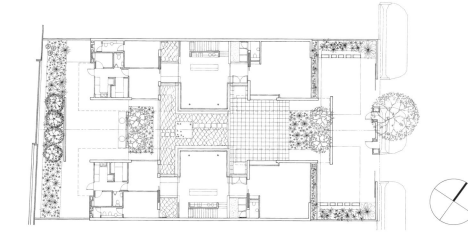

Cricket has never enjoyed a high profile in Singapore. The governing body of the sport is the Singapore Cricket Association (SCA), who approached Kerry Hill Architects in 1998 to design a pavilion for the national ground. The SCA had little money but a huge amount of enthusiasm and boldly planned to hold an international triangular tournament to which India, Zimbabwe and the West Indies national squads were invited.

THE SINGAPORE CRICKET ASSOCIATION CRICKET PAVILION

Kerry Hill Architects
1999

Right: The pavilion sits elegantly in the landscape. The existing mature trees which encircle the ground contrast with and serve to emphasise the dominant horizontal lines of the building.

Opposite centre:
First storey plan

Opposite bottom: Section

With the international game secured and potential sponsors lining up, plans for the new pavilion had to be hastily pushed forward. The construction period would be five months, and a budget of S$650,000 was set.

The architects' intention was to create a building that would be "simple, economic, and durable". The pavilion consists of two horizontal planes, the larger steel roof plane the dominant element in the composition. A thin, sharply defined line, it projects beyond a raised concrete podium, supported by a regular grid of cruciform-section composite steel

Above left and centre: **Sunlight penetrating through the external louvred screen walls, imbues the spartan space within with a magical quality, but in achieving these poetic qualities, it sacrifices nothing in terms of functional requirements.**

Above right: **A ramp provides access to the field of play.**

columns, so slender in appearance that the roof appears to "float".

Arranged between these two planes are the non-structural walls of the changing rooms. In total, these changing rooms occupy slightly less than half of the rectangular floor plan, the remainder being given up to the open space required for players and officials. Other architectural elements, such as tiered concrete seating for the non-fielding team, the entrance steps and the two offices, are treated as sculptural elements carefully attached to the rectangular form without destroying its integrity. The transition from the raised pavilion to the field of play, traditionally via a flight of stairs, is replaced here by a shallow ramp.

The external walls of the changing rooms are designed as horizontal louvred screens of red balau timber. Above shoulder height the timber strips are quite transparent, allowing natural cross ventilation.

Although the roof of the pavilion is at first perceived as a flat horizontal plane, the parapet conceals a pitched roof designed to throw off the torrential monsoon rain. The parapet of the roof is detached from the roof structure to prevent staining. The extended roof form also provides shade from the sun.

The SCA Pavilion seems to mark the successful outcome of Kerry Hill's search, extending over almost three decades, for an architectural language that affirms his roots in modernism, while expressing the wisdom of Asian precedents in the tropical context. It is stripped to the very essence, without excess or ornament. Every preceding work of Kerry Hill Architects seems to have been a step on the way to achieving this level of refinement and I have a suspicion that, although this is a small project in comparison with the resort hotels and luxury homes he has designed throughout the region, the cricket pavilion has given him a disproportionate amount of pleasure.

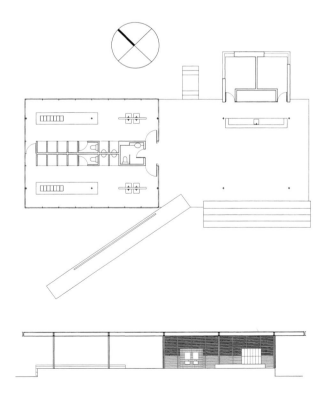

chapter 8

CHANGI
AND TAMPINES

The judges for the United Nations World Habitat Award found in Tampines New Town all the elements that make up a model human settlement. Tampines New Town received the premier award in the Developed Country Category.

TAMPINES NEW TOWN

**The Housing and Development Board
1994**

Opposite: **A typical residential precinct in Tampines New Town, with multistorey car parks, access roads paved with interlocking concrete blocks and extensive landscaping.**

Right: **A neighbourhood primary school is surrounded by distinctively styled high-rise apartment blocks designed by the Housing and Development Board.**

Page 188: **The Market Place**

Page 189:
National Sailing Centre

The largest proportion of land in Tampines New Town is set aside for housing and about one-third is used for roads, utilities and industrial and commercial developments. The rest is reserved for schools, institutions, sports facilities, parks and gardens. High-rise housing is juxtaposed with low-rise schools, neighbourhood centres, large institutions and parks.

A Singapore new town is divided into a number of neighbourhoods. There are currently eight neighbourhoods in Tampines; each has between 5,000 and 6,000 apartments and covers an area of 80–100 hectares (198–247 acres). Within each neighbourhood, a centre with retail shops, eating places and markets provides residents with their daily needs. This neighbourhood centre is located within a ten-minute walking distance from all apartments in the neighbourhood. Planning by neighbourhoods ensures that facilities and amenities, such as schools, parks, playgrounds and bus stops, are easily accessible.

A neighbourhood is further subdivided into smaller components known as housing precincts. Precincts are intended to foster the growth of smaller and more intimate communities. In a precinct, four to eight residential blocks are arranged in such a way as to frame an open space known as a precinct centre. A network of footpaths leads to this space, which is intended to be the focal point for

Above: **Covered walkways connect all the blocks in a precinct.**

Right: **A typical residential precinct in Tampines New Town.**

activities within the precinct.

Generally, there are eight to twelve precincts in a neighbourhood. These are linked together by pedestrian malls and are also connected to the neighbourhood centre.

At the heart of the new town is the town centre. Centrally located amidst the surrounding neighbourhoods, it contains the main commercial and social facilities, including supermarkets, emporiums, restaurants, cinemas, a library, banks, offices, an HDB branch office, a town park, a swimming complex, sports stadium or indoor training hall. The Tampines Town Centre also functions as a node

in Singapore's transportation network. An MRT station and a bus interchange are located in the town centre.

Tampines New Town is a regional centre, serving not only the new town but the whole northeastern sector of the island. It will eventually have facilities such as a cultural centre and hotels, and there are plans to make it a mini-downtown.

Greenery is planted in open spaces, which are linked. Together with trees in surface car parks and road sides, the open spaces help create a green environment. Green connectors, consisting of interlinked walkways and open spaces along

which are shelters and playgrounds, unite the precincts in the neighbourhoods and encourage people to interact with one another.

Criticism of earlier HDB housing centred around the repetitive environment and the homogeneity of spaces. Tampines New Town is an attempt to address some of this criticism. Some precincts are much more compact and "urban" as a result of multi-storey car parks. After 40 years of housing by a centralised authority, which accommodates almost 90 percent of the population, the impression of an overall monotony in housing provisions across the island is rapidly being modified.

Above: **A children's play area, set in landscaped open space overlooked by residential units.**

Left: **The HDB New Town structure model**

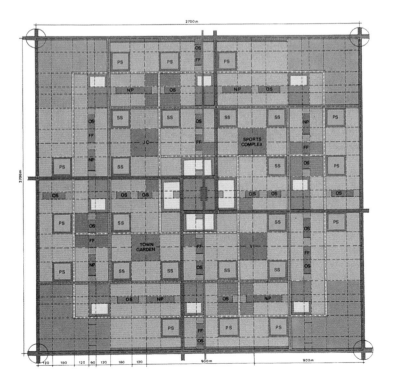

With its strong formal expression, Tampines Neighbourhood 4 looks monumental, but it also challenges the prevalently accepted image of public housing. The containment of space and the tall "gateways" to the courtyards create "defensible space". The segregation of vehicles and pedestrians removes one of the more unsatisfactory images of public housing.

TAMPINES NEIGHBOURHOOD 4

P & T Consultants Pte Ltd
1994

The exploitation of "thresholds" and "private courtyards" recalls some of the best public housing in the Netherlands and Germany.

The Tampines Neighbourhood 4 project marked a significant new direction in public housing in Singapore. For over 25 years, the Housing and Development Board (HDB) was the sole agency involved in public housing. Tampines Neighbourhood 4 was the first tender by private sector architects for the Design-and-Build type of public housing. From a short list of ten teams invited to submit proposals, this scheme was selected based on design and estimated costs.

The overall plan is straightforward; three interlocking octagons enclose three huge courtyards with a central connecting axis. Car parks are integrated in a $1\frac{1}{2}$-storey semi-basement beneath the two outer courtyards, while the central courtyard is extensively landscaped, with sheltered gazebos.

The architectural language employed is post-modern, with a two-storey podium expressed in horizontal panels and a strong horizontal "cornice" and "parapet" expressed again by utilising horizontal panels of patterned brickwork. The hierarchy of privacy that is established is a major departure from previous public housing schemes. The exploitation of "thresholds" and "private courtyards" recalls some of the best public housing in the Netherlands and Germany.

The Tampines Neighbourhood 4 project was a ground-breaking innovation in the Singapore context and led to other public housing projects being put out to Design-and-Build tender. More innovations can be expected from future collaborations between public and private sector architects.

Above: **The architectural language employed is post-modern, with a two-storey podium expressed in horizontal panels and a strong horizontal "cornice" and "parapet".**

Left: **Section**

The Changi Airport Terminal 1 Expansion (T1E) is the latest addition to this global hub and it marks a new phase in the airport development. It represents the most substantial shift in design sensibility that Changi has witnessed and it points the way forward for the next phase—the building of Terminal 3.

CHANGI AIRPORT TERMINAL 1 EXPANSION (T1E)

PWD Consultants Pte Ltd
1999

BY NIRMAL KISHNANI

The quality of daylighting in T1E gives a dramatic sense of space.

In the evolution of Changi Airport, this little-known project will probably be remembered as the one that signalled change. It is the last of a series of "minor" projects completed in the 1990s, between the completion of Terminal 2 (T2) and the start of Terminal 3 (T3). We could look back and say that it has the brazen boldness of the Terminal 2 Expansion, or that it has the skill of transition and continuity that the Terminal 1 Refurbishment embodied. And perhaps, later on when T3 is on line, that it was Changi's testbed of new sensibilities in airport design.

In that sense, it's worth is more than a question of size. T1E is actually an ensemble of three components—one renovation and two extensions—in each half of the symmetrical terminal. In total, the six areas make up 14 additional boarding gates, two new zones for shops and cafes and the renovation of T1's Transfer Counters.

The renovation is the most discreet of the lot and perhaps the least significant. It's a smart new look for the counters, one that blends with the old and says little about the undercurrents of change. The new extensions, which are startlingly bold and speak volumes are, oddly enough, harder to find. The largest of the new areas are the extensions to finger piers—where the new gates are located—along the northerly arms of the H-shaped terminal. As the furthermost points in T1, even passengers are unlikely to pass them accidentally.

The thinking behind this design by PWD Consultants' Airport Development Division (ADD) seems to be that it was time to shift the paradigm. Passenger expectations have also moved on. The comparisons are no longer with Schiphol or Bangkok; there is a new breed of airports setting

the standard. And this standard is as much about the appearance of airport terminals, now integral to the pleasure of travel, as it is about service.

T1E will go down as a new chapter in Changi Airport. The first thing that hits you when you cross from old to new is the level of transparency and daylighting. There is a dramatic change in the sense of space. The ceilings in the new finger piers are much higher than any in T1 or T2. Winged aluminium panels cap the main circulatory route and this "flighty" ceiling is punctuated by a series of skylights.

With the level of natural light the new envelope affords, almost half the electrical lights can be switched off during the day. Even the once utilitarian air-bridges are no longer dark tunnels linking aircraft with building. A lengthwise steel truss on both sides of the new bridge doubles up as structure and window.

The biggest operational change is the creation of larger gate lounges. At the far end of each pier, three boarding gates share a common waiting area and security-screening channel. There are obvious economies of scale to be had with this, but this amalgamation also gave the designers more leeway in terms of layout, landscaping and light.

The pièce de résistance of the pier-extensions occurs at the junction between old and new. The link, which involved turning the finger by 30 degrees and dipping the floor level by

1 metre (3.3 feet), is essentially a large connector space. A matrix of steel frames and fritted glass, some held up with spidery fittings, folds over this space. As you emerge from the old pier, you enter a space that is awash with soft light and offers an enticing view to the far end of the pier, with its bright splashes of colours. The transition is unapologetic and quietly defiant.

The other new area under T1E takes place further back along the building at the junction of the finger piers and the terminal. The flashy shopfronts of this new commercial corner draw you in with the promise of yet another bargain.

As you approach the shops, another level comes into view. Up the escalator, one enters what must be one of the most breathtaking new spots in Changi—a café under large tree-shaped steel trusses that hold up a glass roof, lined with soft rollaway sunscreens. With its views to the waiting aircraft, towering indoor palms, timber floors and a pervasive sense of calm, this is panacea to the stress of travel.

A certain "pragmatic ecleticism" rules the day in Changi. The airport keeps trying new things in an effort to stay ahead of the competition. In that regard, it differs—for now, at least—from the newer airports in the region, which seem aesthetically more coherent. But that judgement is premature, for how will the terminals of Kuala

Lumpur and Hong Kong cope with change, which is endemic to any building that is designed to last for decades? To the critical eye, Changi seems busy. But it also has a quiet confidence and, judging from T1E, a newfound maturity with just the right blend of functionality and romance. There is a certain irony in the fact that it's easy to miss this project they call Terminal 1 Expansion (T1E). It costs over $170 million and represents the most substantial shift in design sensibility Changi Airport has seen. And yet, to experience the new spirit, you have to consciously look for it.

The Market Place, located off Bedok Road, is within an ordinary suburban shopping complex; not the sort of place you would drive the length of the island to visit. Indeed, it was once so nondescript, it would have been possible to pass by without giving it a second glance. But not anymore. The place leaped into the 21st century with the arrival of a new kid on the block.

THE MARKET PLACE

Tangguanbee Architects
1994

The huge span of the roof is not immediately realised. Instead, a feeling of lightness is experienced as one moves around the place.

A brilliant investment decision by Far East Organisation and the unique skills of architect Tang Guan Bee have combined to produce a place that fizzles with energy. This is exactly the right sort of brief to utilise the capricious talents of Tang, who has been steadily compiling an oeuvre outside the mainstream architectural tastes in Singapore that is deserving of international recognition.

No. 11 Institution Hill (1988), the Picture House (1990), Abelia Apartments at Ardmore (1994), Eastpoint (1996), Windsor Park House (1997) and Fortredale (1998) attest to a certain artistic genius who refuses to follow the conventional Singaporean architectural tastes.

The Market Place was built on a shoestring budget of $3 million (a bungalow in District 11 would set the owner back by about the same

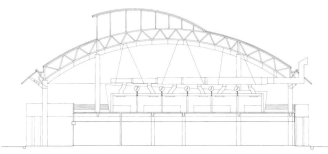

amount). Between two parallel rows of existing, unspectacular post-war shophouses, Tang has inserted a brightly coloured, two-storey, open-sided "decorated shed" with a huge arched roof.

The Market Place takes its siting and planning from the existing layout of the shophouses and pedestrian movements. Occupying the central space configured by the existing rows of shophouses, the plan of the first storey is longitudinal to parallel the five-foot way and reinforce the open green between The Market Place and the shophouses.

The huge size of The Market Place (66 metres by 33 metres; 217 feet by 108 feet) is not immediately realised. Instead, a feeling of lightness is experienced as one moves around the place. This is achieved structurally by reducing the number of reinforced concrete columns to the minimum,

using long span truss beams and by expressing the metal roof structure. Various techniques are used, for example, by tearing the vault roofing to introduce clerestory glazing, by using perforated metal panels and wire mesh to enhance a layering effect, by introducing a coloured lean-to polycarbonate roof to the main metal decking to soften enclosures, by treating the stalls/exhaust system ductings as elements to break down the scale of the second storey, and by using colours and finishes to focus or diffuse sensory perceptions.

The first storey is given over to shop units, while a food court is located on the second storey. The Market Place invigorates the surrounding area and is a brilliant piece of urban surgery.

The creation of an environment for nurturing children's inherent creative energy has always posed a demanding design problem. Schools are children's first experience of society and, as such, they have to be friendly and reassuring and simultaneously show discipline and have a sense of order.

ELIAS PARK PRIMARY SCHOOL

Akitek Tenggara
1995

Akitek Tenggara has taken, as the generating idea for Elias Park Primary School, the notion of a school as "A Small Village"—a microcosm of the larger community. The intention of the architect is to diminish the scale of the building so that it is perceived as a place for children. This is not an entirely new idea. In the 1960s, architect Herman Hertzberger used the idea of streets and courts in the design of the Montessori School at Delft in Holland. Hans Sharoun's unbuilt but seminal design for a primary school at Darmstadt also has a village-like configuration that stresses the engagement of the interior with the exterior. Much of their thinking, and perhaps Akitek Tenggara's, was influenced by the writings of Jean Piaget in *Dreams and Imitation in Childhood* (1962) and Maria Montessori in *The Absorbent Mind* (1967).

The plan of Elias Park Primary School is internalised to give a protected world, one that is in dynamic contrast to and yet obviously part of the context of mass housing in which it is located. The teaching blocks and ancillary facilities are expressed as a series of pavilions. The village scale is thus emphasised against the backcloth of high-rise HDB slab-blocks. The school is fronted by the playing field, while the assembly hall and canteen block (i.e. the large volume spaces) are deliberately placed at the "rear", in close proximity to the multi-storey housing.

This challenges the notion that a school ought to have an imposing or even monumental entrance. The contrary logic is to reduce the impact of the hall and to emphasise horizontality. In theory, this gives a more friendly and welcoming building.

The idea of a small village is expressed most convincingly in the plan arrangement. Upon entering the administration block, one encounters a modest "galleria". Its delightful spatial quality comes as a surprise, for it is not over-emphasised in the external form. It is a civic space and from here, one progresses via a two-level, shel-

Above and left: **The details of the school place the building firmly in the tropics. There are wide sun shading devices, deep overhangs and in-between spaces which are the stuff of tropical architecture.**

Below: **Birds-eye view of the school.**

Opposite: **An open-to-sky court takes the form of a forum with a raised platform upon which an outdoor performance might be staged.**

tered corridor or "street" through a series of open-to-sky courts of various configurations. One takes the form of a forum, with a raised platform from which the principal might address a group of children or a small outdoor performance might be performed. Another "village square" is punctuated by a "tower". Along the street, several alcoves, almost like small shop spaces, invite the imagination of the school children.

"You will notice that this school looks so much smaller than equivalent schools, but this is not because we are providing less floor area," says the architect, Tay Kheng Soon. There is a conscious effort to build a "place" for children. For example, cill heights throughout are kept low and the con-

crete wall alongside the canteen, which is tall and potentially overpowering, is "stepped" and finished in a horizontal ribbed pattern.

The details and the section of the school place the building firmly in the tropics. There are wide concrete sun shading devices, deep overhangs and in-between spaces—the stuff of tropical architecture. The classrooms are one-room deep to encourage natural ventilation, soft landscaping is introduced to reduce insolation (heat gain from radiated heat) and the roof design of the assembly hall permits only diffused daylight to enter. It is a successful fusion of modernism with the traditional vernacular response to the climate.

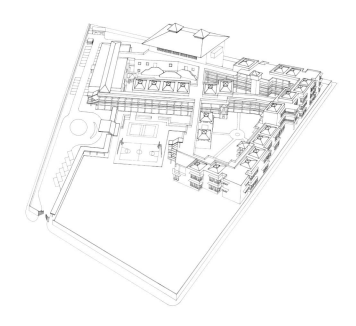

Temasek Polytechnic was the last major building by the late James Stirling, who worked in partnership with Michael Wilford. The project was carried out in association with DP Architects Pte Ltd. The project exhibits many of Stirling's design philosophies: clarity in organisation and composition, exploration of formal geometry, coherent circulation systems and a limited palette of material and colour.

TEMASEK POLYTECHNIC

**James Stirling and Michael
Wilford Associates;
in association with
DP Architects Pte Ltd
1995**

BY LOOK BOON GEE

Below left: **At the centre
of the plan is a horse-
shoe shaped library
and administration block
which surround a huge
interactive plaza.**

Below right: **The grand
promenade resembles a
traditional five-foot-way.**

The overall planning of Temasek Polytechnic exhibits a masterly touch of simplicity and a sense of inevitability. It is located on a 30-hectare (74-acre) wedge-shaped site at the fringe of an HDB estate—an axis is drawn from the town centre to the heart of the new campus, an urban gesture that is both embracing and sensitive. The group of buildings is orientated towards the reservoir to the south and to the distant city. At the centre is a horse-shoe shaped library and administration block, from which four individual schools (Business, Design, Engineering and Information Technology and Applied Science) radiate into the surrounding gardens.

The administration block embraces a central plaza, where the ceremonial ramp, stairs, covered promenade and a *porte cochere* give rise to a truly spectacular and evocative space. A giant "window" has been created beneath the administration block to frame a vista of the reservoir beyond the triangular garden.

Other buildings on the campus have separate identities, each treated as parts belonging to a greater whole. An overall integrity in architectural composition that is illusively simple is bestowed upon the site. The clear organisation of spaces, understandable by their strong forms and memorable character, allows the buildings and activities to be easily comprehensible; thus encouraging greater social communication and interaction among students and academic staff. This notion works well in a large educational institution perceived as "a city for learning", which might otherwise be confusing and impersonal.

A strong sense of unity exists in both the architectural forms and the character of spaces. The unity of the spatial experience is achieved by the explicit order and logic. When criticised about the monumentality of these forms and strict geometry, Michael Wilford explains, "Buildings are monumentally informal in the monumental tradition of public building, but also they acknowledge the populist character of today's places of public culture and entertainment."

Above: **Two memorable images of Temasek Polytechnic are its pre-patinated green copper roof and the strong colours used to code the circulation spine.**

Below: **Campus plan**

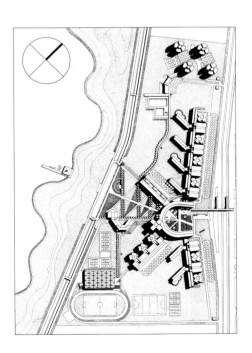

The memorable images of Temasek Polytechnic are its pre-patinated green copper roof, its lilac painted brickwalls and the large swathes of strong colours used to code the circulation spine. The main concourse is covered in marine blue, while secondary concourse spaces employ cadmium yellow, orange, raspberry and aquamarine. The use of a limited range of materials and colours avoids visual confusion.

Despite initial studies to understand the climate, weather-control devices such as sun-shading have not been incorporated. Perhaps the subjugation of the technological and structural aspects of the building is to avoid visual complexity, but it results in the greatest shortcoming of the building. Though the grand promenade vaguely resembles the traditional five-foot-way, the problem is that its two- and three-storey-high openings and breezeway give little protection from the harsh tropical weather.

Nevertheless, there are important lessons to be learnt from the English master. The legacy James Stirling left behind on the local architectural scene has yet to be fully appreciated but he has wittily demonstrated how an assemblage of buildings can be imbued with strong character and communicative spaces.

The design of the Japanese Primary School does not depart from the concept of the school as an institution. It does not ruffle expectations, like Zvi Hecker's Jewish School in Grunwald Forest, Germany. It states, in no uncertain terms, an authoritarian nature and certainly, its architecture does not seem to want to dispel the prescribed, disciplinary style of education that makes you think, in a general way, "Japanese system". However, the architecture of the Japanese School is not frighteningly formidable.

THE JAPANESE PRIMARY SCHOOL

**Architects Vista
in association with Pacific
Consultants International
1996**

BY VINCENT LIM

Fundamentally, the architecture of the Japanese School, which was designed by Pacific Consultants International in association with local practice Architects Vista, is about geometry—though not simply a rudimentary use of it to pat the programme into an easily buildable shape. In a sense, you can call this deeper alliance with geometry a rule-based approach to the use of shapes. It can be read as a purist's game with squares.

The first of the squares is invoked for the massive main entry foyer. From there, the basic shape is stretched and translated in a northwest direction to form a staggered trail of main building blocks. Below the main blocks, a matrix of squares grows in a northerly direction, like a gridded rug, towards the open field to mark the open ter-race. The effect is like a Cartesian grid of squares spreading out to take over the trapezoidal site.

The squares also creep upwards. The most dominant manifestation of squares in the vertical dimension is found in the sunscreens, where it is arrayed to a near dizzying effect. The intense play of light and shadow on the square filigree sunscreen, which covers almost the whole of the school

The intense play of light and shadow on the square filigree, which covers almost the whole of the school, adds a phenomenological depth to the abstract white image of the architecture.

Left: **Even though much of the design of the building is based on abstract geometry, the learning environment is neither cold nor unfriendly.**

Above: **The 45-degree pitched roof shape of the sports hall can be seen as the rotation of a square about one of its corners.**

Below: **The squares of the sunscreen recall traditional Japanese screens, except in the Japanese Primary School, the screens are made of concrete instead of timber and paper.**

(in fixed modules), adds a phenomenological depth to the abstract white image of the architecture.

This modular strategy of patterning the sunscreens and then repeating them is rooted in Japanese tradition—the traditional Japanese house plan is proportioned by tatami mats, which come in fixed modules. It thus becomes a relevant strategy to forge a Japanese identity for the school. This is, however, a touch of Japanese-ness at an abstract and conceptual level.

More concretely, the modulation of squares and modularity of the sunscreen recalls traditional Japanese screens, except the screens in the school are made from concrete instead of timber and paper. But even then, the result is surprisingly delicate and porous. It reinvents the gentle experience of looking through screens but with masonry as the material.

The sunscreens are definitely helpful in cutting down the harsh glare of tropical sunlight. Plus, they allow breezes to penetrate.

Less obvious but no less important is the logical argument of the square into the roof design. The 45-degree pitched roof shape of the classroom blocks can be seen as the rotation of a square about one of its corners. This argument is substantiated by the rhomboid pattern applied on the end elevations just below the roofs. The roof of the main foyer is also a logical projection of the square plan into a pyramid.

It is clear by now that every design decision follows from a logical line of reasoning to invoke, retain, reinforce and restate the square. This rootedness in the central concept clarifies and defines the parameters within which the architects can wander with his creativity and yet conform.

Even though much of the design of the building is based on abstract geometry, the learning environment, it has to be said, is not cold and unfriendly. The internal streets flanked by the classroom blocks are glazed over, natural light floods in and the two ends of the streets are left open for natural cross-ventilation. It is a cheerful and comfortable meeting space for children.

In seeking privacy, the three-storey Lem House turns its back on its immediate neighbours. This is not an uncommon response in the suburban landscape of Singapore. A number of contemporary houses express "difference" and "individual identity" in this manner.

LEM HOUSE

Mok Wei Wei
William Lim Associates
1997

Lem House rejects a nostalgia for the traditional vernacular and the architectural language is that of "second order" modernism.

Lem House looks north and east over a tidal drainage canal known as Sungei Bedok and is cooled by diurnal breezes that penetrate from the coast. The parti is a simple orthogonal plan which, in order to fit on the site, has been split along a "fracture line". One part of the plan slides along this fracture to be accommodated on the wider part of the tapering site. This notion of fracture is emphasised in the formal massing. The view from the north suggests multiple fracture lines as vertical wall planes are expressed as projections.

The house plan and section are in part a pragmatic response to the site constraints and regulations imposed by the Building Control Department. Statutory requirements stipulate a 2-metre (6.6-foot) set-back along both sides of the house, a 3-metre (9.8-foot) set-back for the rear of the plot and a 7.5-metre (24.6-foot) set-back for the front of the plot facing the cul-de-sac.

Mok Wei Wei has designed the house primarily to take advantage of the unique views. The northeast facing elevation and a considerable proportion of the northwest and southeast facing elevations are glazed with aluminium framed windows and doors. The 2-metre (6.6-foot) projection to the roof slab and the 1-metre (3.3-foot) wide perforated-metal sunshading devices at the level of the first- and second-storey floor slabs are designed to deal with the problem of early morning solar radiation. Solid walls facing west and southwest ensure that the house is well shaded from the afternoon and evening sun.

The use of floor-to-ceiling sliding aluminium window frames and curtain-walling results in the house having maximum transparency, so it enjoys magnificent views in both directions along the banks of the canal and to the northeast over the currently undeveloped land on the opposite bank.

The reverse is also apparent.

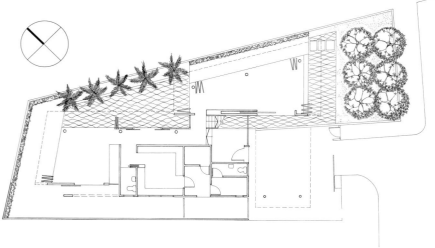

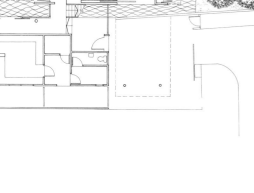

Above right: **The bathroom has white painted walls with white marble floors, large mirrors and etched glass doors.**

Below left and right: **Lem House opens itself to public scrutiny of the occupants. It is a paradox of contemporary urban life that there is often a simultaneous desire for recognition and anonymity.**

Pedestrians and cyclists using the canal-side promenade, just 10 metres (32.8 feet) away from the house, look directly into the study and the dining room at the first storey, which is elevated 1.5 metres (4.9 feet) above the adjacent ground. Glancing upwards, passers-by also have an oblique view into the living room and the bedrooms on the second and third storeys. By its very transparency, Lem House opens itself to public scrutiny of its occupants and their lifestyles. It reflects a paradox of contemporary urban life where there is often a simultaneous desire for recognition and anonymity.

The house is entered from the car porch. A shallow pond alongside the entrance lobby extends beneath an etched glass window to the garden in front of the study and in the opposite direction, alongside the dining room. This "moat" brings the immediate context into the interior but it simultaneously imposes a conceptual distance between the house and its surroundings and makes the appearance of accessibility an illusion.

The house rejects a nostalgia for the traditional vernacular and the architectural language is that of modernism. Flat roofs and planar forms are employed, in contrast to the transparency of the aluminium framed windows. Many of the windows are sliding-folding doors, French windows or side-hung casements, so that, when desired, the house functions well without air-conditioning.

For Mok Wei Wei, the design represents a development beyond the more overtly double-coded deconstructivist language of Tampines North Community Centre, also designed by him in 1986. In this instance, he utilises a restrained palette. The client, interior designer Alice Lem, is responsible for the minimalist interiors which contribute to the success of the design. The interior is almost entirely white—white painted walls with white marble floors, large mirrors and etched glass doors in the bathrooms. White marble was chosen for its cooling effect and as a backcloth for the appreciation of artwork.

In the late capitalist economy where the rapid flow of capital requires spaces for flexible accumulation, Eastpoint's strong urbanistic ethos and its regenerative spatial intelligence will stand it in good stead as the resilient anchor within the fluidity. Such an innovative shopping complex in Singapore may well continue to become a key crucible for a new collective urbanity and the new civic expression of an evolving civil society.

EASTPOINT SHOPPING CENTRE

**Tangguanbee Architects
1996**

BY LEONG TENG WUI

Below left: **Eastpoint offers a certain "dirty realism" in its overall ambience and character, which suggests the complexity, imperfections and the anonymity of the contemporary city.**

Below right: **The virtual "mall" will never be able to replicate the material experience of the crowds, the browsing, the spectacle, the smell and the sound of physical shopping.**

Since the 1991 Urban Redevelopment Authority (URA) Concept Plan to decentralise Singapore into a polycentric network of regional and sub-regional centres built around key Mass Rapid Transit (MRT) hub stations, a new urban landscape has emerged. More significantly, the polycentric nexus radically reconfigures the pattern of centrality across the landscape and undermines the traditional idea of the city as the dominant centre with a subservient suburban periphery. A good barometer of these changes is

the proliferation of what are called regional shopping centres. These are built around MRT stations in the public housing heartlands to optimise the value of the land and also to stimulate urban growth around the stations. While the resulting conurbation brought an unprecedented degree of convenience and accessibility to the region, there also seems to be an increasingly recursive monotony and homogeneity of experience in many of these shopping centres.

Eastpoint Shopping Centre, located beside the Simei MRT station in the

eastern region, stands out as an important counterpoint to the serial homogeneity found in many shopping developments in Singapore. It is a compact but highly charged project, pregnant with many inventive possibilities that have important lessons for the development of a place-specific, urbane and yet innovative modern architecture for a global city.

The modern malls are often "sanitised", "Disney-fied" and "exclusionary" thematic environments. Eastpoint, by contrast, suggests the complexity, imperfections and anonymity of a contemporary city. Common industrial materials and off-the-shelf details were used to create "pulp fiction" architecture that challenges the dominant bourgeois architectural pretensions of many shopping centres. There is a conspicuous absence of "fine" detailing and no over fetishised designer details. Instead, the details are simple, economical and, at times, even "brutal" in their resolution. The mixed "tech" look helps to create a refreshing nonchalance in its overall ambience. Eastpoint comes across as a more

Above: **Eastpoint Shopping Centre stands out as an important counterpoint to the impoverished civic quality often found in many shopping developments in Singapore.**

Below: **Eastpoint taps into a rich and inventive carnivalesque tradition for site-specific and time-specific place-making.**

"socially accessible" space in that it lacks the exclusionary image of the other more pretentious and "class-conscious" shopping developments. This is attested to by the diversity of users and the richness of public life that one finds at Eastpoint.

Indeed it is this "publicness" of shopping that often heightens the sense of the "carnivalesque" atmosphere—the physical proximity, the sensory pleasures and the spectacle of display, exchange and consumption have all contributed towards the programme of shopping as one of the more resilient contemporary phenomena where the sense of the "collective" is still viable and visible. Eastpoint's clever spatial layout and programmatic mix offers many inven-

tive possibilities. Global fast-food restaurants and large franchise chains co-exist and interact surreptitiously with "localised" ones, such as the air-conditioned wet market, the trade union club, the rooftop children's pool and the cineplex. The resultant programmatic density and intensity creates a heady brew, a kind of modern and yet local "carnivalesque" bazaar that is in the mould of Singapore's old Great World or Beauty World shopping bazaar—an often surreal experience of ever changing sight, sound and smell that strongly assaults the senses; a hybrid social space where the profane coexists with the profound; the emergent modern confronting the disappearing old; and where the global intersects the local in unprecedented

and unanticipated ways.

Eastpoint taps into this rich and inventive tradition. The resulting collage of events, images, elements and forms is both familiar and yet uncanny. A green terrazzo wall and floor inlaid with anglo-chinese symbols in the cinema foyer, a roof deck children's playpool overlooking the HDB estates, an air-conditioned wet market next to Starbucks, a Sri Dewa Hair Salon next to Vidal Sassoon, and even "embalmed" palm trees with cleverly inserted fire sprinklers all contribute to a surreptitious and compressed sense of multiple "times" and "places". Here, we are vividly reminded why shopping is such an interesting collective experience.

The National Sailing Centre (NSC), conceived primarily as a facility to accommodate the Singapore Sports Council's growing sailing needs, negotiates the ideas and imagery of its subject matter—that is, sailing and the idea of a sailing club—in ways that are at times contradictory and at others complimentary, but always interesting and arresting.

NATIONAL SAILING CENTRE

Akitek Tenggara II
1998

BY PETER SIM

Above: **The design of the National Sailing Centre demonstrates that to be meaningful, architecture has to be equally about people, place and experience.**

Right: **Site plan**

Page 212: **Institute of Technical Education (ITE), Bishan**

Page 213: **Golden Village Multiplex Yishun 10**

On initial acquaintance, Akitek Tenggara's National Sailing Centre (NSC) at the East Coast Park, seems wrought with contradictions. Consisting primarily of two gleaming white masses of corrugated steel and concrete, the geometric, pristine and modernist forms appear to posit themselves a little uncomfortably on a stretch of the Singapore coast that perhaps most resembles the popular notion of a tropical idyll.

Instead of adopting the language of chalet architecture for a programme and site of this nature, the NSC almost defiantly assumes a modernist, streamlined and formalistic expression. Through doing this, the design develops its experimental edge and is able to investigate several issues of not only climate, but also of how to make an architecture that is appropriate to the larger issues of identity, sense of place and meaning.

The problem of the site was a fundamental factor in the placement and interrelation of building masses. The design had the unenviable task of being more or less in-the-round, with canal, sea, beach and the road creating fronts on all sides. The ideas of

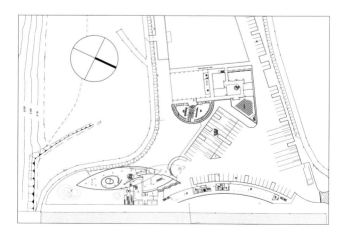

public/private and front/back have been treated as sequential layered experiences, mediated by degrees of opacity. As one proceeds into the building, this opacity dissolves into a space with overlapping boundaries between functions and between interior and exterior, into a space of shade and comfort.

The imagery that the disparate forms conjure up is at once layered and intriguing. The most obvious is that of the image of a boat as an autonomous entity. The masses asymmetrically balanced on the site can be likened to sail boats in the midst of a race, a sculptural manifestation of this water dance of delight. Such nautical imagery is further enhanced through the use of curved surfaces with horizontal corrugations that form the external walls, reminding one of the ribbed hulls of watercraft. Contradictory to the seemingly watertight "hull" however, these walls frequently reveal themselves as entirely porous screens that serve as filters for privacy and light while allowing cross ventilation. Likewise, the space may be akin to traditional boat sheds where

Above and below: **The building masses asymmetrically balanced on the site can be likened to sail boats in the midst of a race.**

boats and fishing nets were tended to and which also formed a focus for social interaction.

If the composition of forms in space are to mirror the different yet irreplaceable position that each sailor has in a crew, then the NSC is unfortunately missing its skipper. For reasons so frequently out of the hands of the designer, a proposed third block was omitted in the final realisation of the centre. This ship-shape mass was meant to locate itself seaward of the other two on a finger of land that extended towards the water's edge. And so it is, that for all the good things that the building does, it does not fully address one crucial factor—the sea.

The end result reveals as much about the creative abilities of the designer as about the popular conceptions and misconceptions of what architecture in the tropics, in particular, and what architecture, in general, should concern itself with. Although the NSC responds to the elements and is "climatically correct" (if there is such a thing), it appears but a minor concern. The design of the NSC demonstrates more importantly that to be sufficiently meaningful, architecture has to be equally about people, place and experience.

chapter 9

THE
NORTH AND CENTRE
OF THE ISLAND

From the inception of his practice in the 1980s, Tang Guan Bee has been acknowledged as the most avant-garde of Singapore architects. His designs are attention capturing and idiosyncratic—witness recent projects such as Eastpoint Shopping Centre and Fortredale. His work, to quote one critic, "exhibits planned incongruities...common to the literary and performance arts which reflect our current lifestyle". These very qualities are exhibited in the Windsor Park House.

WINDSOR PARK HOUSE

Tang Guan Bee
Tangguanbee Architects
1997

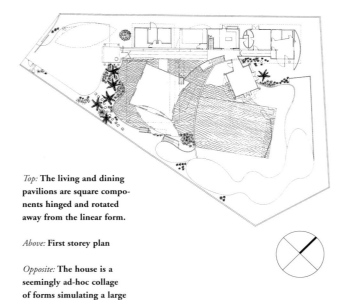

Top: **The living and dining pavilions are square components hinged and rotated away from the linear form.**

Above: **First storey plan**

Opposite: **The house is a seemingly ad-hoc collage of forms simulating a large art installation.**

Set on a steep hill and overlooking a suburban housing estate, Windsor Park House occupies a commanding position. It is a situation that the architect has exploited, with a seemingly ad hoc collage of forms scattered across the hilltop, simulating a large art installation. Viewed from afar, Windsor Park House stands out from its conventional neighbours with its sail-like roof, transparent walls, primary colours and copper-clad pavilions.

Despite its apparently random plan, the house is a rational response to the triangular site configuration. The bulk of the accommodation is arranged in a two-storey "tube" parallel to the northwestern boundary. This is almost the ideal orientation from the point of view of protection from solar insolation. Attached to the south facing side of the tube are the dining and living pavilions, square components that are hinged and rotated away from the linear form, opening up views to the horizon. The resultant plan has a remarkable resemblance to

a MIR space station that has grown by accretion of modules at various times in its orbital course around the earth. Many meanings have been attributed to the house. Tang Guan Bee described it as an art gallery and entertainment hub for the clients.

After the initial glimpse of the house, it disappears from view as the road dips, to reappear, seen now from a different angle, close up and in silhouette. The impression of a cacophony of elements is even stronger. In the foreground is an elliptical car porch, its roof suspended on cables from a single column. Beyond is a huge curved roof over a glazed transparent box that contains the living module. Sandwiched between them is a larger-than-life pivoted entrance door that gives access to an arrival "runway", complete with "landing lights". The imagery of an orbital space capsule is again strongly conveyed as the visitor walks across the crunching gravel to enter this "intergalactic docking bay". The house which, from a distance, appeared to be integrated into the

Above left: **A larger-than-life pivoted entrance door gives access to a linear circulation space.**

Above centre and right: **A viewing gallery is suspended over the living platform.**

Below: **The large amount of glass used for external walls gives the owner a panoramic view of the skyline of the city and of the neighbouring housing estate.**

hillside, in fact sits on a level platform above the surrounding terrain. This emphasises its alienation from the neighbouring houses and demonstrates a recurring sub-theme in this book of the desire to express difference in an increasingly homogenised world. It is a form of escape to another reality. The source of the architect's inspiration is difficult to pinpoint exactly, but all these images are not inappropriate given that the owner of the house is in the film industry.

A linear circulation space, referred to earlier as a runway, is the key organising device in the plan. Other accommodation is attached to this communications corridor, which starts at the entrance pavilion and terminates at the guest bedroom suite. To the north of the corridor are the "servant" spaces—the maid's room, kitchen, yard and service stair. To the south are the "served" spaces—the living pavilion surrounded by water, the dining pavilion and the subter-

ranean audio-visual room with underwater views of the swimming pool.

The notions of viewing and exposure surface in the form of the house. The large amount of glass used for external walls gives the owner a panoramic view of the skyline of the city and of the neighbouring housing estate. Simultaneously, the lifestyle of the household is exposed to the view of these same neighbours. The living room is designed as a "stage" surrounded by water upon which the "performance" of daily life is enacted. It is almost a public space. Suspended above the living platform is a catwalk, which is simultaneously a viewing gallery to the activities below and evocative of a fashion runway for those looking up. One writer has suggested that the sloping glazing is symbolically a big movie screen and that the living platform, although public in nature, is surrounded by a body of water which reinforces the idea of detachment and solitude.

This duality is not limited to the living space. In the subterranean audio-visual room, the owners and guests can view films or can, like voyeurs, see the activities of the half-naked swimmers underwater. The swimmers can simultaneously view the activities of those entombed in the audio-visual room and revel in their own freedom. And again, in the ceiling of the dining room is a circular glazed void through which diners can be observed from the second-storey room overhead. It is not difficult to imagine the cinematic possibilities implicit in all these relationships.

The architect has articulated the transition between spaces to heighten difference. The entrance to the house is through a tall pivoted door that appears to be unsupported. The action of entering the house is thus dramatised, as the heavy door smoothly rotates. Likewise, to gain access to the living platform, one crosses a glass bridge spanning a body of water,

just before the space expands vertically into a two-storey living area. Instinctively, one glances down, stepping timorously on the transparent surface, before refocusing on the double-height space. The difference between materials signals the threshold between activities.

The boundary between the inside and outside spaces is blurred by the extensive use of clear glass and the almost even quality of daylight, which eliminates shade and gives a feeling of being outdoors. It focuses attention on tectonic qualities rather than spatial articulation.

The house is a reflection of many aspects of our contemporary lived experience in an urban location—being visible yet anonymous, being in the public arena and yet retaining a private self, expressing difference and yet yearning for solitude, being open and yet detached.

Tang is at the cutting edge in expressing, through architecture, the

various contradictions in life. The conventional notion of the house is inverted, the innermost workings are revealed. The house exhibits none of the whims associated with an individual house and it eschews the nostalgia associated with pseudo-classical villas. The apparent contradictions and chaos achieve a unity through a strong conceptual framework and an underlying tension that holds the fragments together.

Above: **The apparent contradictions and chaos in Windsor Park House achieve a unity through a strong conceptual framework and an underlying tension that holds the fragments together.**

Bottom: **A strong conceptual framework binds the disparate elements of the spatial composition.**

In the past, it was often the town hall, the church or the mosque that provided the cultural focus of a town. In today's largely secular society, it is building types, such as the cineplex, which are the symbols of our urban culture. Golden Village Multiplex at Yishun 10 is an example of this relatively recent urban building typology.

GOLDEN VILLAGE MULTIPLEX YISHUN 10

Geoff Malone
Geoff Malone International (GMI)
1992

218

Top: **The Multiplex attracts patrons from a wide catchment area and projects an image of a vigorous and enterprising New Town.**

Right: **The architect's detail of a light fitting.**

Below: **The central two-storey atrium with its sci-fi lighting.**

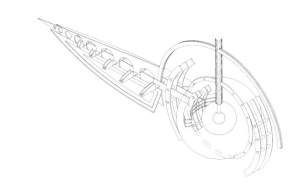

The Golden Village Multiplex is located in close proximity to Yishun MRT Station and the Yishun Central bus terminus. It was designed by Geoff Malone of Geoff Malone International (GMI) who has been a prominent figure in the organisation of the Singapore Film Festival for many years. Car parking is located beneath the building and an arcade around the perimeter at first storey ties the building into the main pedestrian circulation routes. The Multiplex is flanked by Northpoint, a major shopping complex on an adjoining site, and together, they create a feeling of urbanity necessary for a new town to take root and act as a magnet for a wider catchment area.

The building is a simple three-storey box, with the main cinema entrances arranged on diagonally opposite corners. Once the functional criteria were met, the architect was able to give full rein to his innovative talents in the design of the façade of the cinema and the interior foyer.

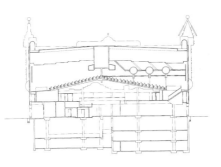

Above: **Section through two of the cinemas**

Far left: **An arcade ties the Multiplex into the main circulation routes in the town centre.**

Centre and left: **The detailing of the external cladding is reminiscent of the Kirin Building in Osaka by Shin Takamatsu.**

The detailing of the external cladding is reminiscent of the Kirin Building in Osaka by Shin Takamatsu, with meticulously constructed junctions of stainless steel and profiled cladding juxtaposed with lighting tubes. Unlike Takamatsu's monochromatic façades, however, the colours used in Yishun 10 are predominantly red, white and silver, with "splashes" of other primary colours—all evoke the excitement and magic of "a night at the movies". Interestingly, the Kirin Building houses a film institute and cinema buffs will recall it being used for location filming of the movie *Black Rain*.

A central two-storey atrium has numerous restaurants arranged around its perimeter at first-storey. The auto-mated ticket office is located in this central space. An escalator and stair-cases give access to the spacious second-storey foyer and thence to the ten individual cinemas on the third storey. A stair-lift permits access to the disabled.

In the main foyer, aside from the functional planning, the architect obviously derived much pleasure from the task of designing the sculptural sci-fi light fittings and multi-coloured fluorescent tube lighting in an otherwise slightly dimmed interior. Floor lighting beneath laminated glass blocks and multiple television monitor screens, with constantly changing images, all contribute to the "escapism" that is an integral part of a visit to the cinema.

For a brief interlude, the cinema-goer is transported out of the HDB township and the frantic rush of economic activity into a world of fantasy, glamour and enchantment.

The Multiplex is "both a centripetal and a centrifugal force" in the urban landscape; it attracts patrons from a wide catchment area and projects an image of a vigorous and enterprising new town. It is ironic that, until the early 1990s, cinemas in Singapore were closing down for lack of patronage and some were being converted to churches. Now we see not only a revival of the genre, but as exemplified in the Golden Village Multiplex Yishun 10, it can create a special urban focus.

From huge distriparks to smaller factories, architects are now integrating design with the industrial process. Located at Sungei Kadut Way, a factory designed by LOOK Architects for Lam Chuan Import-Export reflects this current trend. Consciously steering away from the conventional metal-clad shed, the architecture attempts to create a new identity for the owners. At the same time, it reflects an earnest attempt to be more energy-efficient.

LAM CHUAN INDUSTRIAL BUILDING

LOOK Architects
1995

BY TAN HOCK BENG

A curved front wall with skewed canopies is juxtaposed with flat planes to create a strong visual interest on the front elevation.

Factories and industrial facilities were, in the past, regarded as "non-glamorous" projects, to be designed in the shortest time, using the most cost-effective construction method. Largely based on functional requirements, they ended up as simple sheds with few aesthetic qualities.

As Singapore positions itself in the international marketplace, clients and architects are taking a different approach towards the design of this building type. Many firms now pay more attention to the public faces of their facilities—after all, they are often the first impressions that buyers get of the company's operations.

The Lam Chuan Industrial Building, designed by LOOK Architects, reflects this trend. It is an invigorating building with none of the stultifying blandness that characterises most industrial buildings in Singapore. With a total gross floor area of about 4,600 square metres (49,514 square feet), the $5 million factory is feisty in spirit. This is immediately apparent as the visitor enters the premises and is greeted by an exuberant design for the guardhouse and the covered car park.

The architecture achieves a strong presence and a degree of controlled playfulness, while a need to respond to the climate appears as a subtext. One of the building's most prominent elements is the various sun-shading devices which effectively shield the building on the east and west façades. These are not mere "tack-ons", but are integrated with the curtain wall system, thus achieving a unique vertical building component. Using laminates manufactured by the factory, the architect demonstrates innovative ways to use the products as sun-shading fins.

The architecture is accomplished in its external expression. A curved front wall with skewed canopies is juxtaposed with flat planes to create a strong visual interest on the front elevation. These elements reflect the different functional spaces behind the two-storey façade. Internally, the control is also evident. In its spatial disposition, the first storey consists of a voluminous lobby, several meeting rooms and sales and production offices, while the second storey comprises the managerial office and other administrative spaces. This office floor is enhanced by skylights, where the luminosity imparts a pleasant atmosphere to the entire space. Behind this office space is the huge factory space.

Far left: **The first storey consists of a voluminous lobby, several meeting rooms, sales office and production offices.**

Top: **The visitor is greeted by an exuberant design for the guardhouse and the covered car park.**

Left: **Sun-shading devices effectively shield the building on the east and west façades.**

Bottom: **Perspective of the entrance foyer**

Here, the architect has chosen to keep all aspects of the building simple.

Structures and materials are employed to make the large production spaces under the roof as light and open as possible. A system of ventilators and service walkways, together with a curved metal roof with deep protective eaves, are designed to facilitate cross-ventilation. This facility reflects an emerging interpretation for factory design, which is adventurous yet thoughtful.

This is a mature piece of work that focuses upon the search for new expressions for industrial buildings.

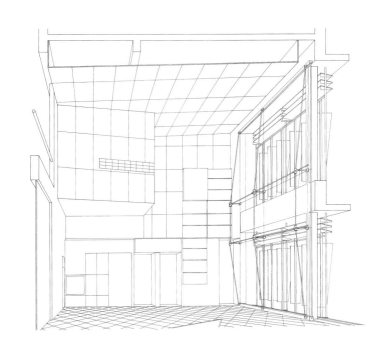

Choa Chu Kang Housing is a residential Design-and-Build project with 607 dwelling units. It was won in competition, and constructed for the Housing and Development Board of Singapore (HDB). The award of the contract showed that Akitek Tenggara had submitted a highly innovative approach to public housing, incorporating many ideas that Tay Kheng Soon had been developing since 1967.

CHOA CHU KANG HOUSING

Akitek Tenggara
1997

The project is conceptualised as a perimeter block with an increased block depth. Through the introduction of a single variable in the morphology, a number of important spatial and formal variations resulted.

When the public housing authority opened its doors to private architects, it gave an opportunity to test new geometries within the strict design constraints specified by the HDB. Choa Chu Kang housing is conceptualised as a perimeter block with an increased block depth. Through the introduction of a single variable in the morphology, where the conventional block depth of 11 metres (39 feet) is increased to 13.6 metres (45 feet), a number of important spatial and formal variations resulted. Firstly, the increased depth necessitated a reconfiguration of the internal floor plan of the units where the usual location of the living room alongside the public access corridor could now be relocated to the opposite side of the plan,

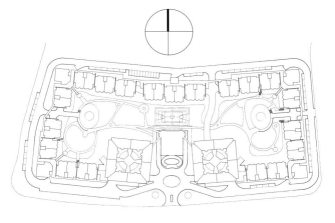

Above left: **Most units have views into the large communal open space. The plan arrangement, with its two covered pavilions and a playspace for children, allows "community" to develop naturally.**

Above right: **Covered access walkways link all parts of the site.**

Left: **Site plan**

thereby gaining an unobstructed view of the internal public garden.

Secondly, the increased depth yielded a shorter total block length while fulfilling the gross floor area requirements of a minimum plot ratio of 2.8:1. The density efficiency of the new proposal was such that a great deal of height variation could be introduced since the total floor space could be accommodated relatively easily. The average height of the blocks became 12.1 storeys, the lowest being seven storeys and the highest 18 storeys. This is in contrast to the almost uniform 19 storeys of the adjacent HDB blocks built to a slightly lower density. A plot ratio of 3:1 was achieved with a building site coverage of 40 percent. The latitude in heights gave rise to the optional addition of more floor space, if required, through infilling some of the lower blocks. A higher plot ratio of 3.5:1 would be possible while still retaining some degree of height variation. The bonus was the extensive size of the central integrated communal open space in the scheme.

Most units have views into the large communal open space. All car parks are located under the blocks and exposure to street noise is minimised. The relative calm in this inner space is remarkable although it can be disturbed by inconsiderate households playing music loudly, which is amplified by the building configuration. Children can play in relative safety, senior citizens can walk without having to negotiate steps or cars, while joggers can circle the garden court.

Akitek Tenggara has incorporated aspects of March and Steadman's built form studies carried out at Cambridge University under Leslie Martin in the United Kingdom in the 1960s and 1970s. The ideas of Dutch-born theorist Prof John Habraken have also influenced the intention to give the end-user some flexibility in internal room arrangements. The column structure allows for maximum flexibility of room layout to the end-users' requirements. Rooms can be added, removed or varied in size within the apartment perimeter. The architects passionately believe that there are many other configurations that could be explored, with benefits accruing.

Corfe Place House raises a number of questions about prevailing values in the suburbs of a rapidly developing tropical city in Asia. It is located in Serangoon Gardens, one of the private estates on the outskirts of Singapore that changed little before the 1990s. The estate embodied many of the values of its counterparts in the English suburbs.

CORFE PLACE HOUSE

KNTA Architects
1997

Opposite: **There is a clear distinction between the constructed and the natural world. Water is the only connection, flowing from inside to outside, defining activity areas on plan.**

Right: **After demolition, the Corfe Place House was rebuilt and transformed to express not conformity but difference and a breaking away from convention.**

The semi-detached house type was probably transported as a housing type to the colonies in Southeast Asia in the early part of the 20th century. In Singapore, one can see examples of such housing built for colonial civil servants and commissioned army officers from the lower ranks. Thereafter, it found favour with developers of private estates, as it saved costs through the reduction of one external wall and the land area needed for development. The image associated with such housing remained remarkably stable until recent years. It resisted the rapid social and economic changes that transformed the land-

Difference is expressed not only in the increased height of Corfe Place, which dwarfs its single-storey neighbour, but also in the deliberate choice of a modern aesthetic and materials that are commensurate with this aesthetic.

scape of Singapore after independence. But rising aspirations of the population, pressure on land and re-zoning at higher plot ratio inevitably reached Corfe Place.

The house, designed by KNTA Architects, was formerly one half of an identical pair of semi-D's. After demolition, it was rebuilt and transformed to express not conformity but difference and a breaking away from convention. The party wall has become not a "common" wall but a wall of separation, of demarcation, of defining one's own space. The deference of former times gives way to the assertive expression of one's individual identity.

Difference is expressed not only in the increased height of Corfe Place, which dwarfs its single-storey neighbour, but also in the deliberate choice of a modern aesthetic and materials that are commensurate with this aesthetic. There is greater transparency in the elevations compared with its older neighbour. The roof form contributes to the expression of difference. A metal clad pod containing mechanical services equipment and water tanks projects above the flat concrete roof. Provision was also made for solar panels for hot water heating.

The plan further emphasises difference by the manner in which geometry is manipulated in the newer house. A sharp incision has been made in the front elevation and a second incision in the side elevation. With the delicate skills of a surgeon, the architect has cleaved the living space from the rest of the dwelling, which is aligned with the party wall, and twist-

Above, left and right: **The house is remarkable for the precision of the details and the delicate, almost fastidious, attention to tectonics. KNTA has produced a delightful minimalist statement with a limited palette of materials.**

ed it. A fissure has been created in the plan, a crevasse through which light streams down from a glazed aperture in the roof. The narrowness of the site limits this fractional shift of geometry to just 5.5 degrees.

The displacement of the living "platform" is further emphasised by its isolation within a shallow pond. The principal vertical circulation element, a steel staircase, is located within the fissure. It is hinged around a vertical steel column and negotiates a route through the pressing sides of the crevasse to the upper level. Four bridges, like stretched tendons, provide the link between the functional elements and exploit tightly compressed vistas from within the crack.

The main living space opens out to the perimeter garden, but nature is not welcomed within. There is a clear distinction between the constructed and the natural world. The sliding doors can be opened to allow breezes to enter, but this house is not primarily concerned with climatic response. There is another agenda. The house is an internalised experience. Water is the only connection. It flows from inside to outside, defining activity areas on plan.

The house is an exquisite object. It is remarkable for the precision of details and the delicate, almost fastidious, attention to tectonics. KNTA has produced a delightful minimalist statement with a limited palette of materials. In the Asian metropolis of the 21st century, the ability to create such drama in a tight suburban setting is invaluable.

The Institute of Technical Education (ITE) at Bishan continues the development of Akitek Tenggara's exploration of a modern architectural language for the tropics. Climatically, the design emphasises transparency and permeability in the spatial structure. The sheltering effect of the overhangs over the passageways creates an architecture of shade rather than an architecture of mass.

INSTITUTE OF TECHNICAL EDUCATION (ITE), BISHAN

Akitek Tenggara II
1994

Throughout ITE Bishan, there is consistent architectural language. The building celebrates technology in a poetic manner.

ITE Bishan's two 250-metre (820-foot) long parallel blocks of accommodation are separated by an 18-metre (59-foot) wide strip of landscape. They are gently bent to a curve with an inside radius of 170 metres (558 feet). The four-storey-high blocks are punctured at intervals along the façade to permit prevailing breezes to pass through the structure.

The curved roof has a wide overhang which gives protection from the rain and sun. The overhang is supported on a secondary steel frame which also carries broad metal louvres that shield the external walls. The building has a striking image of raw technology, with steel bridges across the gap between the two blocks. The building is stripped to the essentials. Decoration is superfluous; every component either has a structural reason or is an essential climate controlling device.

The building is entered on the west side, into a soaring naturally-ventilated atrium and open-to-sky auditorium. The roof is a high, curved steel frame with open sides, not entirely suitable for its users in a tropical thunderstorm but, at other times, the atrium is the hub of the complex. An industrial finished glass lift ascends within this atrium space, which is connected by flying bridges to the intermediate floors of the teaching blocks. The multi-purpose hall is at the south end of the block, with exhaust ducting from the kitchen beneath elegantly deployed.

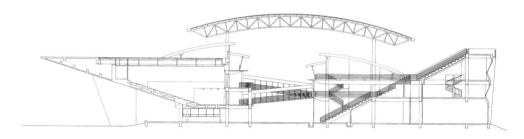

Above left: **Section**

Above right: **An industrial finished glass lift ascends within the atrium space.**

Left: **Two 250-metre (820-foot) long parallel blocks of accommodation are bent to a curve with an inside radius of 170 metres (558 feet).**

Bottom: **The building has a striking image of raw technology.**

Consistent architectural language is evident throughout the building, which celebrates technology in a poetic manner. The central "street" is reminiscent of Tay Kheng Soon's concept for Kampong Bugis DGP (1990); it is high and narrow with overhanging roofs that give shade throughout the day. Non-reflective landscape helps to cool the building.

Architecturally, the design emphasises changeability in the usage and adaptability in the fabric of the building. The design strategy is to be able to accommodate modifications in an aggregative manner rather than adopt a finite design composition which resists additions or alterations.

Ang Mo Kio Avenue 3 is, on first acquaintance, a curious location for the French international school in Singapore. This is HDB "heartland" and the school is in close proximity to an industrial estate to the north and to Serangoon North HDB estate to the east, while to the south is Serangoon Gardens Estate, a bastion of Singapore's affluent middle-income group. It is far from the popular expatriate enclaves in and around Holland Village or along the East Coast.

LE LYCÉE FRANÇAIS DE SINGAPOUR

Kumpulan Akitek
1999

The administration area, the huge gymnasium and the four-storey secondary school are aligned along the highway, protecting and acoustically sheltering the primary and infant areas.

The French international school in Singapore, or Le Lycée Français de Singapour, immediately stands out in this context as "something foreign". Its form, architectural language and spatial qualities betray its origins and the immediate conclusion that one might leap to is that this is the work of a French consultant architect. But that conclusion is wrong. The design is in fact the work of a young archi-

tectural team from Kumpulan Akitek and the contract for the school was won in a limited "Design-and-Build" competition in conjunction with Neo Corporation Pte Ltd.

The "French-ness" in the project may be derived in part from the very precise programme that was prepared by the client. The school was to be divided into three departments, namely kindergarten, primary and secondary. The scale reflected these age

groups—i.e. low, medium and tall—while the materials used ranged from the intimate scale and texture of timber to the tactile quality of brick and finally to the more universal attributes of concrete and steel. The different materials do suggest an intentional non-conformity. This brief immediately sets the French school apart from other Singapore schools.

This programme would not in itself guarantee a French identity so one must look further for this elusive quality. It is perhaps to do with the spaces in the school, though these are not specifically French. They simply seem to have a sense of freedom and a certain "panache". It is as though one were meeting an expatriate and one discerned by his or her bearing, manner and attire that he or she was from France. Perhaps it is the roof profile, set like a beret at a jaunty angle.

Unlike Singapore schools, Le Lycée Français de Singapour does not have a sense of a clear hierarchy. There is no parade square or distinction between classroom blocks and specialist teaching blocks, such as one

Above left: **A faceted façade protects the school from the noise of traffic along Ang Mo Kio Avenue 3.**

Above right: **Le Lycée Français de Singapour is an intriguing and stylish addition to the local landscape.**

Bottom: **Boundaries between the different departments are blurred.**

finds in the ubiquitous PWD model. The entrance is not dominant and boundaries are blurred, although there are obviously clear distinctions between the different departments. Perhaps it is the lack of a distinct hierarchy which gives the school a unique identity in the local context.

At another level, the building is simply a response to the site. The administration area, the huge gymnasium, with its climbing wall, and the four-storey secondary school are aligned along the highway, the faceted façade protecting and acoustically sheltering the primary and infant areas. The four-storey secondary school block forms a backcloth to the daily life of the school. It has a certain monumentality with its tall square columns that split at the top into four steel struts which in turn support the oversailing roof structure.

The running track and football field are "shoehorned" into the tight site in approximately the correct orientation to avoid the setting sun. In the final analysis, this is an intriguing and stylish building that fits into the Singapore landscape without any hint of aloofness or self-importance.

UNDER
CONSTRUCTION
AND UNBUILT
ARCHITECTURE

Singapore is the most densely populated country in the world, with 4 million people on a current land area of 660 square kilometres (254.8 square miles). By the end of the year 2000, the density will reach 6,060 persons per square kilometre. In 2001, the Urban Redevelopment Authority (URA) will reveal a revised Concept Plan for the island, with an estimated population of 5.5 million by the year 2040—that will work out to 7,237 persons per square kilometre (assuming an additional 100 square kilometres, or 38.6 square miles, of land is reclaimed).

KAMPONG BUGIS DEVELOPMENT GUIDE PLAN

**Tay Kheng Soon
Akitek Tenggara II
and the Singapore Institute
of Architects (SIA)
1990**

Opposite: **Aerial view of a model of the Kampong Bugis DGP.**

Below: **The model demonstrates the use of solar collector panels and rain water collection in addition to the use of dense morphologies.**

Page 232: **The Esplanade—Theatres on the Bay**

Page 233:
Expo 2000 MRT Station.

One of the key questions confronting Singapore architects is how to build in this evolving situation. Architect Tay Kheng Soon has been an outspoken critic of conventional planning approaches and he has developed the Tropical City Concept which, in the context of existing cities in the tropics, emphasises re-urbanisation. This view is within a larger thesis that the city's relationship with the countryside is to be considered as one and not two realms, for the sustainability of both. The conservation of bio-diversity and natural landscape is best achieved by limiting human encroachment into nature and eco-agriculture. The priority is to limit the existing curtilage of the city by better utilisation of existing urban land through better planning and compact spatial morphologies.

In 1990, the then Minister of National Development S. Dhanabalan invited Tay to demonstrate the Tropical City Concept in the form of a Development Guide Plan for Kampong Bugis. It was the first time that private architects were involved in urban planning in this manner. As the Singapore Concept Plan was undergoing a statutory review at that time, the team took it upon itself to contextualise its study of the site within its own review of the Singapore Concept Plan.

Tropical cities are fundamentally dissimilar to city planning models in temperate climates in that the reduction of the need to travel or to move about is predicated by the discomfort experienced in hot humid conditions.

Cities should be compact since suburban sprawl generates reliance on private vehicles and greater fuel use. This means the emission of more carbon monoxide, which contributes to the greenhouse effect. Furthermore, the rain and the sun should be considered positively rather than negatively because at relatively high densities, economies of scale allow solar energy and rain water collection and recycling to be incorporated into the infrastructure of the city. Better bio-climatic synergy can be achieved.

The primary aim in urban design and architecture in the dense city centres of the tropics should therefore aim at reducing the temperature of the city as a whole and to make the reliance on air-conditioning optional

Above: **Overview of the model with a gross plot ratio of 4.8:1.**

Below: **Conceptual model of a high-rise "tropical" tower.**

rather than mandatory. Single buildings cannot solve the problems of heat retention, dust and noise pollution which air-conditioning alleviates. These conditions can only be resolved through large scale redevelopment.

The first strategy in such redevelopment is to introduce high level shading to prevent the heating up of the city fabric. These high level shading devices would simultaneously be rain and sun energy collectors. The second strategy is to green the city both horizontally and vertically to absorb radiant and ambient insolation. This requires legal enactment. Tay proposed the introduction of two taxes—the green and the blue tax. The green tax is based on the notion that every building is deemed to have removed biomass from nature, which existed prior to urbanisation. To the extent that a building owner reintroduces biomass back to a site, the tax is reduced. No tax is payable if the entire biomass is put back. The blue tax works in a similar manner. Every building has to retain rainwater as much as possible so as not to burden the city's

storm drainage system. To the extent that water is retained, the tax is reduced. If all is discharged, the full tax is payable.

In the Singapore context of available re-urbanisable urban central area land, Tay calculated that, in 1990, an additional 1 million people, including the necessary non-residential floor space, could be accommodated if mixed-use developments were planned at appropriate nodes, transit stations, on decks over highways, on obsolete industrial sites and on reclaimed land adjacent to the city centre. The implication of this is significant as it is possible that five new towns of the current New Town model (see page 191) need not have been built in the outskirts of the city. Many semi-rural areas and undeveloped farmland could have been preserved for nature and future recreational uses.

THE KAMPONG BUGIS DEVELOPMENT GUIDE PLAN

The Kampong Bugis site is some 72 hectares (177.9 acres) of cleared land at the confluence of two rivers at the

fringe of the city centre. In contextualising the design parameters of the subject site, all available urban land in the central planning area was quantified. Next, the pattern of floor space generated over the years was analysed from statistics. From this, it was possible to quantify the residential and non-residential floor space pattern of demand. It was then a simple matter to compute the total floor area in relation to a projected population. The next task was to compute the average plot ratio on the available land to be developed for the projected population. Disused railway yards, oil-storage tank farms, disused gas or abandoned engineering works, etc., when added together, could easily accommodate the extra million people projected without building any more new towns. The proposed plot-ratio of 4.8 was not high by any metropolitan standards. It was therefore judged to be entirely realistic.

A number of other conclusions can be drawn. Firstly, it is feasible to increase the city centre population greatly, without undue stress. Secondly, with the possibility of housing a large population in the city centre, the need for the outward expansion of new towns which, in 1990, were typically built at a net residential density of only 2.8, could be halted and thereby the outer natural fringes of Singapore island could be preserved and kept intact for nature and for future generations. Thirdly, the compactness of the nodal clusters allows for the interconnection of buildings at basement level and at podium level. The need to travel could

be reduced through the mixing of residences with work place, shopping, entertainment and social and cultural facilities. Through heavy planting on roof decks and on the building surfaces, a conducive micro-climate could be created. The shielding of the interiors of building sites from the dust and noise of roads, enhanced by interconnecting car parking decks below the buildings, would basically create a quiet and dust-free environment.

The use of air-conditioning for comfort in the tropics becomes optional rather than obligatory, the need to obviate heat discomfort having been dispelled through local planning and design. It was reasoned that air-conditioning is a permanent feature of a more affluent way of life in the tropics, but a strategy was evolved to enhance options for its use and to introduce energy-saving technologies. The principal technology is a decentralised energy production policy. In this policy, the waste heat, which would have to be otherwise discharged, can be recovered for district-cooling through heat absorption refrigeration. Furthermore, the transmission losses of power generation can also be saved. The feasibility depends entirely on the compactness of the urban morphology.

The Tropical City Concept was conceived in the context of an island-city-state. When the thinking is applied to a larger context, other factors come into play. Factors such as rural to urban migration, ecological protection of landscapes and natural features, water and soil conservation, and preservation of bio-diversity have

to be factored into the concept.

All cities came about because of the need to transact ideas, goods and services. Increasingly, these transactions are speeded up through the use of telecommunications and information technology (IT). Such networks will be further intensified with additional features that will enable remote working, shopping and even automated manufacturing. A degree of decentralisation of the workplace has become possible.

Simultaneously, the demand for intensive human face-to-face interaction increases. Face-to-face communication has advantages over electronic communication systems in that it is unpredictable and unplanned. In research centres around the world, restaurants and bars are important meeting places which researchers frequent to exchange ideas. This has important implications for the planning of cities where the location of social nodes must provide scope for a wide range of human transactions. The combination of Electronic Information Systems and intensive human interface creates a challenge to consider an enhanced role for the city. The city

can be a place wherein lifelong learning is feasible and residence, work, study and research become closely inter-related. These spatial implications challenge architecture and urban planning.

The Kampong Bugis Development Guide Plan interprets the conceptual idea and agenda for the Tropical City into a strategy awaiting implementation. It represents the critical alternative to current planning policies.

In January 1991, the Minister for National Development chaired a public participation seminar, the first of its kind ever to be held in Singapore and in retrospect, it can be seen as a historic event. Unfortunately, the vision proposed by Tay Kheng Soon was deemed to be too radical.

In 2000, the predicted population for Singapore was revised upwards to 5.5 million by the year 2040. Perhaps the time has come to build Kampong Bugis, along the lines of Tay Kheng Soon's Tropical City Concept.

The Kampong Bugis Concept Plan

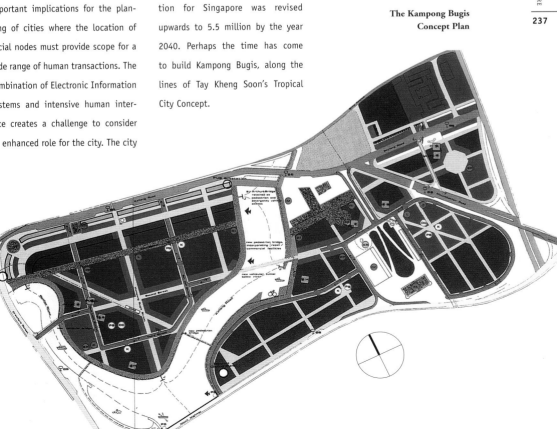

Historically, Asian cultures have designed their significant buildings in rational response to their geographic, climatic and cultural context and they built them with the most advanced technology currently available. Where possible and appropriate, new architectural vocabularies have been explored.

THE ESPLANADE—THEATRES ON THE BAY

**DP Architects Pte Ltd
in association with Michael Wilford
and Partners London
2002**

Below and opposite bottom:
**The Esplanade—Theatres
on the Bay project attracted
immense controversy when
first unveiled to the public,
as it is seen, by virtue of
its prominent waterside
location, as the symbolic
equivalent of the Opera
House in Sydney.**

Opposite top: **The Concert
Hall and the Lyric Theatre
are shaded by devices that
change in shape and form as
they extend across the surfaces of the two glass shells.**

The Esplanade is being built on the edge of Singapore's historic Civic District. A waterfront walkway under the Esplanade bridge joins the Esplanade Park. From the Concert Hall and Lyric Theatre, there are views across the Padang and towards Victoria Theatre and the National Monument. The design is intended to respond to this historic setting. It will be highly visible from the high-rise commercial towers of the CBD.

Climatically, the architects argue that it is inappropriate to have a naturally ventilated structure since we have come to expect the comfort of air-conditioning in our public buildings. The architects have thus attempted to reconcile the inherent conflicts that arise between the exploitation of views, the exclusion of direct sunlight and consequent high insolation, and the need for efficient air-conditioning. The solution involves the use of glass "shells" around the foyers of the two major performance venues, shaded by a unique system of sunshades configured in a mesh pattern that evokes geometries in nature, as well as Asian traditional craft and art. The sunshading devices change in shape and form and the extent of cover they provide also changes as they extend across the surfaces of the shells. In terms of design and construction, the arrangement of the sunshades has been made possible by the use of advanced computer software.

The architects have contrived to give the two shells a feeling of light-

ness juxtaposed against the solid appearance of the base of the building. Clad in granite in earth tones, this base acts as a strong counterpoint. The two main performance spaces are designed to be visually rich, in contrast with the relative restraint of the foyers. The Concert Hall is finished in wood, fabric covered panels and textured concrete. It has to be acoustically sensitive and can be fine-tuned, with the aid of an acoustic canopy, to suit a variety of performances ranging from a solo flute to a large symphony orchestra.

The Lyric Theatre is a versatile general purpose space that is intended to accommodate performances ranging from traditional drama to amplified musical performances. This venue has a fly tower above the main stage and an orchestra pit.

In addition, there are two smaller venues, the Chorus Room and the Drama Room. Finally, a large courtyard, doubling as an outdoor performance space, opens out to Marina Bay. The Esplanade project will doubtless be closely scrutinised and all aspects critically reviewed when it is completed in 2002.

The National Library Board (NLB) building is an externalised play of surfaces and textures which conceals two blocks that are separated by a day-lit internal street and connected by zigzagging bridges. The larger block sits astride a civic plaza, with promises of "outdoor" events and café culture. The elevations are an elaborate play of materials and sunshading devices that are brought together as much for their aesthetic qualities as for climatic performance.

THE SINGAPORE NATIONAL LIBRARY BOARD BUILDING

Ken Yeang, TR Hamzah and Yeang and Swan and Maclaren
2003

The Singapore National Library Board (NLB) Building is one of the most important institutional projects in progress. Aware that this project will affect how he is judged, Ken Yeang describes it as one that will be "seriously simulated, consulted and advised". Yeang has worldwide recognition as an advocate and practitioner of Bioclimatic Design—and he has expanded the canvas of Bioclimatic Design to an ecological level.

Backing him on this project is an international team of experts from Australia, the United Kingdom and Singapore, who will provide input on everything from airflow simulations to embodied energy. This level of multi-disciplinary input has become affordable only in the last few years. And so this project is as much a question of "how to achieve" as it is of "what to achieve".

The NLB project is the most prestigious public commission of a large institutional building since the Esplanade: Theatres on the Bay. The National Library Board seems to know that it is merely the custodian of a building that will belong to all Singaporeans, one that could well become a benchmark in Southeast Asia. The client's approach goes beyond creating a functional library. They also want a significant piece of architecture—a world class design.

At the public exhibition of the shortlisted competition entries, the Swan and Maclaren submission (in association with TR Hamzah and Yeang) stood out for the breadth of its environmental agenda. No one promised to deliver Tropical Excellence quite the way Yeang did. No other submission argued for an environmental agenda quite as clearly, with performance-based explorations of what "tropical" means exactly.

What is remarkable about this submission is not that it offers anything radically new. Rather that it

does not. It promises instead to deliver an integration of all we know so far on the climatic design and ecological impact of buildings. While the principles have been in place for years, implementation capability has lagged behind. In the last ten years, design and simulation tools have come into the picture, for everything from energy simulation to daylighting design. This gives "designer intuition" a lot more bite.

Looking at the submission itself, the principles of passive design are all there—daylighting, solar orientation, sunshading, natural ventilation and landscaping—pieced together into a collective strategy for low energy and high comfort. Most of the library workspaces and collection areas will operate in the Active Mode (artificial light and air-conditioning), a clear acknowledgement that comfort is as much a question of lifestyle and perception as it is about cost and energy.

Into this blend of the Active and

Top, bottom left and right:
Three views of the submission models for the National Library Board Building. The NLB stresses that this will not be the exact appearance of the final design. The design is a work-in-progress.

[CHAPTER 10] UNDER CONSTRUCTION AND UNBUILT ARCHITECTURE

241

Passive, Yeang has worked in a third strategy—the Mixed Mode, where natural ventilation is supported by mechanical means, such as fans, in certain transitional spaces (lobbies, foyers, courtyards). The strategy is supported by airflow and energy simulations, along with predictions on comfort. Yeang then layers these issues with ecological concerns, such as material recyclability, carbon dioxide emissions, waste management, embodied energy, etc.

The NLB building is an externalised play of surfaces and textures which conceals two blocks that are separated by a day-lit internal street and connected by zigzagging bridges.

The blocks are a clever juxtaposition of formality and asymmetry—a curved block for noisier public activities (exhibitions, auditorium, multimedia) sits alongside a larger, rectilinear entity that will house the library collections. The division of the brief into two halves generates spatial ambiguities of what's inside, outside and on the other side. It sublimates the message that the "once serious" library culture can be more fun; that building has become urban catalyst; that a library can be a "place for the people".

Clearly a lot rides on the project. As client, the National Library Board will settle for nothing less than a national and civic institution that functions well. If the building delivers on all its green promises, it will also become a "lever" in the quest for "knowledge-based design".

More than just a station on a line, the Expo 2000 MRT station by Foster and Partners is *the* station on a line. By importing Norman Foster's oeuvre for his now ubiquitous design of stunning structural premise, Singapore has bagged another heavyweight in the international architectural circle.

EXPO 2000 MRT STATION
CHANGI AIRPORT LINE

Foster and Partners
2001

BY CHEE LI LIAN

This is a speculative piece of writing about the Expo Station on the new Changi Airport line. It is not a fictitious work by any means; the point of this piece is essentially to raise questions as to what this station may achieve when it is finally completed and fully operational. At the time of writing, the great titanium toroidal roof peeks from behind the temporary hoarding fronted by a strange surrealistic landscape of pyramidal piles of sand.

Operating in a condition of tabula rasa, the new Expo Station literally grew out of nowhere—an empty site with few constraints and fewer still credible contexts to confer with. It is a void that is to be filled with a sub-city; self-sufficient and self-generative in its appeal, with infrastructure provided physically by way of transportation links and facilities, coupled inevitably with a belief in the power of architecture to engender pulsating life into a featureless site. The choice of Foster and Partners as architects for this station justifies a fundamental need to psychologically "anchor" a reputation to this less-than-neutral space. As if to provide an impetus, the decision has, to a large extent, drawn attention to the project.

As is expected, Foster and Partners have delivered the goods. The station, although still incomplete, evokes an imposing presence despite being hidden from Upper Changi Road East by the larger Expo building. In the evening light, the bronze reflection thrown off the massive three-dimensional curved roof catches one's eye and announces emphatically the station's most significant feature. The roof is the first of its kind here on our island and is a study in rigorous geometry and structural ingenuity. Derived from the section of a torus (a shape

Although incomplete, the Expo 2000 MRT Station has an imposing presence.

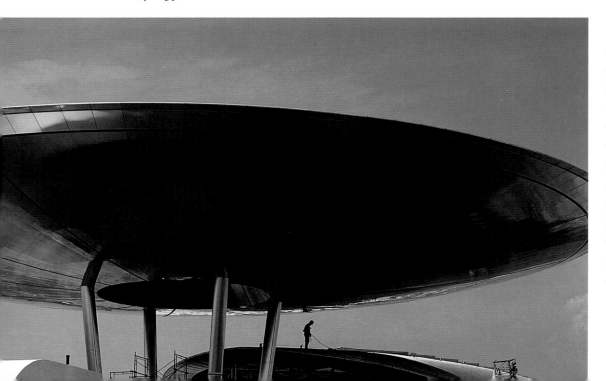

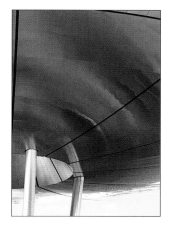

Above left and right: **The ticket hall is marked by a circular, stainless steel disc as a roof.**

Bottom: **The torus-shaped roof over the concourse has a clear span of 70 metres (230 feet), a grand gesture unrivalled by any other station.**

defined by two radii), the three-dimensional curve gains from the double curvature of the shell lattice structure and the eventual shape is a cylindrical cut perpendicular to the torus. The whole roof is nimbly supported by just two pairs of "V" twin columns separated by a huge 70-metre (230-foot) span between. Visually emphasising the sweeping curvature of the roof and the great expanse of its location's open space, the clear span is a grand gesture still unrivalled by other stations. The free-standing ticket hall, with a circular stainless steel disc as roof, overhangs and terminates one end of the toroidal curved roof form.

The life of the Expo Station now depends on the periodic wave of fairs that descends upon it sporadically throughout the year. The only way in which any life can perpetually vivify this site is by way of a sound programmatic plan. Fortuitously, it is still early days for the Expo Station and perhaps there are plans to let the station run as though it were an independent sub-city. That potential remains to be tapped.

A larger query would be this: How does the station legitimise itself as part of a distinct selection of sites representing Singapore and set itself apart from the mind-boggling choices of meaty destinations that pepper the globe? This question must be answered since the point of the Expo is to pose as a surrogate city to the downtown core and the station, as an extension of the airport, is the gate by which impressions are made or broken. An imageable design, such as Foster and Partners have furnished, and the beauty of efficacy, are plus points. But considering the stiff competition, what else can we offer as a "destination" above all others?

In the end, we need to be reassured that the substantial resources spent on good design, engineering prowess and big names will generate returns in terms of spin-offs. There is more at stake here, beyond the "shell", as one hopes to discover with the passing of time.

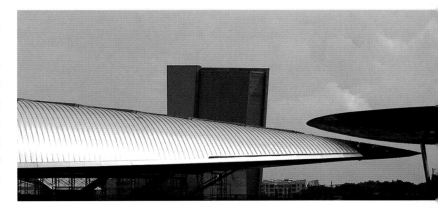

CONTRIBUTORS

CHEE LI LIAN graduated from the National University of Singapore in 1997 with the degree of Bachelor of Architecture (Honours). She was awarded the Lee Kuan Yew Medal, the Singapore Institute of Architects Medal, the Board of Architects Prize and Gold Medal in the same year. She worked with DP Architects prior to joining the School of Architecture at NUS as a member of staff. She is currently pursuing graduate studies at University College, London.

CHEW I-JIN (MSIA) graduated with a B Arch from the University of Cambridge, UK. She is a registered architect in Singapore and is in practice with Kumpulan Akitek.

CAMPBELL IAIN CUMMING is a B. Arch (Hons) graduate of the University of Newcastle upon Tyne, UK. A former exchange student at NUS, he returned to Singapore after graduation and joined the practice of William Lim Associates. He is currently in practice with Han Yip Lee Architects (HYLA).

ANN ISABELL-SCHOELLES GERONDELIS (B.Sc. (Arch), M.Arch, AIA, ACSA) is a freelance writer in Singapore and is a registered architect in the State of Georgia, USA. She served previously as assistant professor in the School of Architecture, National University of Singapore, and as design instructor in the College of Architecture, Georgia Institute of Technology, Atlanta, Georgia, USA. She was winner of the 1985 SGF Prize for design excellence.

HEE LIMIN (MSIA) graduated with a B Arch (Hons) from the School of Architecture at the National University of Singapore in 1990. She was awarded the SIA Medal in the same year. She is a registered architect who worked for six years with the PWD and is currently an assistant professor in the School of Architecture, NUS.

NIRMAL KISHNANI is an honours graduate in architecture and holds an MSc in Environmental Pschology from Surrey University (UK), where he studied under Professor David Canter. He is currently reading for a PhD at Curtin University, Australia.

ANAND KRISHNAN graduated from the University of New South Wales with a B Arch (Hons) and went on to obtain a Graduate Diploma in Urban Design from Sydney University. He subsequently worked with Kerry Hill Architects, the URA and with Teo A Khing Design Consultants. He is currently pursuing graduate studies at Harvard University.

LEONG TENG WUI graduated from the National University of Singapore in 1995 with the degree of Bachelor of Architecture (Honours). He was awarded the Singapore Institute of Architects Medal. He went on to Harvard University, where he was awarded the degree of Master of Architecture in Urban Design. He is currently working with the URA.

VINCENT LIM (MSIA) graduated from the School of Architecture at the National University of Singapore with a B Arch (Hons) in 1994. He was the winner of the SIA Medal and the Board of Architects Prize in the same year. He is currently an architect in practice with B+S+T Architects.

LOOK BOON GEE (MSIA) graduated with B Arch (Honours) from the University of New South Wales. He is principal of LOOK Architects.

PETER SIM WEI CHIANG graduated from the School of Architecture at the National University of Singapore with a B Arch (Hons) in 1997. He was the winner of the ICI Dulux Gold Medal in the same year. He is currently in practice with Alsop and Stormer in London (UK).

TAN BOON THOR graduated from the School of Architecture at the National University of Singapore with the degree of Bachelor of Architecture (Hons) in 1995. He was awarded the Board of Architects Prize in the same year. He is now in practice with PWD Consultants Pte Ltd.

TAN HOCK BENG (MSIA) graduated from the School of Architecture at NUS with the degree of Bachelor of Architecture (Hons) in 1989. He was awarded the Singapore Institute of Architects Medal in the same year. He is the principal of MAPS Design Studio and the author of several books on Southeast Asian architecture, including *Tropical Architecture and Interiors* (1994), *Tropical Resorts* (1995) and *Tropical Romantic* (2000).

PROJECT DATA

UOB Plaza

Address	80 Raffles Place
Client	United Overseas Bank Ltd
Architect	Architects 61 Pte Ltd
Consultant	Concept and Master Planner: Kenzo Tange Associates
Project Manager	UOB Property Management Pte Ltd
Civil & Structural Engineer	Ove Arup & Partners
Mechanical & Electrical Engineer	J Roger Preston Pte Ltd
	(now known as Rust JRP Pte Ltd)
Quantity Surveyor	Rider Hunt Levett & Bailey
Main Contractor	Nishimatsu Lum Chang Joint Venture (Plaza I)
	Wimpey Woh Hup Environmental Engineering (Plaza II)
Interior Design	Kohn Pedersen and Fox Conway
Lighting Engineer	Sarner Grundy Lighting Design (Lighting Consultant)
Acoustic Engineer	Acviron Acoustics Consultants Pte Ltd
Landscape Architect	Belt Collins & Associates International
Curtainwall Consultant	Arup Facade Engineering

Hitachi Tower/ Caltex House

Address	16 Collyer Quay/30 Raffles Place
Client	Savu Investments Pte Ltd
Architect	Architects 61 Pte Ltd
Design Consultant	Murphy Jahn Architects
Civil & Structural Engineer	Steen Consultants Pte Ltd
Mechanical & Electrical Engineer	Ewbank Preece Engineers Pte Ltd
	(now known as PCR Engineers Ptd Ltd)
Quantity Surveyor	Rider Hunt Levett & Bailey
Main Contractor	Obayashi Corporation
Lighting Engineer	Francis Krahe & Associates Inc
Acoustic Engineer	Acviron Acoustics Consultants Pte Ltd
Curtainwall Consultant	Curtain Wall Design & Consulting Inc Texas

OUB Centre

Address	Raffles Place
Client	Overseas Union Bank
Architect	SAA Partnership
Design Consultant	Kenzo Tange Associates/Urtec
Civil & Structural Engineer	Bylander Meinhardt Partnership
Mechanical & Electrical Engineer	Bylander Meinhardt Partnership
Quantity Surveyor	WT Partnership
Main Contractor	Kajima-Hazama-JDC Joint Venture

Republic Plaza

Address	9 Raffles Place
Client	CDL Properties Ltd
Architect	RSP Architects Planners & Engineers Pte Ltd
Design Consultant	Kisho Kurokawa Architects & Associates
Project Manager	City Project Management Pte Ltd Pte Ltd
Civil & Structural Engineer	RSP Architects Planners & Engineers
Mechanical & Electrical Engineer	Squire Mech Pte Ltd
Quantity Surveyor	Rider Hunt Levett & Bailey
Main Contractor	Shimizu Corporation
Interior Design	RSP Interiors Pte Ltd
Lighting Engineer	Francis Krahe & Associates Inc
Acoustic Engineer	Acviron Acoustic Consultants Pte Ltd
Landscape Architect	Cicada Pte Ltd
Curtainwall Consultant	Arup Facade Engineering

Telok Ayer Market

Address	Raffles Quay
Client	Renaissance Properties Pte Ltd
Architect	Quek Associates
Civil & Structural Engineer	Ng Wee Meng & Associates
Mechanical & Electrical Engineer	Elsad Associates
Main Contractor	Golden Design Decor Enterprises

South Boat Quay Conservation Area

Address	South Boat Quay
Architect	Urban Redevelopment Authority
Project Manager	Urban Redevelopment Authority
Civil & Structural Engineer	Urban Redevelopment Authority
Mechanical & Electrical Engineer	Urban Redevelopment Authority
Quantity Surveyor	Urban Redevelopment Authority
Main Contractor	Hon Construction Pte Ltd
Landscape Architect	Urban Redevelopment Authority

One Fullerton

Address	No.1 Fullerton Road, Fullerton Square
Client	Precious Treasure Pte Ltd
Architect	Architects 61 Pte Ltd
Project Manager	DP Architects Pte Ltd
Civil & Structural Engineer	Oscar Faber Pte Ltd
Mechanical & Electrical Engineer	PCR Perdana Consulting Pte Ltd
Quantity Surveyor	KPK Quantity Surveyors (1995) Singapore Pte Ltd
Main Contractor	Dragages Singapore Pte Ltd
Acoustic Engineer	Acviron AccousticsConsultants Pte Ltd
Landscape Architect	Belt Collins International

Capital Tower

Address	168 Robinson Road
Client	Pidemco Land
Architect	RSP Architects Planners & Engineers Pte Ltd
Project Manager	Pidemco Land
Civil & Structural Engineer	Maunsell Consultants (S) Pte Ltd
Mechanical & Electrical Engineer	Parsons Brinkerhoff Consultants Pte Ltd
Quantity Surveyor	Northcroft Lim Consultants Pte Ltd
Main Contractor	Ssangyong Engineering & Construction Co Ltd
Interior Design	Gensler
Lighting Engineer	Vision Design Studio
Acoustic Engineer	Acviron Acoustic Consultants Pte Ltd
Landscape Architect	PDAA Design Landscape Architects
Curtainwall Consultant	Arup Facade Engineering

Millenia Tower

Address	1 Temasek Avenue
Client	Pontiac Marina Pte Ltd
Architect	DP Architects Pte Ltd
Design Consultant	Kevin Roche John Dinkeloo and Associates USA
	(Structural Design Consultant)
	Weiskopf & Pickworth USA
Project Manager	Masahiro Tomita
Civil & Structural Engineer	Bylander Meinhardt Partnership
	Bylander Meinhardt Partnership
	(Consulting Engineer)
Mechanical & Electrical Engineer	Bylander Meinhardt Partnership
	Cosentini Associates
	(Consultant Mechanical and Electrical Engineer)
Quantity Surveyor	Davis Langdon and Seah (S) Pte Ltd
Main Contractor	Dragages Et Travaux Publics (S) Pte Ltd
Interior Design	Hirsch/Bedner & Associates
Lighting Engineer	HM Brondston and Partners Inc
Acoustic Engineer	Shen Milsom and Wilke Inc
Landscape Architect	Aspinwall Clouston Pte Ltd
Curtainwall Consultant	R A Heintges Architects Consultants

Singapore Suntec City

Address	Raffles Boulevard
Client	Suntec City Development Pte Ltd
Architect	DP Architects Pte Ltd
Design Consultant	Tsao & McKown
Project Manager	Suntec City Project Management
Civil & Structural Engineer	Maunsell Consultants (S) Pte Ltd
Mechanical & Electrical Engineer	Parsons Brinckerhoff Consultants Pte Ltd
Quantity Surveyor	Davis Langdon and Seah
Main Contractor	Hyundai Engineering & Construction Co Ltd
Interior Design	Richard Basmajian Pte Ltd
Lighting Engineer	Fisher Marantz Refro Stone Architectural Lighting Design
Acoustic Engineer	CCW Acoustics Pte Ltd
Landscape Architect	Aspinwall Clouston
Curtainwall Consultant	R A Heintges Architects Consultants

Millenia Walk

Address	Raffles Boulevard
Client	Pontiac Marina Pte Ltd
Architect	DP Architects Pte Ltd
Design Consultant	Philip Johnson and John Burgee Architects
Project Manager	Masahiro Tomito (Kajima Overseas Asia Pte Ltd)
Civil & Structural Engineer	Leslie E Robertson Associates
Mechanical & Electrical Engineer	Cosintini Associates
Quantity Surveyor	Davis Langdon & Seah
Main Contractor	Dragages et Travaux Public
Lighting Engineer	Claude Engle Lighting
Landscape Architect	Aspinwall Clouston

Ritz Carlton Millenia

Address	1 Temasek Avenue
Client	Pontiac Marina Pte Ltd
Architect	DP Architects Pte Ltd
Design Consultant	Kevin Roche John Dinkeloo and Associates USA
Project Manager	Masahiro Tomita
Civil & Structural Engineer	Bylander Meinhardt Partnership
Mechanical & Electrical Engineer	Bylander Meinhardt Partnership
Quantity Surveyor	Davis Langdon &Seah
Main Contractor	Dragages Et Travaux Publics
Interior Design	Hirsch/Bedner & Associates
Lighting Engineer	Claude R Engle Lighting Consultant
Acoustic Engineer	Shen Milsom and Wilke Inc
Landscape Architect	Aspinwall Clouston Pte Ltd
Curtainwall Consultant	R A Heintges Architects Consultants

Raffles Hotel

Address	1 Beach Road/328 North Bridge Road
Client	Raffles Hotel (1886) Pte Ltd
Architect	Architects 61 Pte Ltd
Project Manager	DBS Property Services Pte Ltd
Civil & Structural Engineer	Steen Consultants Pte Ltd
Mechanical & Electrical Engineer	Steen Consultants Pte Ltd
Quantity Surveyor	Davis Langdon & Seah
	(now known as Davis Langdon and Seah (S) Pte Ltd)
Main Contractor	Ssangyong Engineering & Construction Co Ltd
Interior Design	Bent Severin & Associates Pte Ltd
Lighting Engineer	Philips (S) Pte Ltd
Acoustic Engineer	CCW Acoustics Pte Ltd
Landscape Architect	Belt Collins & Associates International

Singapore Art Museum

Address	71 Bras Basah Road
Client	National Heritage Board
Architect	PWD Consultants Pte Ltd
Project Manager	PWD Consultants Pte Ltd
Civil & Structural Engineer	PWD Consultants Pte Ltd
Mechanical & Electrical Engineer	PWD Consultants Pte Ltd
Quantity Surveyor	PWD Consultants Pte Ltd
Main Contractor	Kimly Construction Pte Ltd
Interior Design	PWD Consultants Pte Ltd
	Keir & Yeo Design Consultants
	(for Patrons' Club, Shop and Library)
Lighting Engineer	PWD Consultants Pte Ltd
Landscape Architect	National Parks Board

CHIJMES

Address	Victoria Street
Client	CHIJMES Investment Pte Ltd
Architect	Ong & Ong Architects Pte Ltd
Design Consultant	Didier Repellin
Project Manager	Ong & Ong Architects Pte Ltd
Civil & Structural Engineer	Ove Arup & Partners Singapore
Mechanical & Electrical Engineer	United Project Consultants Pte Ltd
Quantity Surveyor	Choy & Associates
Main Contractor	Low Keng Huat (S) Ltd
Interior Design	Keir & Associates
Lighting Engineer	Project Lighting Design Pte Ltd
Acoustic Engineer	CCW Associates Pte Ltd
Landscape Architect	Aspinwall Clouston Pte Ltd

The Substation

Address	45 Armenian Street
Client	The Ministry of Information and the Arts (MITA)
Architect	PWD Consultants Pte Ltd
Project Manager	PWD Consultants Pte Ltd
Civil & Structural Engineer	PWD Consultants Pte Ltd
Mechanical & Electrical Engineer	PWD Consultants Pte Ltd
Quantity Surveyor	PWD Consultants Pte Ltd
Main Contractor	Batae Engineering Pte Ltd
Lighting Engineer	PWD Consultants Pte Ltd
Acoustic Engineer	PWD Consultants Pte Ltd

Asian Civilisations Museum

Address	Armenian Street
Client	National Heritage Board
Architect	PWD Consultants Pte Ltd
Civil & Structural Engineer	PWD Consultants Pte Ltd
Mechanical & Electrical Engineer	PWD Consultants Pte Ltd
Quantity Surveyor	PWD Consultants Pte Ltd
Main Contractor	Singa Development Pte Ltd
Interior Design	PWD Consultants Pte Ltd
Lighting Engineer	PWD Consultants Pte Ltd
Landscape Architect	Ren Matsui Landscape Design / Ms Eng Tow
	(Landscape Design Services)

Wheelock Place

Address	Orchard Road /Scotts Road
Client	Everbilt Developers Pte Ltd
Architect	Wong and Ouyang & Associates Pte Ltd
	RSP Architects Planners & Engineers Pte Ltd
Design Consultant	Kisho Kurokawa Architects & Associates
Civil & Structural Engineer	RSP Architects Planners & Engineers Pte Ltd
Mechanical & Electrical Engineer	Wong and Ouyong & Associates Pte Ltd
Quantity Surveyor	Davis Langdon & Seah (S) Pte Ltd
Main Contractor	Pents Ocean – LKH JV
Interior Design	Walker Group/CNI New York
Lighting Engineer	WGFS (Asia) Pte Ltd
Landscape Architect	Belt Collins & Associates (International)
Curtainwall Consultant	Heitmann & Associates Inc (USA)

Cineleisure Orchard

Address	8 Grange Road
Client	Cathay Organisation Pte Ltd
	and Cathay Cineleisure International Pte Ltd
Architect	Architects 61 Pte Ltd
Design Consultant	Mitchell Giurgola and Thorp Associates Australia
Civil & Structural Engineer	HCE Engineers Partnership
Mechanical & Electrical Engineer	Beca Carter Hollings & Ferner (SE Asia) Pte Ltd
Quantity Surveyor	Davis Langdon and Seah (S) Pte Ltd
Main Contractor	Sato Kogyo Co Ltd
Interior Design	Designphase Pte Ltd

Lighting Engineer	Sarner Grundy Lighting Design Pte Ltd
Acoustic Engineer	Acviron Acoustics
Landscape Architect	Tierra Design

Nassim Jade

Address	Nassim Road
Client	Allegro Investments Pte Ltd
Architect	Chan Sau Yan Associates (CSYA)
Structural Consultant	Trigram Partnership
Civil & Structural Engineer	Harris & Sutherland
Mechanical & Electrical Engineer	Beca Carter Hollings & Ferner (SE Asia) Pte Ltd
Quantity Surveyor	Rider Hunt Levett & Bailey
Main Contractor	San Bee Building & Civil Consultants
Lighting Consultant	Isometrix Lighting + Design
Landscape Consultant	Belt Collins International

Abelia Apartments

Address	Ardmore Park
Client	Malayan Credit Properties pte Ltd
Architect	Tangguanbee Architects
Civil & Structural Engineer	HCE Engineers Pte Lyd
Mechanical & Electrical Engineer	Servitech Consultants Pte Ltd
Quantity Surveyor	OTN Building Cost Consultants Pte Ltd
Main Contractor	Assoland Construction Pte Ltd
Interior Design	Tangguanbee Architects
Landscape Architect	PDAA Design

The Heeren

Address	268 Orchard Road
Client	Heeren Properties Pte Ltd
Architect	Architects 61 Pte Ltd
Project Manager	Swee Cheng Management Pte Ltd
Civil & Structural Engineer	Steen Consultants Pte Ltd
Mechanical & Electrical Engineer	Technocon Engineers Pte Ltd
Quantity Surveyor	Davis Langdon and Seah (S) Pte Ltd
Main Contractor	Shimizu Corporation
Interior Design	DI Design & Development Pte Ltd
LightingConsultant	Lightsource Incorporated, HK/Seattle
Acoustic Engineer	CCW Acoustics Pte Ltd
Landscape Architect	PDAA Design Pte Ltd
Curtainwall Consultant	Robert Heintges Architects & Consultants, NY USA
	March Heinlein, Italy (Stone Consultant)

Goei House

Address	95 Emerald Hill Road
Client	Magdeline Goei
Architect	SCDA Architects
Civil & Structural Engineer	KH Consultants
Mechanical & Electrical Engineer	OSV Consultants Pte Ltd
Quantity Surveyor	Barton Associates Pte Ltd
Main Contractor	LSL Building Construction
Interior Design	SCDA Architects
Landscape Architect	SCDA Architects
	Nyee Phoe Flower Garden Pte Ltd

77 Emerald Hill

Address	77 Emerald Hill Road
Client	Richard Helfer
Consultant	KKS Consultants Pte Ltd

158 Emerald Hill

Quah House

Address	158 Emerald Hill Road
Client	Mr and Mrs Quah
Architect	HYLA Architects
Civil & Structural Engineer	Maunsell Consultants (Singapore) Pte Ltd
Mechanical & Electrical Engineer	OSV Consultants Pte Ltd
Main Contractor	Ee Chiang Construction Pte Ltd
Interior Design	HYLA Architects
Lighting Engineer	Lighting Technologies Pte Ltd
Pond Specialist	Aquateigna
Landscape Consultant	Nyee Phoe Flower Gardens Pte Ltd

62 Emerald Hill

Address	62 Emerald Hill Road
Architect	WoHa Design / WH Architects
Civil & Structural Engineer	SLP Consulting Engineers
Mechanical & Electrical Engineer	Mechelect Engineering Services
Quantity Surveyor	CS Toh & Sons & Associate Consultancy
Interior Design	WoHa Design / WH Architects
Lighting Engineer	WoHa Design / WH Architects

Scotts 28

Address	28 Scotts Road
Client	HPL Properties Pte Ltd
Architect	Architects 61 Pte Ltd
Project Manager	HPL Properties Pte Ltd
Civil & Structural Engineer	Meinhardt (S) Pte Ltd
Mechanical & Electrical Engineer	Meinhardt (S) Pte Ltd
Quantity Surveyor	KPK Quantity Surveyors
Main Contractor	Hyundai Engineering & Construction Co Pte Ltd
Interior Design	KKS Consultants & Designers Pte Ltd
Lighting Engineer	Isometric Lighting and Design
Acoustic Engineer	Acviron Acoustics Consultants Pte Ltd
Landscape Architect	ACLA Pte Ltd
Curtainwall Consultant	Robert Heintges Architects & Consultants, NY USA

Paterson Edge

Address	Paterson Road
Client	Sembawang Land Pte Ltd
Architect	Mok Wei Wei of William Lim Associates
Civil & Structural Engineer	Steen Consultants Pte Ltd
Mechanical & Electrical Engineer	Bescon Consulting Engineers Pte Ltd
Quantity Surveyor	Rider Hunt Levett & Bailey
Main Contractor	Kian Hiap Construction Pte Ltd
Interior Design	William Lim Associates
Landscape Architect	Beh Two Design Pte Ltd
Curtainwall Consultant	ALT Cladding & Design Inc

Morley Road House

Address	4 Morley Road
Client	Mr and Mrs Loo
Architect	Mok Wei Wei of William Lim Associates
Mechanical & Electrical Engineer	AE & T Consultants
Quantity Surveyor	Barton Associates Pte Ltd
Main Contractor	Pekson Construction & Engineering Pte Ltd
Interior Design	William Lim Associates
Landscape Architect	Tierra Design

Camden Medical Centre

Address	Grange Road
Client	Pontiac Land Pte Ltd
Architect	DP Architects Pte Ltd
Design Consultant	Richard Meier Architect
Civil & Structural Engineer	Ove Arup and Partners Singapore
Mechanical & Electrical Engineer	J Roger Preston (S) Pte Ltd
Quantity Surveyor	Davis Langdon & Seah
Main Contractor	Kajima Overseas
Lighting Engineer	Fisher Marantz Renfro Stone Inc
Landscape Architect	Belt Collins International
Curtainwall Consultant	R A Heintges Architects Consultants

Crescent Girls School

Address	357 Tanglin Road
Client	The Ministry of Education
Architect	PWD Consultants Pte Ltd
Project Manager	PWD Consultants Pte Ltd
Civil & Structural Engineer	PWD Consultants Pte Ltd
Mechanical & Electrical Engineer	PWD Consultants Pte Ltd
Quantity Surveyor	PWD Consultants Pte Ltd
Main Contractor	Kwan Yang Construction Pte Ltd
Lighting Engineer	PWD Consultants Pte Ltd

Burkill Hall

Address	Singapore Botanic Gardens
	Tyersall Avenue
Client	National Parks Board
Architect	PWD Consultants Pte Ltd
Project Manager	PWD Consultants Pte Ltd
Civil & Structural Engineer	PWD Consultants Pte Ltd
Mechanical & Electrical Engineer	PWD Consultants Pte Ltd
Quantity Surveyor	PWD Consultants Pte Ltd
Main Contractor	San Ho Huat Construction Pte Ltd
Lighting Engineer	PWD Consultants Pte Ltd
Landscape Architect	National Parks Board

Reuter House

Address	Ridout Road
Client	Reuters Southeast Asia
Architect	William Lim of William Lim Associates
Civil & Structural Engineer	R J Crocker, C T & Partners
Mechanical & Electrical Engineer	J Roger Preston & Partners
Quantity Surveyor	PIBS- Brechin Pte Ltd
Main Contractor	Fourways Pte Ltd
Interior Design	William Lim Associates
Landscape Architect	Garden & Landscape Centre

Eu House I

Address	Belmont Road
Client	Geoffrey Eu
Designer	Ernesto Bedmar . Bedmar and Shi Designers Pte Ltd
Civil & Structural Engineer	Tham & Wong
Mechanical & Electrical Engineer	Woo & Associates
Quantity Surveyor	Yow Peng Choon & Partners
Main Contractor	Fourways Pte Ltd
Interior Design	Bedmar and Shi Pte Ltd

Eu House II

Address	Bishopgate
Client	Geoffrey Eu
Designer	Ernesto Bedmar . Bedmar and Shi Pte Ltd
	in association with B+S+T Architects
Civil & Structural Engineer	TH Ng Management Pte Ltd
Mechanical & Electrical Engineer	Mechelect Engineering Pte Ltd
Quantity Surveyor	George Low Co.
Main Contractor	Actus Builders Pte Lyd
Interior Design	Bedmar and Shi Pte Designers Pte Ltd
Landscape Architect	Tierra Design

Victoria Park House

Address	Victoria Park
Designer	Ernesto Bedmar . Bedmar and Shi Designers Pte Ltd
	in association with B+S+T Architects
Civil & Structural Engineer	Cericon Consultants
Mechanical & Electrical Engineer	Gims & Associates
Quantity Surveyor	BKP Associates Pte Ltd
Main Contractor	Actus Builders Pte Ltd
Interior Design	Bedmar and Shi Pte Ltd
Landscape Architect	Tierra Design

Coronation Road West House

Address	178 Coronation Road West
Client	Mr and Mrs Lee Mon Sun
Architect	Chan Soo Khian. SCDA Architects
Civil & Structural Engineer	Web Structures
Lighting Consultant	Million Lighting
Quantity Surveyor	Barton Associates
Main Contractor	Builders Trends
Interior Design	SCDA Architects
Landscape Architect	SCDA Architects, Nyee Phoe Flower Garden Pte Ltd

Kandang Kerbau Hospital

Address	Kampong Java Road / Bukit Timah Road
Client	Ministry of Health
Architect	Akitek Tenggara II
Principal Consultant	PWD Consultants Pte Ltd
Design Consultant	McConnell Smith & Johnson
	(also Hospital Planning Consultant)
Project Manager	PWD Consultants Pte Ltd
Civil & Structural Engineer	PWD Consultants Pte Ltd
Mechanical & Electrical Engineer	PWD Consultants Pte Ltd
Quantity Surveyor	PWD Consultants Pte Ltd
Main Contractor	Ssangyong Engineering & Construction Co Ltd
Interior Design	Davenport Campbell & Partners (S) Pte Ltd

Genesis

Address	170 Bukit Timah Road
Client	Tan, Moses and Chee/TID Associates Pte Ltd
Architect	Kerry Hill Architects
Civil & Structural Engineer	Fraser Worley
Mechanical & Electrical Engineer	Donnelly Simpson Cleary & Oehlers (SE Asia) Pte Ltd
Quantity Surveyor	Rider Hunt Levett & Bailey
Main Contractor	Pekson Construction & Engineering Pte Ltd
Interior Design	Kerry Hill Architects/Total Integrated Design (Pte) Ltd
Lighting Engineer	Elsdale Lighting Design – Exterior
Interior	Kerry Hill Architects/Total Integrated Design (Pte) Ltd

Alliance Française de Singapour

Address	1 Sarkies Road (off Bukit Timah Road)
Client	Alliance Française de Singapour
Architect	Point Architects
Design Consultant	Dominique Perrault
Civil & Structural Engineer	De Consultants Pte Ltd
Mechanical & Electrical Engineer	M&P Consulting Engineers (S) Pte Ltd
Main Contractor	Pan Pacific Builders Pte Ltd
Interior Design	Katherine McKay
Lighting Engineer	Mike Thomsett/Leisure Works Pte Ltd
	(Auditorium Acoustic & Lighting Consultant)
Curtainwall Consultant	Doru Tofan von Maldiny
	(Texture Walls Finish & Mosaics)

Check House II

Address	8 Cluny Park
Architect	KNTA Architects
Civil & Structural Engineer	Ronnie and Koh Partnership
Quantity Surveyor	W K Choy
Main Contractor	Patson Marketing and Construction Pte Ltd
Interior Design	KNTA Architects
Landscape Architect	Cicada Landscaping Consultants

Bukit Timah Nature Reserve Interpretation Centre

Address	Hindhede Drive
Client	National Parks Board
Architect	PWD Consultants Pte Ltd
Project Manager	PWD Consultants Pte Ltd
Civil & Structural Engineer	PWD Consultants Pte Ltd
Mechanical & Electrical Engineer	PWD Consultants Pte Ltd
Quantity Surveyor	PWD Consultants Pte Ltd
Main Contractor	Ban Lee Hoe Engineering & Construction
	Tan Tse Chin Construction Pte Ltd
Lighting Engineer	PWD Consultants Pte Ltd
Landscape Architect	National Parks Board

Cluny Hill House

Address	Cluny Hill
Architect	Kerry Hill Architects
Civil & Structural Engineer	Frazer Worley
Mechanical & Electrical Engineer	Lincolne Scott Ng Pte Ltd
Quantity Surveyor	Davis Langdon & Seah Singapore Pte Ltd
Main Contractor	Hern Yang Construction Pte Ltd
Interior Design	Kerry Hill Architects
Landscape Architect	Tierra Design

King Albert Park House

Address	King Albert Park
Architect	Akitek Tenggara II
Civil & Structural Engineer	HCE Engineers Pte Ltd
Mechanical & Electrical Engineer	Ewbank Preece Engineers Pte Ltd
Quantity Surveyor	Davis Langdon & Seah Pte Ltd
Main Contractor	Kwan Yong Construction Pte Ltd
Interior Design	Bedmar and Shi Design Pte Ltd

Lighting Engineer	Kwan Yong Electrical
Landscape Architect	Kernteck Design Pte Ltd

The French Embassy in Singapore

Address	Cluny Park Road
Client	French Ministry of Foreign Affairs
Architect	ZD-R with Dubois- Richez (Paris)
	and TSP Architects+ Planners Pte Ltd
Civil & Structural Engineer	B & T Consultants Pte Ltd
Mechanical & Electrical Engineer	Bescon Consulting Engineers Pte
Quantity Surveyor	Choy & Associates (1992)
Main Contractor	Glauser International and Seng Fah
	Construction Pte Ltd JV
Interior Design	Dubus-Richez and TSP Architects + Planners Pte Ltd
Landscape Architect	Dubus-Richez and TSP Architects + Planners Pte Ltd

Gentle Road House

Address	Gentle Road
Architect	Tan Hock Beng . Maps Design Studio
Structural Consultant	MSE Engineering & Management Consultancy
Main Contractor	CCH Construction System

The Institute of Southeast Asian Studies

Address	Heng Mui Keng Terrace
Client	The Institute of Southeast Asian Studies
Architect	PWD Consultants Pte Ltd
Project Manager	PWD Consultants Pte Ltd
Civil & Structural Engineer	PWD Consultants Pte Ltd
Mechanical & Electrical Engineer	PWD Consultants Pte Ltd
Quantity Surveyor	PWD Consultants Pte Ltd
Main Contractor	Toh Seng Sit Construction Pte Ltd
Interior Design	DP Design Pte Ltd
Landscape Architect	PT Wijaya Tribwana International
	(Landscape Consultant)

28 Eng Hoon Street

Address	28 Eng Hoon Street
Architect	Look Architects
Structural Consultant	BK Tan Consultants
Main Contractor	Chye Hiap Seng Construction Pte Ltd

Ayer Rajah Community Club

Client	People's Association
Architect	Akitek Tenggara II
Civil & Structural Engineer	Maunsell Consultants (Singapore) Pte Ltd
Mechanical & Electrical Engineer	OSV Consultants Pte Ltd
Quantity Surveyor	RJ Consultants Pte Ltd
Main Contractor	Jacklie Construction Pte Ltd
Interior Design	Akitek Tenggara II

UE Square

Address	179 River Valley Road
Client	United Engineers Pte Ltd
Architect	Architects 61 Pte Ltd
Design Consultant	(Concept and Master Planner) Kenzo Tange Associates
Project Manager	United Engineers Pte Ltd
Civil & Structural Engineer	HCE Engineers Partnership
Mechanical & Electrical Engineer	United Engineer (S) Pte Ltd
Quantity Surveyor	Davis Langdon and Seah (S) Pte Ltd
Main Contractor	Kajima Overseas Asia Pte Ltd
Interior Design	Design Minoko
Lighting Engineer	Project Lighting Design
Acoustic Engineer	Ccw Accoustics Pte Ltd
Landscape Architect	Garden & Landscape Centre
IT Building Consultant	IT Division Of United Engineers Pte Ltd and
	NTT International Corporation
Wind Study Consultant	Vipec Engineers & Scientists Ltd
Curtainwall Consultant	Arup Facades

The Beaufort Sentosa

Address	25 Bukit Manis Road
Client	Beaufort International Hotels
Architect	Kerry Hill Architects
Civil & Structural Engineer	Ove Arup & Partners
Mechanical & Electrical Engineer	J Roger Preston & Parners Pte Ltd
Project Manager	Project Systems International Pte Ltd
Main Contractor	Takenaka Corporation
Interior Design	Ed Tuttle . Design Realisation
Lighting Design	TSLE

The SAFTI Military Institute

Address	500 & 510 Upper Jurong Road
Client	Ministry of Defence (MINDEF)
	Joint Operations & Planning Directorate (DJOPD)
Architect	DP Architects Pte Ltd
Design Consultant	Mitchell Giurgola & Thorp Associates
Project Manager	Lands & Estates Organisation
Civil & Structural Engineer	Steen Consultants Pte Ltd
Mechanical & Electrical Engineer	Ewbank Preece Engineers Pte Ltd
	(now known as PCR Engineers Ptd Ltd)
Quantity Surveyor	Rider Hunt Levett & Bailey
Main Contractor	Lee Kim Tah Construction (Phase 1)
	Singapore Piling & Civil Engineering Pte Ltd
	(Phases 2 and 3)
Interior Design	Mitchell Giurgola & Thorp Associates
Lighting Engineer	Corbett Design Associates Pte Ltd

Acoustic Engineer	Acviron Acoustics Consultants Pte Ltd
Landscape Architect	Aspinwall Clouston Pte Ltd

Singapore Discovery Centre

Address	Upper Jurong Road
Client	Ministry of Defence (MINDEF)
Architect	DP Architects Pte Ltd
Design Consultant	Mitchell Giurgola & Thorp Associates
Project Manager	Lands & Estates Organisation
Civil & Structural Engineer	Steen Consultants Pte Ltd
Mechanical & Electrical Engineer	Ewbank Preece Engineers Pte Ltd
	(now known as PCR Perdana Pte Ltd)
Quantity Surveyor	Rider Hunt Levett & Bailey
Main Contractor	Deenn Engineering Pte Ltd
Acoustic Engineer	Acviron Acoustics Consultants Pte Ltd
Landscape Architect	Aspinwall Clouston Pte Ltd

Henderson CC and the Bukit Merah West Neighbourhood Police Centre

Address	500 Bukit Merah View
Client	Peoples Association
Architect	Forum Architects
Civil & Structural Engineer	Ronnie and Koh Partnership
Mechanical & Electrical Engineer	Belmacs Consulting Engineers
Quantity Surveyor	RJ Consultants
Main Contractor	Union Contractors Ltd (Singapore Branch)
Lighting Engineer	Forum Architects
Acoustic Engineer	Acviron Acoustics Consultants
Landscape Architect	Forum Architects

Gallery Evason

Address	Gallery Evason Hotel at Robertson Quay
Client	Robertson Quay Investments Pte Ltd
Architect	William Lim Associates and Tangguanbee Architects
Civil & Structural Engineer	Steen Consultants Pte Ltd
Mechanical & Electrical Engineer	J Roger Preston Pte Ltd
Quantity Surveyor	Rider Hunt Levett & Bailey
Main Contractor	Great Earth Construction Pte Ltd
Interior Design	William Lim Associates and Tangguanbee Architects
Lighting Engineer	Vision Design
Acoustic Engineer	CCW Accoustics Pte Ltd
Landscape Architect	Tierra Design

Marine Parade Community Centre

Address	Marine Parade Road
Client	Peoples Association
Architect	William Lim Associates
Artist/ Mural Designer	Surachai Yeamsiri
Civil & Structural Engineer	JHA Partnership
Mechanical & Electrical Engineer	Bescon Consulting Engineers Pte
Quantity Surveyor	Rider Hunt Levett & Bailey
Main Contractor	SAL Construction Pte Ltd
Interior Design	William Lim Associates
Lighting Engineer	Vision Design Studio
Acoustic Engineer	Acviron Acoustics Consultants
Landscape Architect	William Lim Associates
Building Technologist	Promanco Kenman Singapore

Singapore Indoor Stadium

Address	2 Stadium Road
Client	Singapore Sports Council
Architect	RSP Architects Planners & Engineers Pte Ltd
Design Consultant	Kenzo Tange Associates
Civil & Structural Engineer	RSP Architects Planners & Engineers Pte Ltd
Mechanical & Electrical Engineer	Preece Cardew & Rider
Quantity Surveyor	Langdon Every & Seah
Main Contractor	Ssangyong Construction
Interior Design	Total Integrated Design Pte Ltd
Acoustic Engineer	Yamaha Architectural Accoustics Laboratory

The Gateway

Address	116 Beach Road
Client	Gateway Land Pte Ltd
Architect	Chua Ka Seng & Partners Chartered Architects
Design Consultant	IM Pei & Partners
Civil & Structural Engineer	TY Lin (SEA) Pte Ltd
Mechanical & Electrical Engineer	J Roger Preston Pte Ltd
	(now known as Rust JRP Pte Ltd)
Quantity Surveyor	Rider Hunt Levett & Bailey
Main Contractor	Turner (East Asia) Pte Ltd
Acoustic Engineer	Cheah Carl Wilkinson
Landscape Architect	BCP Pte Ltd
	Moh & Associates Pte Ltd (Geotechnic engineer)

The Concourse

Address	298 and 300 Beach Road
Client	Hong Fok Land Pte Ltd
Architect	Architects 61 Pte Ltd
Design Consultant	Paul Rudolph Architect
Project Manager	Hong Fok Land Pte Ltd
Civil & Structural Engineer	Steen Consultants Pte Ltd
Mechanical & Electrical Engineer	PCR Engineers Ptd Ltd
Quantity Surveyor	Rider Hunt Levett & Bailey
Main Contractor	Maincon (Building) Pte Ltd
Interior Design	Richards Basmajian Ltd
Lighting Engineer	HM Branston

Acoustic Engineer	CCW Acoustics Pte Ltd
Landscape Architect	Aspinwall Clouston Pte Ltd
Curtainwall Consultant	Curtain Wall Design & Consulting Inc

Peoples Association HQ/Kallang Airport Terminal

Address	Stadium Link Road
Client	People's Association
Architect	Architects 61 Pte Ltd
Project Manager	People's Association
Civil & Structural Engineer	KL Tham Engineering Consultants
Mechanical & Electrical Engineer	Besplan Maintenance Engineers Pte Ltd
Quantity Surveyor	KPK Quantity Surveyors
Main Contractor	Pekson Construction & Engineering Pte Ltd
Interior Design	Architects 61 Pte Ltd

LaSalle-SIA College of the Arts

Address	Goodman Road
Client	LaSalle-SIA College of the Arts
Architect	William Lim Associates
Civil & Structural Engineer	Steen Consultants Pte Ltd
Mechanical & Electrical Engineer	YP Chee & Associates
Quantity Surveyor	Rider Hunt Levett & Bailey
Main Contractor	Teow Aik Realty (S) Pte Ltd
Acoustic Engineer	CCW Accoustics Pte Ltd
Landscape Architect	Martin Lee Designs

Khoo House

Address	115 Dunbar Walk
Client	Steven Khoo and Dawn Poh
Architect	Ken Lou Architects
Civil & Structural Engineer	MTech Consultants
Quantity Surveyor	RJ Consultants Pte Ltd
Main Contractor	BST Construction Pte Ltd
Interior Design	Ken Lou Architects
Landscape Architect	Kern Teck Design Pte Ltd

ITE Balestier

Address	114 Balestier Road
Client	Institute of Technical Education
Architect	Architects Vista Pte Ltd
Civil & Structural Engineer	Meinhardt Singapore Pte Ltd
Mechanical & Electrical Engineer	Squire Mech Pte Ltd
Quantity Surveyor	KPK Quantity Surveyor (1995) Singapore Pte Ltd
Main Contractor	Chiu Teng Construction Pte Ltd

Cambridge Road Housing

Address	Cambridge Road
Client	The Housing and Development Board
Architect	CESMA International Pte Ltd
Civil & Structural Engineer	The Housing and Development Board
Mechanical & Electrical Engineer	The Housing and Development Board
Quantity Surveyor	The Housing and Development Board
Main Contractor	Spandeck Engineering (S) Pte Ltd
Landscape Architect	CESMA International Pte Ltd

Bugis Junction

Address	Bugis Junction, Malay Street/Bugis Street
Client	Bugis City Holdings Pte Ltd
Architect	DP Architects Pte Ltd
Project Manager	Steamship Investment & Development (Keppel Land)
Civil & Structural Engineer	Meinhardt (S) Pte Ltd
Mechanical & Electrical Engineer	Beca Carter Hollings & Ferner (SEA) Pte Ltd
Quantity Surveyor	Rider Hunt Levitt & Bailey
Main Contractor	Nishumatsu Lim Chang JV
Interior Design	Rifenberg Associates (Thailand) – Hotel
Lighting Engineer	T Kondos Associates (USA)
Acoustic Engineer	Acviron Acoustics
Landscape Architect	Studio Land Inc. (USA)

Bournemouth 8

Address	70 Bournemouth Road
Client	Asia Sky (Bournemouth) Pte Ltd
Architect	Chan Sau Yau Associates
Civil & Structural Engineer	CP Lim and Partners
Mechanical & Electrical Engineer	Lincolne Scott Ng Pte Ltd
Quantity Surveyor	JK Consultants
Main Contractor	Pan Pacific Builders Pte Ltd
Landscape Architect	Nyee Phoe Flower Garden Pte Ltd

Fortredale

Address	2 Tanjong Rhu Road
Client	T3 Investments Pte Ltd
Architect	Tangguanbee Architects
Civil & Structural Engineer	P&T Consultants Pte Ltd
Mechanical & Electrical Engineer	P&T Consultants Pte Ltd
Quantity Surveyor	KPK Quantity Surveyors
Main Contractor	Projection Pte Ltd
Interior Design	Alice Lem Design
Aluminium Consultant	Merdeka Construction Pte ltd

Sennett House

Address	39A & 41 Sennett Lane
Client	Mr & Mrs K S Tan and Mr & Mrs Robert Law
Architect	Chan Soo Khian. SCDA Architects
Civil & Structural Engineer	Web Structures
Mechanical & Electrical Engineer	Emac Pte Ltd
Stone Specialist	Builders Shop

Main Contractor — Shining Construction
Interior Design — SCDA Architects
Landscape Architect — SCDA Architects, Nyee Phoe Flower Garden Pte Ltd

The Singapore Cricket Association Cricket Pavilion
Address — 31 Stadium Crescent
Client — Singapore Cricket Association
Architect — Kerry Hill Architects
Civil & Structural Engineer — Harris and Sutherland (Asia)
Mechanical & Electrical Engineer — Lincolne Scott Ng
Quantity Surveyor — Davis Langdon and Seah Singapore
Main Contractor — Hern Yang Construction
Interior Design — Kerry Hill Architects

Tampines New Town
Address — Tampines New Town
Client — The Housing and Development Board
Architect — The Housing and Development Board
Civil & Structural Engineer — The Housing and Development Board
Mechanical & Electrical Engineer — The Housing and Development Board
Quantity Surveyor — The Housing and Development Board
Landscape Architect — The Housing and Development Board

Tampines Neighbourhood 4
Address — Tampines Neighbourhood 4
Client — The Housing and Development Board
Architect — P&T Consultants Pte Ltd
Civil & Structural Engineer — P&T Consultants Pte Ltd
Mechanical & Electrical Engineer — P&T Consultants Pte Ltd
Quantity Surveyor — KPK Quantity Surveyors
Main Contractor — Kajima Oversesa (Asia) Pte Ltd
Landscape Architect — Keikan Sekkei (S) Pte Ltd

Changi Airport Terminal 1 Expansion (T1E)
Address — T1 Boulevard
Client — Civil Aviation Authority of Singapore
Principal Consultant — PWD Consultants Pte Ltd
Project Manager — PWD Consultants Pte Ltd
Civil & Structural Engineer — PWD Consultants Pte Ltd.
Mechanical & Electrical Engineer — PWD Consultants Pte Ltd
Quantity Surveyor — PWD Consultants Pte Ltd.
Main Contractor — Tanenaka Corporation

The Market Place
Address — Bedok Road
Client — Far East Organisation
 — Lucky Realty Co Ltd (Developer)
Architect — Tangguanbee Architects
Civil & Structural Engineer — Sim Bee Teck & Associates
Mechanical & Electrical Engineer — United Project Consultants Pte Ltd
Quantity Surveyor — Perspective Engineering Management Consultants (Pte) Ltd
Main Contractor — Jie Yu Construction Pte Ltd

Elias Park Primary School
Address — 11 Pasir Ris St 52
Client — Public Works Department
Architect — Akitek Tenggara II
Civil & Structural Engineer — Ove Arup & Partners
Mechanical & Electrical Engineer — Beca Carter Hollings & Ferner (SE Asia)
Quantity Surveyor — Davis Langdon & Seah
 — (now known as Davis Langdon and Seah (S) Pte Ltd)
Main Contractor — San Ho Huat Construction Pte Ltd
Interior Design — Akitek Tenggara II

Temasek Polytechnic
Address — 21 Tampines Avenue 1
Client — Ministry of Education
Architect — DP Architects Pte Ltd in association with
 — James Stirling Michael Wilford & Associates
Project Manager — Public Works Department
 — (Now PWD Consultants Pte Ltd)
Civil & Structural Engineer — Ove Arup & Partners International
Mechanical & Electrical Engineer — Singapore – PCR Engineers Pte Ltd
 — UK – Ove Arup & Partners International
Quantity Surveyor — KPK Quantity Surveyors
Main Contractor — Phase 1A: Joint Venture Lee Kim Tah & Woh Hup Pte
 — Phase 1B: Deenn Engineering Pte
 — Phase 2: Singapore Piling and Civil Engineering Pte
Interior Design — James Stirling Michael Wilford & Associates
Lighting Engineer — Ove Arup & Partners
Acoustic Engineer — Acviron Pte Ltd
Landscape Architect — PDAA Landscape Architects (Landscape Design)

The Japanese Primary School
Address — Upper Changi Road North
Client — The Registered Trustees of The Japanese Primary School Singapore
Architect — Architects Vista
Design Consultant — Pacific Consultants International (S) Pte Ltd and Tetsuji Hatano/Pacific Consultants International Tokyo
Civil & Structural Engineer — CMP Consultants Pte Ltd
Mechanical & Electrical Engineer — CMP Consultants Pte Ltd
Main Contractor — Taisei Corporation

Lem House
Address — Eastwood Way
Client — Alice Lem
Architect — Mok Wei Wei of William Lim Associates
Civil & Structural Engineer — JS Tan & Associates
Mechanical & Electrical Engineer — AE&T
Quantity Surveyor — Barton Associates Pte Ltd
Main Contractor — Teo Hee Lai Construction Pte Ltd
Interior Design — Alice Lem Design
Landscape Architect — Tierra Design

Eastpoint Shopping Centre
Address — Eastpoint Shopping Centre, Simei
Client — Simei Properties Pte Ltd
Architect — Tangguanbee Architects and Team Design Architects
Civil & Structural Engineer — Meinhardt (S) Pte Ltd
Mechanical & Electrical Engineer — Rust JRP
Quantity Surveyor — Rider Hunt Levett & Bailey
Main Contractor — Obayashi Corporation
Interior Design — Tangguanbee Architects
Lighting Engineer — Luminor Design Consultants (Lighting Consultant)

National Sailing Centre
Address — East Coast Parkway
Client — Singapore Sports Council
Architect — Akitek Tenggara II
Civil & Structural Engineer — John SW Lee Consultants
Mechanical & Electrical Engineer — OSV Consultants Pte Ltd
Quantity Surveyor — RJ Consultants Pte Ltd
Main Contractor — In Builders (S) Pte Ltd

Windsor Park House
Address — Windsor Park
Architect — Tangguanbee Architects
Civil & Structural Engineer — Meinhardt (S) Pte Ltd
Mechanical & Electrical Engineer — Woo & Associates
Quantity Surveyor — OTN Building Cost Consultants Pt Ltd
Main Contractor — Hup Yew Sen Construction Pte Ltd
Interior Design — Alice Lem Design
Landscape Architect — Tangguanbee Architects

Golden Village Multiplex Yishun 10
Address — 51 Yishun Central
Client — Golden Village Yishun Pte Ltd
Architect — Geoff Malone International (GMI) Singapore
 — and Sofarnos Mousbourgh & Associates Australia
Civil & Structural Engineer — Wholohan Grill & Partners
Mechanical & Electrical Engineer — Vasta and Farmer and Technon Engineers Pte Ltd
Quantity Surveyor — KPK Quantity Surveyors
Main Contractor — Sembawang Construction Pte Ltd
Interior Design — Geoff Malone International (GMI)
Acoustic Engineer — Moss Growcott

Lam Chuan Industrial Building
Address — 12 Sungei Kadut Way
Client — Lam Chuan Import–Export Pte Ltd
Architect — LOOK Architects
Civil & Structural Engineer — SM Wan & Partners (Engineers)
Mechanical & Electrical Engineer — YP Chee & Associates
Quantity Surveyor — P E B Consultants
Main Contractor — New Civilbuild Pte Ltd

Choa Chu Kang Housing
Address — Choa Chu Kang North 6
Client — The Housing and Development Board
Architect — Akitek Tenggara II
Project Manager — The Housing and Development Board
Civil & Structural Engineer — Ove Arup & Partners
Mechanical & Electrical Engineer — Beca Carter Hollings & Ferner (SE Asia)
Main Contractor — Neo Corporation Pte Ltd
Landscape Architect — Nyee Phoe Landscape Designers & Contractors

Corfe Place House
Address — 1 Corfe Place
Client — Mdm Eve Ang
Architect — KNTA Architects
Civil & Structural Engineer — Ronnie and Koh Partnership
Mechanical & Electrical Engineer — AE & T Consultants
Quantity Surveyor — P Q S Consultants
Main Contractor — Exchannel Construction
Interior Design — KNTA Architects
Landscape Architect — Bunga Chantek

Institute of Technical Education (ITE), Bishan
Address — 21 Bishan St 14
Client — Institute of Technical Education Singapore
Architect — Akitek Tenggara II
Civil & Structural Engineer — Ove Arup & Partners
Mechanical & Electrical Engineer — Beca Carter Hollings & Ferner (SE Asia)
Quantity Surveyor — Davis Langdon & Seah
 — (now known as Davis Langdon & Seah (S) Pte Ltd)
Main Contractor — Kimly Construction Pte Ltd
Landscape Architect — Akitek Tenggara II

Le Lycée Français de Singapour
Address — Ang Mo Kio Avenue 3
Client — Lycée Français de Singapour Ltd
Architect — Kumpulan Akitek
Project Manager — Davis Langdon & Seah Project Management Pte Ltd
Civil & Structural Engineer — WR Brown Sinagore
Mechanical & Electrical Engineer — United Project Consultants Pte Ltd
Quantity Surveyor — Davis Langdon and Seah (S) Pte Ltd
Main Contractor — Neo Corporation Pte Ltd
 — Neo Clad Pte Ltd
Interior Designer — Ms Nathalie Tournesac
Landscape Deigner — Geok Lan Landscape

Kampong Bugis Development Guide Plan
Address — Kampong Bugis
Client — Ministry of National Development
Architect — Akitek Tenggara II
 — and Singapore Institute of Architects

The Esplanade—Theatres on the Bay
Address — Raffles Avenue
Client — Ministry of Information and the Arts
Architect — DP Architects Pte Ltd
 — in association with Michael Wilford & Partners
Project Manager — ACDD (PMT), PWD
Civil & Structural Engineer — ACDD (C&S), PWD
Mechanical & Electrical Engineer — ACDD (BS). PWD
Quantity Surveyor — ACDD (CT), PWD
Main Contractor — Penta-Ocean Construction CO.
Interior Design — To be appointed
Lighting Engineer — Vision Design Studio
Acoustic Engineer — Artec Consultants Inc
Landscape Architect — ACLA Pte Ltd

The Singapore National Library Board Building
Address — Victoria Street / Middle Road
Client — Singapore National Library Board
Architect-of-Record — Swan and McClaren
Architect-of-Design — TR Hamzah and Yeang Sdn Bhd
Civil & Structural Engineer of Record — Steen Consultants Pte Ltd
Mechanical & Electrical Engineer of Record — Alpha Engineering Consultant
C&S and M&E Engineer of Design — Buro Happold (M) Sdn Bhd
Quantity Surveyor — Quants Associates
Interior Design — TR Hamzah and Yeang Sdn Bhd
Acoustic Engineer — Total Building Performace Team (NUS)
Landscape Architect — Colin K Okishimo & Associates
Bioclimatic Design Consultant and Wind Consultant — Professor Richard Aynsley
 — James Cook University of North Queensland
Energy/Lighting Consultant — Professor Victor Ogilvay Jr
 — University of Hawaii at Manoa
NLB Cost Consultant — Rider Hunt Levett & Bailey
Technical Coordination and Tender Documentation — Nihon Sekkai Inc
Embodied Energy in Materials Consultant — Nigel Howard BRE (UK)
Curtainwall Consultant — Russell Cole, Arup Facade Engineering (Australia)

Expo 2000 MRT Station Changi Airport Line
Address — Expo 2000 MRT Station
Client — Land Transport Authority (LTA)
Design Consultant — Foster and Partners

GLOSSARY

adaptive reuse: The modification of a building to accommodate a compatible new use. There are no strict rules and the quality of the work is dependent on the skill of the architect. Compatible reuse means a use which involves as little as possible change to the fabric of a culturally significant building.

airwell: A courtyard, open to the sky, which allows air and light to enter a building. A lightwell.

balau: A species of reddish-brown, close-grained timber found in the tropics.

Bauhaus: School of design, building and craftsmanship founded by Walter Gropius in Weimar in 1919. It was transferred to Dessau in 1925 to a new building designed by Gropius, and to Berlin in 1928. It closed in 1933. It was the most significant school of art and design of the 1920s.

black-and-white house: Term used to describe some of the colonial houses in Singapore, built in the 1920s and 1930s to accommodate British civil servants and army officers. They combined the appearance of Tudor cottages with the Malay tradition of raising house on stilts or piles.

Bu Ye Tian (Chinese): In the context used in this book, it means "no night and no day", or in contemporary usage "operates 24 hours".

bungalow: A single-storey house, lightly built, usually with a tiled roof and verandah. The word is derived from the Hindi word *bangla*, meaning "belonging to Bengal". In Singapore, the word is used to describe almost any detached house, irrespective of its form or height.

cantilever: A projecting beam or canopy supported by a downward force behind a fulcrum. It is usually anchored at one end by the weight of the structure above. It appears to be self-supporting.

capital: The upper member of a column.

cladding: The outer "skin" of a building—e.g., architects speak of "curtain-wall cladding" or "brick cladding".

clerestory window: A high level window affording natural daylight. More correctly, it refers to the upper part of the nave of a Basilica or church, rising above the aisle roofs and pierced with windows.

conservation: The process of looking after a building (or an urban space)so as to retain its cultural significance. It includes maintenance, historic preservation, restoration, reconstruction, adaptive reuse and even, on occasions, new buildings which are compatible in scale.

curtain wall: A non-load-bearing wall attached to the exterior of a building structure.

Critical Regionalism: The idea of regionalist architecture being used as a means of criticising post-war modern architecture. The term was first introduced by Alexander Tzonis and Lian Lefaivre in *Architecture in Greece* (1981) and later adopted by Kenneth Frampton in "Towards a Critical Regionalism" (1983).

Doric order: The first form of Greek architecture, also used by the Romans in a simplified form and with a base.

eaves: The lower part of a roof which projects beyond the supporting structure.

elevation: An external face of a building; also a drawing of one made in projection on a vertical plane.

façade: Face or elevation of a building, usually referring to the front elevation.

fenestration: The arrangement of windows in a building.

feng-shui or fung-shui (Chinese): Literally meaning "wind and water", it refers to a system of geomancy employed in China and elsewhere to bring practice into harmony with natural forces. It is used in determining the site or orientation of a city or a house. It is also used to determine the good or bad luck resulting from the siting in relation to cosmic elements.

five-foot way: In Sir Stamford Raffles' proclamation to the Singapore Town Committee in 1822, it was stated that "every house should have a verandah of a certain depth, open at all times as a continued and covered passage on each side of the street". Hence the five-foot way (six-foot way as was inserted in the clauses of all building leases at a later date).

floor plate: An important consideration in the letting of high-rise office towers is the size of the floor plate, or the floor space at each level available for lease after deducting the vertical circulation and service core. The larger the floor plate, and the fewer structural columns, the better its letting potential to large corporate clients.

floor area ratio (FAR): Also known as plot ratio, it is the ratio of floor space to site area. In simple terms, an FAR (plot ratio) of 5:1 means that the floor space provided by a development is five times the site area. This could work out to a 10-storey building built on 50 percent of the site. In reality the formula is slightly more complicated.

Hua Hoi Kak (Chinese): Flower garden corner.

kampong or kampung (Malay): Malay word meaning village or settlement.

kayu manis (Malay): Cinnamon tree.

leitmotif: A recurring theme.

Modern movement: Development in Western art and architecture from the end of the 19th century to its pinnacle in the 1920s and 1930s. Le Corbusier, Mies van der Rohe and Walter Gropius were important figures in a general trend towards simplified and unadorned architectural design.

OTTV: Overall Thermal Transmission Value

parti: The initial design idea, the point of departure for a project.

party wall: The dividing wall between two adjacent properties. Commonly used when referring to the wall between two semi-detached dwellings.

pediment: Term used to describe a low pitched triangular feature above a portico, door or window. When the cornice is discontinuous at the apex, or sometimes at the base, it is called a broken pediment.

pergola: An overhead canopy consisting of an open structure made either of timber or concrete. It is intended to give a feeling of enclosure but also to provide shade and sometimes to support "climbing" plants.

pilaster: Rectangular or semi-circular pier or pillar, attached to a wall. Often with a base and a capital.

podium: A continuous base.

portico: A roofed space, open or partly enclosed, forming the entrance and usually the centrepiece of the façade of a school, hotel or other public building.

preservation: The preservation of an historic building means maintaining the structural fabric in its existing state and retarding deterioration. This is usually appropriate in the case of national monuments.

sala (Thai): A pavilion that is open on four sides.

section: A diagrammatic drawing of a vertical plane cut through a building.

shophouse: Shop with a dwelling above. Shop-houses are usually built as a part of a terrace, often with upper floors overhanging the first storey to form a covered pedestrian arcade. They were characteristic of the 19th and early 20th century commercial centres of Southeast Asian settlements.

shuttering: A term sometimes used to describe "formwork", which is erected to allow concrete to be poured and formed into beams, columns, etc. Shuttering, or formwork, is made of timber, plywood or steel.

soffit: The underside of a beam.

string course: A continuous, horizontal band in, or more usually projecting from, an exterior wall.

tabula rasa: Literally means "a blank table" or "a clean slate". To adopt a tabula rasa approach to development means essentially to clear the site and, in the process, to erase any memories of the past. An approach that is not influenced by outside forces.

terrace: A platform adjoining a building, usually used for leisure activities. An abbreviated expression for a terrace house, which is one of a row of houses sharing common party walls.

tongkang: A small vessel or "lighter" that, until the advent of container ships, carried goods from ships lying at anchor to the Singapore River and thereafter discharged the goods into godowns or warehouses.

venturi effect: Induced movement of air through a building interior by the judicious or calculated placement of large and small apertures (windows, grills, roof openings, etc.) in the external envelope.

verandah or veranda: A large open porch, usually roofed and partly enclosed by a railing, sometimes with the roof supported on pillars, often extending across the front and sides of a house.

vernacular: A form (of architecture) that is indigenous or native to a country or region.

voussoir: A wedge-shaped brick or stone forming one of the units of an arch.

Author's Note
In Singapore, the convention is to refer to the ground floor as the first storey, while the upper floor of a two-storey house is referred to as the second storey. I have adopted this convention throughout.

BIBLIOGRAPHY

Ackerman, James, "The History of Design and the Design of History" in *Culture and Social Vision*, Mark, 1980.
Agrest, Diana, "On Practice, 1979", in *Agrest and Gandelsonas: Works*, Princeton Architectural Press, New York, 1995.
Arcasia, *Contemporary Architecture in Asia*, Korean Institute of Registered Architects, Seoul, 1994.
Archives and Oral History Department, *Chinatown: An Album of a Singapore Community*, Times Books International, Singapore, 1983.
Beamish, Jane and Ferguson, Jane, *A History of Singapore Architecture*, Graham Brash, Singapore, 1985.
Berry, Linda, *Singapore's River, A Living Legacy*, Eastern Universities Press Sdn Bhd, Singapore, 1982.
Burkhill, H.M., "Memories of a House of Character—The Director's House" in *Golden Gardening: Fifty Years of the Singapore Gardening Society 1936–1986*, SGS, Singapore, 1985.
Chan, Vivienne, "Mirror Images: The Sennett House", *SPACE*, 2000/02, Singapore, 2000.
Chew, Ernest and Lee, Edwin, *A History of Singapore*, Oxford University Press, Singapore, 1991.
Chee Li Lian, "Screen Presence: Cineleisure Orchard", *Singapore Architect*, No. 197/98, Singapore, 1998.
Chee Li Lian, "Play it Again SAM: Singapore Arts Museum", *Singapore Architect*, No.198/98, Singapore, 1998.
Chee Li Lian, "Life in Mono: Cambridge Road Housing", *Singapore Architect*, No.199/98, Singapore, 1998.
Chee Li Lian, "Shell Life: Expo 2000 MRT Station", *SPACE*, 2000/04, Singapore, 2000.
Chew I-jin, "Over The Shop: Genesis", *Singapore Architect*, No. 194/97, Singapore, 1997.
Chew I-jin, "158 Emerald Hill", *Singapore Architect*, No. 197/98, Singapore, 1998.
Cumming, Campbell I., "Transcending Typology: Coronation Road West House", *SPACE*, 2000/03, Singapore, 2000.
Cumming, Campbell I., "Bay Watch: One Fullerton", *SPACE*, 2000/04, Singapore, 2000.
Davis, Douglas, *The Museum Transformed: Design and Culture in the Post-Pompidou Age*, Abbeville Press, New York, 1990.
Da Cunha, Derek, "Debating Singapore", ISEAS, Singapore, 1994.
Eco, Umberto, *Travels in Hyper-reality*, Harcourt Brace, San Diego, 1986.
Edwards, Norman and Keys, Peter, *Singapore: A Guide to Buildings, Streets, Place*, Times Books International, Singapore, 1988.
Edwards, Norman, *The Singapore House and Residential Life, 1819-1939*, Oxford University Press, Singapore, 1990.
Frampton, Kenneth, "Towards a Critical Regionalism", in *Anti-aesthetic: Essays on Post-modern Culture*, Bay Press, Seattle, 1983.
Frampton, Kenneth, *Studies in Tectonic Culture*, Cambridge, Massachusetts: MIT Press, 1996.
Fry, Maxwell and Drew, Jane, "Tropical Architecture in the Dry and Humid Zones", Kreiger, 1982.
Gehl, Jan, *Life Between Buildings*, Van Nostrand, New York, 1993.
Gerondelis, Ann, "Big Business: Millenia Tower", *Singapore Architect*, No. 194/97, Singapore, 1997.
Gerondelis, Ann, "Making Connections: UE Square", *Singapore Architect*, No. 196/97, Singapore, 1997.
Gerondelis, Ann, "Katong Community: Bournemouth 8", *Singapore Architect*, No. 199/98, Singapore, 1998.
Government of Singapore, *Singapore: The Next Lap*, Times Editions, Singapore, 1991.
Hall, Peter, *Cities of Tomorrow*, Blackwell, Oxford, 1988.
Hee Limin, "Circumscribing Culture: Ayer Rajah Community Club", *Singapore Architect*, No. 197/98, Singapore, 1998.
Hee Limin, "Rhapsody in White: The Kandang Kerbau Hospital", *Singapore Architect*, No. 200/98, Singapore, 1998.
Hee Limin, "French Accent: The French Embassy in Singapore", *SPACE*, 2000/01, Singapore, 2000.
Hee Limin, "Of Other Spaces: Henderson Community Club", *SPACE*, 2000/03, Singapore, 2000.
Housing and Development Board, *Singapore, Design for Living*, Singapore, 1985.
Housing and Development Board, *Housing a Nation*, HDB, 1985.
Housing and Development Board, *Singapore, HDB Annual Report 1993/94*.
Jencks Mike et al, *The Compact City: A Sustainable Urban Form?*, Spon, UK, 1996.
Khan, Hasan-Uddin, *Contemporary Asian Architects*, Taschen, Cologne, 1995.
Khosla, Jay, "Terminal Expansion: Changi Airport Terminal 1E", *SPACE*, 2000/02, Singapore, 2000.
Khosla, Jay, "Beyond Bioclimatic", *SPACE*, 2000/01, Singapore, 2000.
Knox and Taylor, *World Cities in a World System*, Cambridge, 1995.
Koolhaas, Rem, *S, M, L, XL*, 010, Rotterdam, 1995.
Kostoff, Spiro, *The City Shaped*, Thames and Hudson, London, 1991.
Krishand, Anand, "Pride of Place: The SAFTI Military Institute", *Singapore Architect*, No. 190/96, Singapore, 1996.
Lang, Jon, *Urban Design: The American Experience*, Van Nostrand, Reinhold, New York, 1994.
Lee Kip Lin, *Telok Ayer Market*, Archives and Oral History Department, Singapore, 1983.
Lee Kip Lin, *Emerald Hill*, National Museum of Singapore, Singapore, 1984.
Lee Kip Lin, *The Singapore House 1819–1942*, Times Editions, Singapore, 1988.
Leong Teng Wui, "The Institution and the City: ITE Balestier", *Singapore Architect*, No. 196/97, Singapore, 1997.
Leong Teng Wui, "Shop Effect: Eastpoint Shopping Centre", *Singapore Architect*, No. 197/98, Singapore 1998.
Leong Teng Wui, "Radical Rebuild: 28 Eng Hoon Sreet", *Singapore Architect*, No. 199/98, Singapore, 1999.
Lim, Jon, *The Origin of the Singapore Shophouses*, Architecture Journal, School of Architecture, National University of Singapore, 1992.
Lim, William S.W., "Contemporary Culture + Heritage = Localism", in *Architecture, (Post) Modernity and Difference*, School of Architecture, National University of Singapore, 1993.
Lim, William S.W., *Cities for People*, Select Books, Singapore, 1993.
Lim, William S.W. and Tan Hock Beng, *Contemporary Vernacular*, Select, Singapore, 1997.
Lim, William S.W., *New Asian Urbanism*, Select, Singapore, 1999.
Lim, Vincent, "Square Roots: Japanese Primary School", *Singapore Architect*, No. 193/97, Singapore, 1997.
Lim, Vincent, "Square Cut: The Heeren", *Singapore Architect*, No. 194/97, Singapore, 1997.
Lim, Vincent, "Urban Sanctuary: Nassim Jade", *Singapore Architect*, No. 195/97, Singapore, 1997.
Lim, Vincent, "Journey of Discovery: Singapore Discovery Centre", *Singapore Architect*, No. 198/98, Singapore, 1998.
Lim, Vincent, "Academic Questions: Institute of Southeast Asian Studies", *Singapore Architect*, No. 200/98, Singapore, 1998.
Liu, Gretchen, *Pastel Portraits*, Singapore Coordinating Committee, Singapore, 1984.
Liu, Gretchen, *Raffles Hotel*, Landmark Books, Singapore, 1992.
Liu Thai Ker, "City Planning: Craft or Creed", in proceedings of the Second International Convention on Urban Planning, Housing and Design, Singapore, July 27–29, 1989.
Liu Thai Ker, "Singapore's Experience in Conservation" presented at the International Symposium on Preservation and Modernisation of Historic Cities, Beijing, China, 1990.
Liu Thai Ker, "Public Housing in Singapore: An Architectural Portrait", Housing Design Conference, Singapore, 24–25 September 1992.
Look Boon Gee, "English Lessons: Temasek Polytechnic", *Singapore Architect*, No. 193/97, Singapore, 1997.
Look Boon Gee, "Discordant Harmony: Windsor Park House", *Singapore Architect*, No. 195/97, Singapore, 1997.
Lynch, Kevin, *The Image of the City*, MIT Press, 1960.
Lynch, Kevin, *Good City Form*, MIT Press, 1981.
Maas, Winy et al., *FARMAX*, MVRDV and 010 Publishers, Rotterdam, 1998.
Maas, Winy et al., *METACITY DATATOWN*, MVRDV and 010 Publishers, Rotterdam, 1998.
March, Lionel and Martin, Leslie, *Urban Space and Structure*, Cambridge University Press, 1972.
People's Association, "Community Centre to Community Club" in *People's Association: 1960-1990: 30 years with the People*, Singapore, 1990.
Phua Yue Keng, Roy and Kong, Lily, "Exploring Local Cultures: The Construction and Evolution of Meaning and Identity in Katong", in *Portraits of Places: History, Community and Identity in Singapore*, Ed. Brenda S.A. Yeoh and Lily Kong, Times Editions, Singapore, 1995.
Powell, Robert, "Survival in the City", *Singapore Institute of Architects Journal*, No. 129, pp.38–42, Mar–Apr 1985.
Powell, Robert, "Conservation and the Singapore River", *Singapore Institute of Architects Journal*, No. 132, Singapore, Sep 1985.
Powell, Robert, et.al, "Conservation of Urban Form and Space", IRC, School of Architecture, National University of Singapore, Sep 1986.
Powell, Robert, "Urban Design and the MRT", Singapore Institute of Architects Journal, No.146, pp.36-420 Jan-Feb 1986.
Powell, Robert, "Conservation of Meaning: Development and Conservation in Singapore" in Proceedings of UN Centre for Regional Development Seminar, Kyoto, Japan, 14–17 Nov 1987.
Powell, Robert and Siu-Tracy, Evelyn, "The Urban Morphology of Little India: The Meaning and Values in Urban Form", *PLANEWS, The Journal of the Singapore Institute of Planners*, Vol. 12 No. 1, Singapore, Jul 1989.
Powell, Robert, "Urban Renewal and Conservation in a Rapidly Developing Country: The Singapore Experience", *Singapore Institute of Planners Journal*, No. 175, Singapore, Nov/Dec 1992.
Powell, Robert, *Innovative Architecture of Singapore*, Select Books, Singapore, 1989.
Powell, Robert, *Rethinking the Environmental Filter*, Landmark Books, Singapore, 1989.
Powell, Robert, "The Singapore Report", *MIMAR: Architecture in Development*, No. 43, AKAA/Concept Media, London, 1992.
Powell, Robert, "Ecologically-conscious Design of Cities", in *Environmental Issues in Development and Conservation*, (Eds. Briffet and Sim), SNP Publishers Pte Ltd, Singapore, 1993.
Powell, Robert, et al, "The Last Kampong", *Architecture Journal*, School of Architecture, National University of Singapore, Singapore, 1994.
Powell, Robert, *Living Legacy: Singapore's Architectural Heritage Renewed*, Singapore Heritage Society, Singapore, 1994.
Powell, Robert, "Urban Morphology: Values Embedded in the Singapore Landscape", *Journal of Southeast Asian Architecture*, pages 46–59, 1996.
Powell, Robert, *The Tropical Asian House*, Select Books and Thames and Hudson, Singapore, 1996.
Powell, Robert, *Modern Tropical Architecture: Line, Edge and Shade*, Page One Publishing, Singapore, 1997.
Powell, Robert, "Testing Geometries: Choa Chu Kang Housing", *Singapore Architect*, No. 195/97, Singapore, 1997.
Powell, Robert, "Singapore Country Focus", *World Architecture UK*, No. 56, United Kingdom, 1997.
Powell, Robert, "Pacific Rim Report Malaysia and Singapore", *Architectural Record* 07/97, USA, 1997.
Powell, Robert, "Erasing Memory, Inventing Tradition, Rewriting History: Planning as a Tool of Ideology", chapter in *Contested Urban Heritage: Voices from the Periphery* (editors Shaw and Jones), Ashgate, UK, 1997.
Powell, Robert, *The Urban Asian House: Living in the Tropical City*, Select Books and Thames and Hudson, Singapore, 1998.
Powell, Robert, "95 Emerald Hill", *Singapore Architect*, No. 197/98, Singapore, 1998.
Powell, Robert, "William Lim Siew Wai—Architect", *Monument*, No. 26, Australia, Dec 1998.
Powell, Robert, "The Next Generation: Five Singapore Architects", *Monument*, No. 32, Australia, October 1999.
Powell, Robert, *Rethinking the Skyscraper*, Thames and Hudson, London, 1999.
Powell, Robert, "Out on a Limb", *World Architecture*, No. 86, London, UK, May 2000.
Powell, Robert, "The Singapore Pavilion", *Architecture Australia*, Australia, June 2000.
Powell, Robert, "The Concept of Community: Marine Parade Community Centre", *SPACE*, 2000/02, Singapore, 2000.
Powell, Robert, "Urbanising Suburbia", *Monument: Residential Special Issue*, Australia, 2000.
Powell, Robert, "Living on the Edge", *World Architecture*, No. 90, London, September 2000.
Powell, Robert, *The New Asian House*, Select Books, Singapore, 2000.
Raman, P.G., *Criticism and the Growth of Ideas*, Asia Design Forum (ADF), Singapore, 1992.
Ricouer, Paul, "Universal Civilisation and National Cultures", in *History and Truth*, Evanston, 1966.
Ritchie, Ian, "The Museum as Public Architecture", *Museum Builders*, James Steele ed., Academy Editions, UK, 1994, p. 12.
School of Architecture, *Urban Study of Mohamed Sultan Road*, Unpublished Work of Year 4 students, National University of Singapore, 1986.
Seow Eu Jin, *Architectural Development in Singapore*, unpublished doctoral thesis, University of Melbourne, 1974.
Sharp, Ilsa, *There is Only One Raffles*, Souvenir Press, London, 1981.
Sheldon, Garth, "Letting the Past Serve the Present: Restoration in Singapore", *Towards the Excellence in the Built Environment*, REDAS, Singapore, 1988.
Sim, Peter, "Gentle Transformation", *SPACE*, 2000/01, Singapore, 2000.
Sim, Peter, "Ship Shape: The Singapore National Sailing Centre", *SPACE*, 2000/02, Singapore, 2000.
Sim, Peter, "Urban Chic: Gallery Evason", *SPACE*, 2000/04, Singapore, 2000.
Singapore Institute of Architects, *Rumah: Contemporary Architecture of Singapore*, Singapore, 1982.
Sorkin, Michael, *Exquisite Corpse*, Vers, New York, 1991.
Tan Boon Thor, "Civilising Influences: Asian Civilisations Museum", *Singapore Architect*, No 198/98, Singapore, 1998.
Tan Hock Beng, *Tropical Architecture and Interiors*, Page One, Singapore, 1993.
Tan Kok Meng (ed.), *Asian Architects*, Vol. 1, Select Books, Singapore, 2000.
Tange, Kenzo, "Recollections" in *Kenzo Tange 1946–1996 Architecture and Urban Design*, ed. Massimo Bettinotti, Electra Publisher, Milan, 1996.
Tay Kheng Soon, *The Intelligent Tropical City*, briefing notes for student elective, Year 4, School of Architecture, National University of Singapore, 16 Jan 1988.
Tay Kheng Soon, *The Intelligent Tropical City as a Framework for Architecture and Planning* in a seminar, Heritage and Change in South-East Asian Cities, South-East Asian Study Group and the Aga Khan Program at Harvard University and MIT, Singapore, Jan 23–24, 1988.
Tay Kheng Soon, *Mega Cities in the Tropics: Towards an Architectural Agenda for the Future*, Institute of South-East Asian Studies, 1989.
Tay Kheng Soon and Powell, Robert, "The Tropical City: A Resource Conserving Approach to Planning", proceeding of the second International Convention on Urban Planning, Housing and Design, Singapore, Jul 27–29, 1989.
Tay Kheng Soon, *The Intelligent Tropical City*, Vols. I and II, Student Workshop, School of Architecture, National University of Singapore, IRC, Nov 21–Dec 9, 1989.
Tay Kheng Soon, Powell, Robert and Chua Beng Huat, *Kampong Bugis Development Guide Plan*, Singapore Institute of Architects, Singapore, Feb 1990.
Tay Kheng Soon, "The Architectural Aesthetics of Tropicality", in *Modern Tropical Architecture: Line, Edge and Shade* by Robert Powell, Page One Publishing, Singapore, 1997.
Turnbull, C.M., *A History of Singapore 1819–1975*, Oxford, 1977.
Tzonis, Alexander and Lian Lefaivre, "Why Critical Regionalism Today?" in *Theorising a New Agenda for Architecture: An Anthology of Architectural Theory (1965–95)*, Princeton Architectural Press, New York, 1995.
URA, *Revised Concept Plan*, Singapore 1991.
URA, *Conservation Guidelines for Emerald Hill Conservation Area*, Singapore, 1991.
URA, *Conservation Guidelines for Boat Quay Conservation Area*, Singapore, 1991.
URA, *Conservation Guidelines for Beach Road Conservation Area*, Singapore, 1991.
URA and HDB, *Punggol 21—A Waterfront Town of the 21st Century*, Singapore, 1996.
Van Schaik, Leon, "Social Condensers: The Club as a Social Force" in *Community Clubs 1986-1999 Exhibition Catalogue*, William Lim (ed.), RMIT University, Australia, 1997.
Van Schaik., Leon, "Between Abstraction and Cultural Reference", *Singapore Architect Singapore Institute of Architects Journal*, 200/99, Singapore, December 1999.
Van Schaik, Leon, "Singapore Architects: Mok Wei Wei", in *Architectural Review Australia*, Autumn 1995.
Vidler, Anthony, "Refiguring the Place of Architecture", in an introduction to *Agrest and Gandelsonas: Works*, Princeton Architectural Press, New York, 1995.
Wong, A. and Yeh, Stephen, ed., *Housing a Nation*, Housing and Development Board, Singapore, 1986.
Yeang, Ken, *The Tropical Verandah City*, Longmann, Kuala Lumpur, 1987.
Yeoh, Brenda, *Contesting Space*, Oxford University Press, New York, 1996.
Yong Mun Cheong, *Asian Traditions and Modernisation*, Times Academic Press, Singapore, 1992.

PICTURE CREDITS

Albert Lim KS
Jacket (front and back), 2, 3, 4, 9, 12, 22, 24 (left), 28, 29, 30, 31, 32, 33, 34, 35 (right), 36, 37 (top right, centre and bottom), 38 (left and right), 42, 44, 45 (centre, right and bottom), 51 (left), 53 (top and left), 54 (left and right), 55 (left and right), 56, 62, 68, 69, 70, 71 (left and right), 78, 79 (top), 80 (top and bottom: courtesy of HYLA), 81 (courtesy of HYLA), 90, 97 (bottom right), 100, 108 (courtesy of SCDA), 109 (left and right: courtesy of SCDA), 111 (courtesy of Akitek Tenggara), 112 (courtesy of Akitek Tenggara), 113 (courtesy of Akitek Tenggara), 114 (top right), 117 (left, centre and right), 118, 119, 124 (courtesy of Kerry Hill Architects), 125 (top and bottom: courtesy of Kerry Hill Architects), 130, 131 (left and centre), 132, 133 (courtesy of Forum Architects), 134, 136 (left and right), 137 (top and bottom), 140 (top and bottom), 141 (right), 142 (courtesy of Akitek Tenggara), 143 (top and bottom), 144 (courtesy of Kerry Hill Architects), 145 (top left, bottom left and right: courtesy of Kerry Hill Architects), 146, 147 (left and right), 148 (top), 149, 151 (top and bottom), 152 (top and bottom), 153 (left, centre and right), 154, 155 (top left, top centre, top right and bottom), 156, 157, 158, 159, 160, 161, 174 (courtesy of Architects Vista), 175 (right, centre and left: courtesy of Architects Vista), 176, 177 (left, centre and right), 179 (left and right), 180 (courtesy of CSYA), 181 (left, top right and bottom right: courtesy of CSYA), 182, 183 (top, far left, left top and left bottom), 184, 185 (right and left), 186, 187 (left, centre and right), 196, 197 (top and bottom), 201 (left and right), 202 (left and right), 203, 204, 205 (left, top right and bottom right), 206, 207 (top, bottom left and bottom right), 208 (left and right), 209 (top and bottom), 212, 214, 215, 216 (top left, top centre, top right and bottom), 217 (top and bottom), 222, 223 (left and right), 224, 225, 226, 227 (left and right), 228, 229 (top, centre and bottom), 230, 231 (top right and bottom), 233, 234, 235, 236 (top and bottom), 242, 243 (top left, top right and bottom)

Robert Powell/Akimedia
8, 10 (left and right), 13, 16, 17, 24 (right), 35 (left), 45 (left), 53 (bottom left and right), 57 (top left, top right and bottom), 74, 75 (top and bottom), 77 (centre), 79 (bottom), 85 (right), 87 (left, right and bottom), 89, 92 (left and right), 92 (left and right), 94 (left and right), 95, 96, 97 (top and bottom left), 98, 99, 101 (top and bottom), 105 (top left, centre and right), 114 (top left and top centre), 115, 116, 120, 121 (top, bottom left and bottom right), 122, 123, 126, 127 (left and right), 131 (right), 141 (left), 148 (bottom), 150, 165 (top), 166, 167 (top and bottom left), 168, 169 (left and right), 189, 190, 191, 192 (left and right), 193, 194, 195, 198, 200, 210, 211 (top and bottom), 219 (left, centre and right), 231 (top left)

R Ian Lloyd
170 (courtesy of William Lim Associates), 172 (right and left: courtesy of William Lim Associates)

Tan Hock Beng/MAPS Image
26, 110, 128, 129 (top and bottom)

Amir Sultan
19, 40, 48, 49 (top and bottom), 50, 51 (right), 156 (left), 162, 163 (top and bottom), 164, 165 (bottom right and bottom left), 167 (bottom right)

Richard Bryant / ARCAID
46, 47 (centre and right)

Frenchie Cristogatin
60 (left and right), 61 (top and bottom)

Tim Nolan
11 (courtesy of Architects 61), 84 (courtesy of Architects 61 Pte Ltd), 85 (left: courtesy of Architects 61 Pte Ltd), 138 (courtesy of LOOK Architects), 139 (courtesy of LOOK Architects, 220 (courtesy of LOOK Architects), 221 (courtesy of LOOK Architects)

Tim Griffith
63 (courtesy of WoHa Designs), 82 (courtesy of WoHa Designs), 83 (top, centre and bottom: courtesy of WoHa Designs)

Shinkenchiku-Sha Co. Ltd.
67 (left, top and right: courtesy of Kisho Kurokawa)

Dennis Gilbert
72, 73 (left and right: courtesy of Tangguanbee Architects), 188 (courtesy of Tangguanbee Architects), 199 (top and bottom: courtesy of Tangguanbee Architects)

Peter Mealin
76 (courtesy of SCDA Architects), 77 (top and bottom: courtesy of SCDA Architects)

Xiao Photo Workshop
88 (courtesy of Bedmar and Shi), 103 (top and bottom: courtesy of Bedmar and Shi)

Tan Kah Heng
106 (courtesy of Bedmar and Shi), 107 (top left, top right, bottom left and bottom right: courtesy of Bedmar and Shi)

Courtesy of KNTA Architects
15

Courtesy of Murphy Jahn Architects/Architects 61 Pte Ltd.
20, 21, 27 (left, centre and right)

Courtesy of Ong and Ong Architects Pte Ltd.
41, 57 (top centre)

Courtesy of Architects 61 Pte Ltd.
52, 57(top centre)

Courtesy of The Substation
59 (top, centre and bottom).

Courtesy of Wong and Ouyang Architects
64, 65

Courtesy of Ken Lou Architects
172, 173 (right and left)

Courtesy of DP Architects Pte Ltd.
178, 232, 239 (top and bottom)

Courtesy of Geoff Malone International
213, 218 (top and bottom)

Courtesy of Akitek Tenggara
237

Courtesy of T R Hamzah and Yeang Sdn. Bhd. and the National Library Board
240 (top, bottom left and bottom right)

Photograph of the author by Gordon Outhwaite (October, 1999).

INDEX

SINGAPORE ISLAND

Scale 1 : 55 000

km 1 2 3
miles 1 2

LEGEND

Expressway
Main road
Secondary road
MRT
MRT (under construction)
Nature reserve
Land reclamation
MRT station

SEMBAWANG

YISHUN NEW TOWN

Lower Seletar Reservoir

YIO CHU KANG

JALAN KAYU

PUNGGOL

SENGKANG

BUANGKOK

HOUGANG NEW TOWN

PASIR RIS NEW TOWN

LOYANG

CHANGI

ANG MO KIO NEW TOWN

SERANGOON NEW TOWN

THOMSON

BISHAN NEW TOWN

TOA PAYOH NEW TOWN

KOVAN

PAYA LEBAR

DEFU INDUSTRIAL ESTATE

Bedok Reservoir

TAMPINES NEW TOWN

SIMEI NEW TOWN

Changi Airport

KIM CHUAN

BEDOK NEW TOWN

TANAH MERAH

NOVENA

JALAN EUNOS ESTATE

KEMBANGAN

GEYLANG

KATONG

MARINA SOUTH

Pulau Brani

Pulau Sentosa